D1342891

# Critical Criminological Perspectives

## Series Editors

Reece Walters
Faculty of Law
Queensland University of Technology
Brisbane, Queensland, Australia

Deborah Drake
Social Policy & Criminology
The Open University
Milton Keynes, United Kingdom

The Palgrave Critical Criminological Perspectives book series aims to showcase the importance of critical criminological thinking when examining problems of crime, social harm and criminal and social justice. Critical perspectives have been instrumental in creating new research agendas and areas of criminological interest. By challenging state defined concepts of crime and rejecting positive analyses of criminality, critical criminological approaches continually push the boundaries and scope of criminology, creating new areas of focus and developing new ways of thinking about, and responding to, issues of social concern at local, national and global levels. Recent years have witnessed a flourishing of critical criminological narratives and this series seeks to capture the original and innovative ways that these discourses are engaging with contemporary issues of crime and justice.

More information about this series at
http://www.springer.com/series/14932

David Baker

# Deaths After Police Contact

## Constructing Accountability in the 21st Century

David Baker
Coventry University
Coventry, United Kingdom

Critical Criminological Perspectives
ISBN 978-1-349-95478-0      ISBN 978-1-137-58967-5   (eBook)
DOI 10.1057/978-1-137-58967-5

Printed on acid-free paper

This Palgrave Macmillan imprint is published by Springer Nature
The registered company is Macmillan Publishers Ltd. London

*For Ken Baker (1925–2014), who could imagine a life beyond the factory*

# Preface

In June 2011 I was in a café in London with a former colleague. The ubiquitous rolling news played on TV. It announced that PC Simon Harwood, the officer at the centre of the death of Ian Tomlinson in the G20 protests in London in May 2009 was to be charged with his manslaughter. In the weeks that unfolded, I thought more and more about the idea that, so far as the state is concerned, accountability is legitimately constructed in all cases of death after police contact (DAPC). The official narrative is that these cases are investigated independently and rigorously, their findings are made public, and the police no longer 'police the police'. True, numerous cases going back over a long period of time have been highly contentious. Anybody with knowledge of this issue could instantly reel off the names of Blair Peach, Roger Sylvester, Shiji Lapite, Harry Stanley, Jean Charles de Menezes, Ian Tomlinson, Azelle Rodney, or Mark Duggan. There is no institutional denial that the people who die after contact with the police are disproportionately from BME (Black or Minority Ethnic) groups, or that they tend to have issues with mental health or substance abuse. In short, few doubt that people from marginalised groups in our society are disproportionately more likely to die after police contact than any other group of people. There have been numerous cases where a verdict of unlawful killing has been returned by juries in the coroner's court, for example the deaths of Christopher Alder and Ian Tomlinson, albeit that none of these cases went on to be prosecuted successfully in criminal courts. I wanted to know how this state of affairs existed in our society and what that said about society's relationship with police and the state.

This book is not just about the people listed above. It is about a wide variety of people who have died in cases of DAPC, some of whom are barely heard of outside their local area. It is not just about people who are shot dead by police, or hit with batons. It is about people who die drunk or from swallowing drugs while in custody; about people who die in accidents in police pursuit chases; and about people who die as a result of neglect and an absence of care while in custody. Campaign groups and families have long fought for greater police accountability and more transparency in cases of DAPC, citing miscarriages of justice, asymmetrical power in the investigative processes and the failure of police regulators to consider cases of DAPC as potentially being a crime from the outset. The more I thought about these complex issues, I wanted to know: how *is* accountability constructed in all of these cases—because so far as our state and legal system is concerned, accountability *is* manifest, whether we or not we are happy with this.

This book is about deaths after police contact in England and Wales and how accountability is constructed in the aftermath of these cases. That starting point was the genesis of a PhD I began in January 2012. This book represents an updated and reworked version of my PhD. My research uses two documentary datasets, one from verdicts recorded in cases of DAPC by juries in coroners' courts, the other from investigation reports published by the IPCC (Independent Police Complaints Commission) into these cases.

In some ways the book follows a classic social-science approach: it examines a relatively peripheral issue in order to shine a light on wider practices that reflect socio-legal norms and values. In this case, people who die after police contact tend to be labelled as coming from peripheral groups in society, and the issue of death after police contact is relatively peripheral in the wider scheme of police activity in England and Wales. The book aims to show that the issue of DAPC can tell us quite a lot about how policing is and how it might be, in addition to critically examining what we mean when we use the term 'accountability' in relation to public services. It considers the symbolic and practical aspects of policing and accountability in both the wider context but also more specifically in relation to the issue of DAPC.

I do not claim to have written a definitive text, nor do I profess to have an 'answer' to this 'problem'. To paraphrase Brecht in the *Life of Galileo*, academic enterprise is an exercise in ignorance reduction. I hope this book will reduce, in some part, our ignorance of the issue of death after police contact.

# Acknowledgements

First, I am very grateful to Marcia Rigg for her blessing in allowing me to discuss the events leading to the death of her brother, Sean, and the events after his death including the initial IPCC investigation, inquest and subsequent reviews to date in a public forum.

Second, thank you to Helen Shaw and Deborah Coles at *Inquest* for answering endless questions and giving me access to narrative verdicts—without these, there would be no book.

I would like to thank a number of people for advice, guidance and feedback which was invaluable in the production of this book. At the Open University: Louise Westmarland, Steve Tombs, Chris Williams, Deb Drake and Neil Clarke. Steve Savage (University of Portsmouth), Paul Ponsaers (University of Ghent), Andrew Williams (University of Warwick), Jenny Fleming (University of Southampton), Peter Hall (Coventry University), John Woolham (King's College London), Dave Beecham (University of South Australia) and Rachel Nicholas.

At Palgrave Macmillan, thank you to Julia Willan and Dominic Walker for supporting the book from the outset and guiding me through the editing and production process.

Last, but by no means least, to Jane Hinton for love, understanding and putting up with me throughout the process of writing this book. I must have been unbearable to live with at times.

# Contents

# List of Abbreviations

| | |
|---|---|
| ACPO | Association of Chief Police Officers |
| BMA | British Medical Association |
| BME | Black and Minority Ethnic |
| CAD | Computer Aided Dispatch |
| CP | College of Policing |
| DAPC | Deaths After Police Contact |
| DDO | Duty Detention Officer |
| DPS | Directorate of Professional Standards |
| ECHR | European Convention on Human Rights |
| FFLM | Faculty of Forensic and Legal Medicine |
| FME | Forensic Medical Examiner |
| HAC | House of Commons Home Affairs Select Committee |
| HMIC | Her Majesty's Inspectorate of Constabulary |
| HRA | Human Rights Act |
| IAP | Independent Advisory Panel on Deaths in Custody |
| IPCC | Independent Police Complaints Commission |
| JCHR | Joint Committee on Human Rights |
| MDT | Mobile Data Terminal |
| MOJ | Ministry of Justice |
| MPS | Metropolitan Police Service |
| NAO | National Audit Office |
| NCPC | National College of Police Chiefs |
| NGO | Non-Governmental Organisation |

| | |
|---|---|
| NPIA | National Police Improvement Agency |
| ONS | Office for National Statistics |
| PACE | Police and Criminal Evidence Act 1984 |
| PCA | Police Complaints Authority |
| PCB | Police Complaints Board |
| PCC | Police and Crime Commissioner |
| PNC | Police National Computer |
| PSD | Professional Standards Department |
| SLaM | South London and Maudsley Trust |

# List of Figures

# 1

# Introduction: Contextualising Death after Police Contact

Sean Rigg was forty when he died in 'the cage' in Brixton police station on 21 August 2008. He was a rap artist and singer, and had released a CD of his own music and lyrics. He was widely travelled and was considered to be a charming and intelligent person. Sean was black, he had a formal diagnosis of schizophrenia which was controlled by medication. His condition was usually well managed, enabling him to live an active, independent life, but could deteriorate rapidly if he ceased taking medication. Sean lived in a community mental health hostel in south London and was in regular contact with his family, particularly his sister, Marcia, who was considered to be an 'integral' part of his care team (Lakhani 2012). His consultant from the South London and Maudsley Trust (SLaM) considered him to be a physically fit and healthy person.

SLaM, who were responsible for Sean's duty of care stated that from 11 August 2008 he was 'in need of acute treatment and that his placement in the community was unsafe' (Casale et al. 2013: 42–3). SLaM failed to respond to multiple requests from the hostel to meet with Sean in the two weeks prior to his death. Hostel staff called police five times over a period of three hours on 21 August to request officers' attendance due to a relapse in his mental health condition which caused an extreme

© The Editor(s) (if applicable) and The Author(s) 2016
D. Baker, *Deaths After Police Contact*,
DOI 10.1057/978-1-137-58967-5_1

psychotic episode. Police did not attend the hostel, but did respond to an emergency call from a member of the public when Sean was seen acting oddly while semi-dressed outside a residential location. Four officers arrived in a van; they failed to recognise that he had mental health issues. He was arrested at 19.40 for allegedly assaulting a police officer and for an alleged public order offence (IPCC 2012b: 37). Thereafter, he was detained using handcuffs and prolonged prone restraint, following which he was also arrested for the theft of a passport—it was his own expired passport which he kept on his person for identification purposes (Casale et al. 2013: 59). He was then put into the back cage of a police van and driven at speed to Brixton police station. Upon arrival at 19.53 he was left in the van for ten minutes. He was then removed at 20.03 in a collapsed state and placed in a chain metal structure known as 'the cage', adjacent to the custody suite but external to the building. The Forensic Medical Examiner (FME)[1] attended him at 20.13 and requested that an ambulance be called. An ambulance was called at this point, but not an emergency ambulance. At 20.24 the FME was recalled as Sean was not breathing, and at this point an emergency ambulance was called. Officers attempted mouth to mouth resuscitation and used a defibrillator without success. Sean died after less than one hour in police custody. It took more than thirty minutes for anyone to administer medical attention to him.

As per the protocol, the Metropolitan Police Service (MPS) referred Sean's death to the Independent Police Complaints Commission (IPCC). An IPCC team of investigators arrived at Brixton police station around midnight on 21 August. At around 08.00 the following morning it was announced that an independent investigation would be carried out into Sean's death. The investigation report into his death concluded in February 2010 but was not made public until 15 August 2012. A coroner's inquest, heard in public, before a jury, began on 12 June 2012 and concluded on 1 August 2012, nearly four years after Sean's death. The inquest considered evidence that the IPCC did not find, did not seek or did not use. This evidence was gathered principally by Sean Rigg's family. The result was a jury verdict that differed considerably from the findings of the IPCC investigation report. The purpose in opening this book with the death of Sean Rigg

---

[1] Previously known as Police Surgeons. The Metropolitan Police Service (MPS) use the term Forensic Medical Examiner; Kelly et al. (1996) note the wide variation of terms used in this role.

is twofold. First, to illustrate the types of events and issues that may lead to cases of DAPC. Second, to illustrate how different regulatory systems produce different investigations into such deaths, leading to a relational system of accountability construction in these cases. By relational I mean dependent upon the contexts in which accountability is constructed. By accountability construction I mean the processes and mechanisms that are used to produce accountability in cases of DAPC. The following section sets out aspects of both the IPCC investigation report into Sean Rigg's death, and the inquest verdict recorded by the jury.

# Relational Accountability in Cases of DAPC

The jury verdict in the coroner's court ran to three pages compared to the 162-page IPCC investigation report (IPCC 2012b). The IPCC report is striking in its level of empirical detail regarding witness statements and timings of events. Below, there is a brief discussion of issues covered by the jury verdict and IPCC report regarding mental health, restraint, Computer Aided Dispatch (CAD) response and securing evidence. It will become clear that different organisations using different processes construct different types of accountability, underlining the relational aspect of accountability construction in cases of DAPC.

## Mental Health and Restraint

The coroner's jury criticised SLaM for failures or absences in communication, crisis planning, risk assessment and treatment. It stated that SLaM failed to put a crisis management plan into place and that there was inadequate risk assessment of Sean Rigg. Communication between members of Sean's clinical team and also between the team and his family was considered 'less than effective'. Furthermore, they recorded that communications between police, SLaM and Penrose (the hostel provider) were 'inadequate'. The IPCC investigation report makes little comment on SLaM, primarily because the remit of the IPCC is to focus on police action or omission rather than the wider circumstances which contributed to the death of Sean Rigg. Mental health issues are intimately linked with police interactions with marginalised groups, and with the issue of DAPC (Adebowale 2013). For the IPCC not to consider this issue suggests either a lack of knowledge or interest on their part; it suggests that the initial parameters that provide a framework for their investigation of these cases are at best flawed and at worst blinkered. By failing to consider the role of SLaM in the death of Sean Rigg, the IPCC overlooked why police were in contact with Sean in the first place. His death illustrates failings in two public services, as distinct to purely the police, and this is a consistent theme in cases of DAPC.

The jury stated that upon arrival at Brixton police station it should have been reasonable for the police to recognise there was cause for concern about Sean Rigg's physical and mental health, and this should have led to an assessment of these conditions. That this did not occur represented: 'an absence of actions by the Police and this was inadequate'. The failure to acknowledge issues relating to Sean's physical and mental health is linked to the role of police in these cases: are they enforcement officers or peace officers? Do they focus on the criminal justice aspect of their role when dealing with vulnerable groups, or do they focus first and foremost on the preservation of life and the welfare of the individual?

The IPCC report focuses on Sean Rigg's alleged behaviour during transportation to Brixton police station, noting that three of the officers described him spinning around on his back and walking around the sides of the van walls on his feet, leading them to charge him with a public order offence (IPCC 2012b: 54). During the inquest this behaviour was demonstrated to be a physical impossibility by expert witnesses (Casale et al. 2013: 66). The IPCC report spent several pages discussing the inability of officers to acknowledge that Sean had mental health issues, noting that 'it is of some concern' that they did not do so, despite describing his behaviour as 'strange by anyone's standards' (IPCC 2012b: 105). The inability of officers to recognise mental health issues meant they were not procedurally obliged to take into account Standard Operating Procedures (SOP) regarding mental health issues when approaching, arresting, restraining, transporting and caring for Sean Rigg in custody (IPCC 2012b: 110). Had they recognised mental health issues they would have had to conduct a risk assessment and attempted to de-escalate the situation rather than use restraint in the first instance. As noted above, the type of approach determines the type of actions (or omissions) that are adopted by officers.

The jury was critical of the police use of excessive restraint, stating that:

'The length of restraint in the prone position was ... unnecessary. It is the majority view of the Jury that this more than minimally contributed to Sean's death.'

The level of force used during the restraint phase was deemed 'unsuitable'. The jury criticised an absence of leadership and questioned whether: 'police guidelines or training regarding restraint and positional asphyxia were sufficient or were followed correctly'. In the IPCC report, restraint was assessed by an expert from the Association of Chief Police Officers (ACPO) commissioned by the IPCC. He noted that the recognition of 'impact factors' such as mental health issues could have affected the officers use of restraint had they acknowledged the existence of such factors. The section concluded:

'This investigation has uncovered no evidence to suggest that the techniques used by the officers and the level of force applied during the arrest of Mr Rigg was disproportionate or unlawful.' (IPCC 2012b: 113)

The coroner's jury and the IPCC clearly have subjective differences in measurement and this points to one way in which accountability may be seen to be a relational concept. In this case, measurement criteria determining acts as proportionate and lawful might be quite different to those which assess acts in terms of whether or not they are legitimate and desirable.

## Computer Aided Dispatch (CAD) and Scene of Death

The jury criticised CAD responses to emergency calls from the hostel as 'an unacceptable failure to act appropriately'. Furthermore, the police response to these calls was 'unacceptable and inappropriate'. Moreover, they stated that police failed to secure an ambulance as quickly as possible. The IPCC report sets out a detailed description of issues relating to CAD systems and operation. For example, the CAD operator notes on the CAD record, which would have been available to police on their Mobile Data Terminal (MDT): *'he must have mental health issues'* (IPCC 2012b: 77, italics as original). Official reports into cases of DAPC stress the importance of officers referring to existing records to access information when dealing with potentially vulnerable individuals (see, for example Leigh et al. 1998; Best et al. 2004; Hannan et al. 2010; ACPO 2012). A good deal of space is spent in the IPCC report discussing the general principle in CAD of sifting calls into levels of gravity, and of the overall response rates by the local borough police and MPS in general. The IPCC section on CAD response concludes apologetically: 'Unfortunately, in many circumstances it is just not possible for the police performance to match up to the often unrealistic public expectation of them' (IPCC 2012b: 104). One may question how an organisation with a mission statement that states an intention to promote public trust in the police is able to record such an observation.

In the IPCC report, the inability of the police to secure both the scene of the arrest and the scene of death mildly concluded:

'It does appear that little consideration was given to the evidential opportunities that may have existed at the site of the arrest.' (Ibid: 122)

A number of pages discussing the issue of CCTV are prefaced with:

'The whole subject of the CCTV at Brixton police station is an immensely complicated one.' (Ibid: 123)

Yet the family of Sean Rigg were able to secure the CCTV footage from inside Brixton police station while the IPCC were apparently not. The issue of securing evidence is highlighted regarding the independence of the IPCC in a number of academic texts (see Savage 2013a, b; Smith 2009a, b) and official reports (Casale et al. 2013; IPCC 2013; HAC 2010). An independent review into the IPCC's investigation of Sean Rigg's death criticised the eight-month delay in interviewing officers fully about circumstances relating to the death, stating: 'It is difficult to understand the lack of urgency accorded by the IPCC investigation' (Casale et al. 2013: 30).

After fifty-one pages of discussion the IPCC report made two findings, which appears remarkable in the context of a 163-page investigative report. One was that the CCTV at Brixton police station was not in full working order; in fact two cameras were not working, one was in the station yard which would have covered Sean's removal from the van, the other was inside 'the cage' in which he died. The other finding was that officers 'adhered to policy and good practice' during Sean Rigg's transportation by van to Brixton police station (IPCC 2012b: 142). It went on to make two recommendations in respect of these findings. First, that the CCTV system 'should be fully reviewed'. Second, that the carriage of detainees in caged vans should be reviewed.

# A Crisis of Legitimacy

The seven-week inquest produced a verdict partly based on evidence either not found or not considered by the IPCC. Consequently, there were significant disparities in the findings of the IPCC investigation report and the narrative verdict. The most apparent of these was the opening line which stated that Sean Rigg died in Brixton police station, not at King's College Hospital. Criticisms of SLaM, the CAD operators and officers from Brixton police station are not recorded in the IPCC report. The words 'fail', 'failed', 'failing' or 'failure' are recorded on ten occasions in the narrative verdict. They typically relate to actions or omissions in practice, training, communication, risk assessment and duty of care. These words barely feature in the IPCC report. In the jury verdict, the phrase 'more than minimally contributed [to the death of Sean Rigg]' is recorded on three occasions. This did not appear in the IPCC report. The penultimate line of the jury verdict stated:

> 'While Sean Rigg was in custody the Police failed to uphold his basic rights and omitted to deliver the appropriate care.'

The investigation into the death of Sean Rigg represented a crisis of legitimacy for the IPCC. The great disparity between the IPCC investigation report and the jury verdict led Anne Owers, appointed chair of the IPCC in February 2012, to announce that an unprecedented independent review (chaired by Dr Silvia Casale) would be set up to re-examine and critically evaluate the IPCC investigation into Sean Rigg's death in light of the findings from the coronial inquest. Thus, the organisation statutorily founded to independently hold police accountable for their actions decided to refer itself to another independent entity in order to evaluate its processes. The IPCC took this reactive decision because another regulator in the form of the coronial system had uncovered a number of findings and conclusions in Sean's death that the IPCC had either overlooked, not looked for, or simply did not use in their independent investigation report. While the IPCC took four years to publish its investigation report, Silvia Casale was able to publish her report within six months, and the jury inquest in the coroner's court took seven weeks. This book will demonstrate that the content of findings in accountability construction is largely determined by the type of forum that considers the evidence, and the parameters of inquiry and investigation that exist within such a forum. It argues that this is one manifestation of a non-systematised 'system' of police regulation in cases of DAPC.

The death of Sean Rigg is not an isolated case. The book will demonstrate that Sean's death is representative of many cases of DAPC: in terms of the events that led to his death, the way in which the death was investigated, and the type of accountability which is constructed in the aftermath of the death. How can the two organisations tasked with holding police accountable in cases of DAPC produce such wildly different findings? What does this say about the way in which accountability is constructed in these cases, and about the type of police accountability that society and the state accepts or expects in England and Wales? This book examines the processes and mechanisms by which such findings are recorded and demonstrates that the type of forum that produces accountability dictates, to a large extent, the type of accountability that is constructed. It also considers the wider issue of why two different organisations are tasked with investigating and reporting on such deaths and what this might say about the state, police and society in the twenty-first century.

# Death After Police Contact in England and Wales

Between 2004 and 2015 a total of 1,539 people in England and Wales died after contact with the police (IPCC 2015). The term 'death after police contact' is used throughout this book. This term adopts criteria used by the Independent Police Complaints Commission (IPCC) in regard to 'deaths during or following police contact' as stated in their annual statistical analyses on this issue (see, for example IPCC 2015). It covers the following categories stated by the IPCC: road traffic fatalities, fatal shootings, deaths in, or following police custody, apparent suicides following police custody, and other deaths following police contact (IPCC 2012a: 1).

It is rare that police officers are subject to a criminal trial in cases of DAPC, and extremely rare for them to be prosecuted as a result. Yet the state is legally obliged under Article 2 of the European Convention on Human Rights (ECHR) to investigate cases of DAPC using an independent forum. Each case of DAPC in England and Wales is typically investigated by two independent organisations (the IPCC and the coronial system) and police are held to account for their actions. This book examines how accountability is constructed in cases of DAPC in England and Wales. It argues that there is little overview of the system of accountability construction in cases of DAPC: regulation of these deaths is relatively unregulated. Thus there is limited evidence of lessons being learned to prevent future deaths. While there are processes of regulation that aim to hold police to account in these cases, regulation depends upon a wide range of contexts and factors, and tends to produce relatively arbitrary outcomes.

There is no official denial of the real and symbolic importance of cases of DAPC to society. The capacity of the state and society to hold police to account in these cases is seen as a touchstone for legitimate, transparent and consensual policing in England and Wales. Similarly, there is no official denial that deaths in state custody are significant because the state bears a unique responsibility for the welfare of citizens in their care, and a death in custody can often be viewed with suspicion by the public. Moreover, there is no official denial that a disproportionate number of citizens from marginalised groups in society die in these cases. If you are from a Black and Minority Ethnic (BME) group, have mental health issues, or are dependent on substances then there is a disproportionately large chance that you might die after police contact. None of these issues are disputed by the state. It has made numerous official pronouncements stating how important lesson learning is in reducing the number of deaths after police contact (see, for example Fulton 2008; HAC 2010; JCHR 2004). The central issues are that lessons are not learned, the number of deaths has not reduced, and the level of disproportionality remains stubbornly unchanged. This book examines how this state of affairs continues to exist given that the subject of DAPC is so important to the real, perceived and symbolic relationships between the state, police and society. The death of Sean Rigg in Brixton police station exemplifies many of these issues.

Cases of DAPC in England and Wales are typically investigated by the coronial system and the IPCC.[2] When a person dies after police contact the case is immediately handed over to the relevant force's Professional Standards Department (PSD).[3] The PSD then refers the case to the IPCC who make a decision as to how the case is to be investigated. In Sean Rigg's case, the IPCC decided to undertake an independent investigation into his death; the investigation was undertaken and overseen entirely by IPCC personnel. The IPCC examines the scene of the death, gathers evidence and interviews relevant witnesses. When the investigation is complete a report is constructed which details how events unfolded up to and after the death; it typically includes areas which could be learned from in addition to praise for examples of best practice. Once the IPCC investigation report is concluded the death is then investigated in the coroner's court. This is typically conducted before a jury in public.

The coroner's inquest is inquisitorial, it is a fact-finding exercise and thus not able to ascribe guilt or liability. Inquests aim to examine unexplained and suspicious deaths in order to learn lessons to prevent future deaths. The inquest is able to call witnesses it deems relevant to the case,

---

[2] One example of an exception is the death of Azelle Rodney, shot dead by MPS undercover officers. This case was investigated by judicial inquiry (Holland 2013).

[3] The Metropolitan Police Service (MPS) is an exception, their equivalent unit is called 'The Directorate of Professional Standards' (DPS).

is able to compel witnesses to attend the inquest, and is able to recall witnesses if required. Once the evidence is heard, the jury consider the directions of the coroner and formulate a verdict they feel best describes the death. At the heart of the system that investigates cases of DAPC, then, is a series of relationships between police, state and society; and between police, the IPCC and coroners. This is evidently a complex and multidimensional subject that extends far beyond the individuals involved in a death in custody. As such, these relationships, their interactions with organisational systems and structures, with the law, and societal norms and values need to be examined. Clearly this is not just a question of individual cases, but relates to organisational and systemic issues that affect how and why individuals die after police contact.

## Symbolic Relationships

The police occupy a symbolic position in the relationship between the state and society. Reiner (2013) asserts that they are a physical manifestation of the state to its citizens. As such, they fulfil a number of roles but their function is notable in being relatively ambiguous (see, for example Westmarland 2013; Reiner 2010; McLaughlin 2007). What is less equivocal is their role both as an ultimate emergency service and their ability to legitimately use force in certain circumstances. These twin roles are particularly relevant to this book in that they embody both action and inaction on the part of police. The capacity to preserve life or use force is particularly relevant in police contact with marginalised groups in society, as was evident in the case of Sean Rigg. Numerous sources have noted the disproportionate over-representation of marginalised groups in cases of DAPC (see, for example IPCC 2014; Coles and Shaw 2012; Fulton 2008). This is consistent with statistics from the United States and Australia (see, respectively White et al. 2012; Australian Institute of Criminology 2013).

The symbolic relationship between police, state and society depends on key factors such as consensus, legitimacy and accountability. If the police are able to legitimately occupy such a symbolic position in society, their ability to do so rests on the consent of the population. This means they must be seen to be held accountable. In order to ensure this, a system purportedly exists to provide transparent and rigorous oversight of police action or inaction in cases of DAPC that effectively holds them accountable. Instances of officers being prosecuted in criminal courts as a result of such a death are rare (Smith 2001). Furthermore, there are few known instances of officers being sentenced in these cases (Smith 2009a; Uildriks and van Mastrigt 1991). Thus although the state narrative is that accountability is manifest in such cases, the societal view tends to be that accountability is not always seen to be manifest in all cases of DAPC. This suggests that accountability as a concept is ambiguous and relational, it depends to some degree on how particular audiences view its construction, as is discussed in more detail throughout this book. If society questions the legitimacy of the accountability that is constructed, it seems logical to investigate how accountability is manifest so far as the state is concerned. This may enable a better understanding of the issues involved in the apparent legitimacy gap in many of these cases.

## The Evolution of Discourse: Accountability Construction in the Twenty-First Century

The coronial system upholds the state's responsibilities and obligations to the ECHR in these cases; notably Article 2 which asserts the right to life (see Fig. 3.1). The verdict recorded in Sean Rigg's case clearly identified organisational failures in his duty of care, and this occurred because of obligations imposed on the state by Article 2. Article 2 is identified in the book as being increasingly important in affecting how accountability is constructed in these cases. It has influenced the formulation of different types of processes and outcomes in the coronial system since various precedents (discussed in Chap. 3) were set in the years 2000–02 (Matthews 2011). The major process change in the coronial system is the Article 2 inquest which ensures a significantly more rigorous investigation than was previously the case. In some instances this has produced different outcomes in the form of narrative verdicts recorded by the jury. This book argues that the way in which narrative verdicts are constructed has affected the way in which police are held accountable for these cases in ways that transcend the coronial sphere. Change is effected in the following ways: first, at a macro-level, change is wrought from legal principles external to the state. Citizens' rights in these cases have been secured *from* the state as distinct to *by* the state. At the time of writing, in late 2015, the government has stated that it wishes to withdraw from the ECHR, thus neatly underlining this point (Human Rights Watch 2015). Secondly, at a micro-level, the policies of a growing number of regulatory organisations are increasingly used to assess actions and omissions in cases of DAPC and this affects the content of verdicts and investigation reports recorded by juries and the IPCC respectively.

The IPCC came into being in 2004 and produced the first independent investigation report in the same year. While it does not fulfil a legal obligation to the state in the same way as the coronial system, it typically investigates the same cases. This book demonstrates that changes in the coronial system have affected and effected changes in the way the IPCC investigates and reports on these cases. The existence of two substantively different organisations within the sphere of accountability construction suggests that academic investigation based on discourse analysis is appropriate to this subject. Discourse helps analyse and evaluate the way in which accountability is constructed by the coronial system and the IPCC and the way in which they may, or may not, inter-relate. The discursive relationship that exists between organisations means that knowledge is constructed by different power bases that investigate the same object. Different processes and measurement criteria are used by the coronial system and the IPCC. During the period 2004–15 it has become apparent that the practices they use and the texts they construct have begun to refer to each other's organisational practices and texts as the discourse on the subject of DAPC evolves.

Throughout this book it is argued that the construction of accountability does not occur in a systematic, centralised or planned manner. There is a wide variation in types, styles, content and format within the reporting systems used by both the coronial system and the IPCC. In order to provide a framework within which these texts can be analysed, discourse analysis is used to interrogate how narrative verdicts and IPCC investigation reports are constructed. Discourse analysis considers how language is used by institutions to create and represent reality (see, for example Fairclough 1992). It highlights how specific terms, concepts and combinations of phrases are used in these documents to construct specific types of accountability.

The emergence of Article 2 of the ECHR in the processes of the principal organisations engaged in regulating the police in cases of DAPC has not occurred in a systematic or planned manner. The piecemeal and incremental growth of its usage in documents constructed in the coronial system and the IPCC to some degree reflects Foucault's (1976) belief that relationships of power are not centralised or planned, but diffuse. The enactment of the 1998 Human Rights Act (HRA) in the UK also played a part in cementing the obligation of the state to more thoroughly investigate deaths in custody. Thus the impact of Article 2 on the investigation of these cases has come about partly by precedent, partly by statute. This reflects the lack of central oversight of cases of DAPC and is one reason why lessons are not learned in such cases. Deaths tend to be investigated as individual cases rather than considered as potentially representative of other cases of DAPC in England and Wales. There is little obvious evidence of an analysis of wider organisational or systemic patterns that might result in cases of DAPC. Thus while the death of Sean Rigg might help us understand the manifold issues that are key in cases of DAPC, there is limited evidence of organisational learning from his, or other deaths in cases of DAPC.

## Overview of Chapters

This book will show how accountability is constructed in cases of DAPC in England and Wales. It began by using the representative case of Sean Rigg to illustrate many of the key issues involved in this issue. The book will demonstrate that the findings produced by regulators in cases of DAPC are relational dependent upon the forum that constructs accountability, and the specific processes and parameters used within that forum. It will argue that organisational and systemic issues in the regulation of such deaths means there is little oversight of the accountability constructed by regulators, and consequently there is limited evidence of lessons being learned from these deaths that may prevent future deaths occurring. As such, the 'system' of accountability construction may be said to be non-systematic and lack central oversight. The book will consider why two different regulators examine the same cases of DAPC and what this might say about the nature of regulation and accountability construction in England and Wales. The relevance of Article 2 of the ECHR to the evolution of accountability construction in cases of DAPC will be evaluated throughout the book, and it is identified as being central to the regulation of these cases in the twenty-first century.

Chapter 2 examines the relationship between police, state and society in terms of key issues such as the ambiguous role and function of police, consent, discretion, the use of force and the equivocal concept of accountability. It establishes that policing is both practical and symbolic, and that this affects how legitimacy is constructed. The relationships between different sections of society and the police; between other public services and the police; and between the police and their numerous regulators underline that understanding interdependence and relationships are key to understanding the complex and often multi-causal issues that characterise cases of DAPC. Chapter 3 considers the regulators who hold police accountable in cases of DAPC. The ambiguous roles of the coronial system and IPCC and their uncertain relationship with the police is discussed; similarly, issues of discretion and accountability in their practices are examined. The different practices and policies adopted by each regulator are evaluated and it is established that accountability construction in cases of DAPC is relational and dependent upon a number of contexts. This further underlines that, similar to Chap. 2, understanding relationships in the regulatory sphere is central to understanding how accountability is constructed in cases of DAPC. Chapter 4 moves into an analysis of narrative verdicts recorded in coroners' courts in cases of DAPC and identifies key findings that chart how the construction of accountability is evolving in these cases. It highlights the non-systematic and relational nature of accountability construction within the coronial system. It examines numerous findings from these verdicts; notably the issue of multi-agency involvement in these deaths, the importance of benchmarking criteria in recording findings in these cases, and the relevance of omission as a causal factor in many of these deaths. The chapter also considers police use of force and how juries typically accept its use, albeit with qualification in some cases. Chapter 5 examines IPCC investigation reports from correlate cases used in the narrative verdict dataset. Thus it evaluates the construction of accountability in light of findings in Chap. 4. It finds that the IPCC, similar to the coronial system, has a relatively non-systematic approach to constructing accountability in these cases. Not only is relationality apparent across the two regulators, it is also apparent within each regulatory organisation. Chapter 5 revisits the case of Sean Rigg and argues that it represented a crisis of legitimacy for the IPCC from which it is attempting to reposition itself in terms of investigating and reporting on cases of DAPC. It does this by examining numerous reviews into its practices in the aftermath of Sean Rigg's death. These reviews serve to further illustrate the relational nature of accountability construction and this is taken forward in Chap. 6.

Chapter 6 critically assesses the regulatory domain of accountability construction in cases of DAPC. It discusses how and why the regulatory domain is organised in the way it is, and how this relates to wider trends in governance and regulation in the UK in the twenty-first century. This is contextualised by a discussion of failures in the regulatory sphere of healthcare in the UK in the twenty-first century; illustrating that many of the issues raised in this book go beyond policing and accountability. It is argued that the growing discourse around public services and accountability represents a theatre of construction and consumption of accountable outputs. Chapter 6 begins to consider what this might say about discourse and the evolution of accountability construction in cases of DAPC. Chapter 7 examines the ambiguous concept of accountability in light of findings from Chap. 6 and asks what sort of accountability the state and society might want in cases of DAPC. It considers accountability as a series of types and also of relationships. The chapter discusses how these types and relationships exist within the wider system of regulatory governance in the public sphere. It sets out a conceptual framework that seeks to understand how the current system of accountability construction might function. The book concludes with an overview of key findings and discusses the evolution of accountability and regulation of police in cases of DAPC in the twenty-first century. It considers possible future directions for the system of accountability construction and makes recommendations about how the system could be improved.

# References

ACPO. (2012). *Guidance on the safer detention and handling of persons in police custody* (2nd ed.). Available at: https://www.gov.uk/government/uploads/system/uploads/attachment_data/file/117555/safer-detention-guidance-2012.pdf. Accessed 5 Jan 2014.

Adebowale, V. (2013). *Independent commission on mental health and policing.* Available at: http://news.bbc.co.uk/1/shared/bsp/hi/pdfs/10_05_13_report.pdf. Accessed 23 June 2013.

Australian Institute of Criminology. (2013). 'Police shootings of people with a mental illness.' *Research in Practice, 34.* Available at: http://www.aic.gov.au/publications/current%20series/rip/21-40/rip34.html. Accessed 29 Sept 2013.

Best, D., Havis, S., Gossop, M., Gross, S., Witton, J., Keaney, F., & Strang, J. (2004). The risk of drug swallowing at the point of arrest: An analysis of 24 cocaine-related deaths following police care or custody in England and Wales. *Policing and Society, 14*(4), 380–391.

Casale, S., Corfe, M., & Lewis, J. (2013). *Report of the independent external review of the IPCC investigation into the death of Sean Rigg.* Available at: http://www.ipcc.gov.uk/news/Pages/pr_170513_Riggreview.aspx. Accessed 21 May 2013.

Coles, D., & Shaw, H. (2012). *Learning from death in custody inquests: A new framework for action and accountability.* London: Russell Press.

Fairclough, N. (1992). *Discourse and social change.* Cambridge: Polity.

Foucault, M. (1976). *The will to knowledge: The history of sexuality volume one* (F. Hurley, Trans.). London: Penguin.

Fulton, R. (2008). Review of the forum for preventing deaths in custody: Report of the independent reviewer.

Hannan, M., Hearnden, I., Grace, K., & Bucke, T. (2010). *Deaths in or following police custody: An examination of the cases 1998/99–2008/09* (IPCC research series paper: 17). London: IPCC.

Holland, C. (2013). *The report of the Azelle Rodney Inquiry.* London: TSO.

House of Commons Home Affairs Committee. (2010). *The work of the independent police complaints commission.* London: TSO.

Human Rights Watch. (2015). *The UK government's proposals regarding the Human Rights Act and the European Court of Human Rights.* Available at: https://www.hrw.org/news/2015/05/20/uk-governments-proposals-regarding-human-rights-act-and-european-court-human-rights. Accessed 2 Dec 2015.

IPCC. (2012a). *Deaths during or following police contact: Statistics for England and Wales 2011/12.* Available at: http://www.ipcc.gov.uk/en/Pages/reports_polcustody.aspx. Accessed 7 Nov 2012.

IPCC. (2012b). *IPCC Independent investigation into the death of Sean Rigg whilst in the custody of Brixton police.* Available at: http://www.ipcc.gov.uk/en/Pages/inv_reports_london_se_region.aspx. Accessed 21 May 2013.

IPCC. (2013). *Review of the IPCC's work in investigating deaths: Progress report.* Available at: http://www.ipcc.gov.uk/sites/default/files/Review%20of%20 the%20IPCCs%20work%20in%20investigating%20deaths%20-%20 Progress%20report.pdf. Accessed 10 Dec 2013.

IPCC. (2014). *Review of the IPCC's work in investigating deaths: Final report.* Available at: http://www.ipcc.gov.uk/sites/default/files/Documents/deaths_ review/Review_of_the_IPCCs_work_in_investigating_deaths_2014.pdf. Accessed 17 Mar 2014.

IPCC. (2015). *Deaths during or following police contact: Statistics for England and Wales 2014/15.* Available at: https://www.ipcc.gov.uk/sites/default/files/ Documents/research_stats/Deaths_Report_1415.pdf. Accessed 2 Dec 2015.

Joint Committee on Human Rights. (2004). *Third report: Session 2004–05.* Available at: http://www.publications.parliament.uk/pa/jt200405/jtselect/ jtrights/15/1510.htm#a46. Accessed 17 June 2013.

Kelly, K., Moon, G., Savage, S., & Bradshaw, Y. (1996). Ethics and the police surgeon: Compromise or conflict? *Social Science and Medicine, 42*(11), 1569–1575.

Lakhani, N. (2012, August 15). Sean Rigg investigation: IPCC announces independent review of its own investigation into the death of a mentally ill man in police custody. *The Independent.*

Leigh, A., Johnson, G., & Ingram, A. (1998). *Deaths in custody: Learning the lessons* (Police research series paper 26). London: Crown.

Matthews, P. (2011). *Jervis on the office and duties of coroners: With forms and precedents. Fourth cumulative supplement to the twelfth edition.* London: Sweet and Maxwell.

McLaughlin, E. (2007). *The new policing.* London: Sage.

Reiner, R. (2010). *The politics of the police* (4th ed.). Oxford: Oxford University Press.

Reiner, R. (2013). Who governs? Democracy, plutocracy, science and prophecy in policing. *Criminology and Criminal Justice, 13*(2), 161–180.

Savage, S. (2013a). Thinking independence: Calling the police to account through the independent investigation of police complaints. *British Journal of Criminology, 53*(1), 94–112.

Savage, S. (2013b). Seeking 'civilianness': Police complaints and the civilian control model of oversight. *British Journal of Criminology, 53*(5), 886–904.

Smith, G. (2001). Police complaints and criminal prosecutions. *Modern Law Review, 64*(3), 372–392.

Smith, G. (2009a). Why don't more people complain against the police? *European Journal of Criminology, 6*(3), 249–266.

Smith, G. (2009b). Citizen oversight of independent police services: Bifurcated accountability, regulation creep, and lesson learning. *Regulation and Governance, 3*(4), 421–441.

Uildriks, N., & van Mastrigt, H. (1991). *Policing police violence.* Aberdeen: Aberdeen University Press.

Westmarland, L. (2013). "Snitches get stiches": US homicide detectives' ethics and morals in action. *Policing and Society, 23*(3), 311–327.

White, M., Ready, J., Riggs, C., Dawes, D., Hinz, A., & Ho, J. (2012). An incident-level profile of Taser device deployments in arrest-related deaths. *Police Quarterly, 20*(10), 1–28.

# 2

# Police, State and Society

The fact that the British police are answerable to the law, that we act on behalf of the community and not under the mantle of government, makes us the least powerful, the most accountable and therefore the most acceptable police in the world. (Mark 1977: 56)

## Introduction

The quotation above by the ex-MPS commissioner Sir Robert Mark makes a number of bold claims, many of which would probably be re-asserted by senior police officers and politicians today. It also raises a number of key questions about cases of DAPC. Are police answerable to the law? Do they act on behalf of the community? Are they accountable? This chapter examines these questions and unpicks various issues that underpin them. It highlights the importance of relationships to under-standing these questions and wider issues relating to cases of DAPC. The relationship between police, state and society is examined throughout this book, but this chapter particularly considers the relationship between the symbolic representation and practical reality of policing; it considers

© The Editor(s) (if applicable) and The Author(s) 2016
D. Baker, *Deaths After Police Contact*,
DOI 10.1057/978-1-137-58967-5_2

how discretion plays a significant role in the gap between representation and reality; and it examines how this affects the types of police accountability that might be produced from the perspectives of state, society and the police themselves. These relationships are complex and dynamic, and are inextricably linked with concepts such as legitimacy, consent and ambiguity.

The chapter examines the relationality of concepts such as legitimacy and accountability as it seeks to understand their relevance to cases of DAPC, and the way such deaths are investigated and reported on. A unique power the police have is the use of force, and this is considered in light of the relational aspects of legitimacy and accountability stated above. The use of force often falls disproportionately on marginalised groups in society, as was seen in the death of Sean Rigg, and the chapter discusses how this appears to be legitimate to wider society and what that says about the type of policing society expects. The issue of multi-agency working has been highlighted as being a significant factor in cases of DAPC, as was also noted in the death of Sean Rigg, so the complex dynamics that underpin multi-agency police work are set out in terms of how such deaths occur and also how that affects their subsequent investigation. Finally, all of these issues occur in the 'age of austerity' when public spending is being cut severely, significantly affecting police budgets. The chapter considers what effect such cuts have on the issues set out above. A common axiom is that 'society gets the police it deserves'—what I want to discuss in this chapter is: what sort of police have we got? How do we expect the police to act in complex multi-agency cases involving vulnerable individuals, with an ambiguous role and function, while constantly being exhorted to 'do more with less'? And how does all of this affect accountability in cases of DAPC?

## Roles and Functions: Relationships and Ambiguity

The police occupy a striking diversity of roles. These include: order maintenance, peace keeping, crime prevention, public reassurance and crime control (Reiner 2010; McLaughlin 2007). Police react to a complex variety of events and issues that occur in a variety of contexts. Reactivity is a key part of their role and, to a large extent, what the public expect from the police (Redshaw et al. 1995; Morgan and Newburn 1997). Surrette (2007: 202) and Reiner (2013: 164) assert that what the police actually do compared to what the public perceive they do exists as a 'law of opposites'. Whereas the public commonly perceive of police as crime fighters, the canon of academic literature on policing suggests police have multiple roles with crime fighting being a relatively minor consideration if compared with the issue of maintaining social order. This raises the issue highlighted by numerous authors as to whether police officers are actually 'peace officers' (Reiner 2013: 165). One view from the USA (Shane 2013: 69) is that they might be better conceived of as 'safety officers'. Given the events leading to the death of Sean Rigg the relevance of 'safety' or 'peace' officers is revisited in due course to consider their role in the preservation of life. Evidently the way society, the state and the police themselves view the police role must have an effect on how police act, whether as enforcement officers or 'safety' officers. This could directly affect the issue of DAPC, particularly when, as we have established, the police role is essentially ambiguous.

Legitimacy is widely held to be key in ensuring societal consent for the police function. Legitimacy in police work in its most basic sense relates to being fair, honest and trustworthy (Skogan and Frydl 2004). The public expect the police to fulfil a wide variety of functions that ensure public safety. Conversely, the police rely on public support, both in terms of practical assistance in the form of information, but also in terms of tacit approval by conferring legitimacy on the police to act on behalf of society. This, then, is the basis of consensual policing in England and Wales and underlines the importance of a functional relationship between police and society.

Terpstra and Trommel (2009) believe that police legitimacy may be conceived of in four ways. First, in terms of what the organisation accomplishes. This relates to performance management which they term 'consequential legitimacy'. Second, in terms of presenting themselves as a cultural model that enables the organisation to behave in a way that is meaningful and relevant to society, they call this 'cognitive legitimacy'. This is supported by Tyler and Fagan (2008), who note that legitimacy can be enhanced by having transparent and fair procedures that manifest themselves in positive experiences for the public. Third, Terpstra and Trommel (2009) believe that legitimacy may be produced by the use of socially accepted techniques or procedures, termed '*procedural* legitimacy'. This suggests that deference to the police originates from a public respect of police authority rather than from threats of coercion or sanction (Jackson et al. 2013; Hinds and Fleming 2006). Finally, legitimacy may be simply construed as self-interested calculations made by social groups, and is known as '*pragmatic* legitimacy'. Terpstra and Trommel's (2009) four perspectives of legitimacy are used throughout this book to demonstrate the relational nature of legitimacy as it applies in different contexts to the issue of DAPC.

Legitimacy can be seen from a number of different perspectives and is a relational concept in policing. In any given incident, legitimacy could depend on (but is not limited to) the audience present, the place, the incident itself, the actions or omissions of police, or the prevailing political, social, legal, economic or cultural climate within society. This means that, to a great extent, police do not entirely 'own' legitimacy (Ponsaers 2015). Clearly the relationship between police and society is dynamic (Palmiotto and Unnithan 2011). In cases of DAPC, a continuum of police action that incorporates the use of force and the preservation of life appears to fit the view of numerous authors in the field that policing is a complex activity (Reiner 2010; Punch 2009; McLaughlin 2007; Waddington 1999; Bittner 1975). As the police role is ambiguous and the nature of legitimacy is relational this means that maintaining legitimacy, particularly in cases of DAPC is problematic. It suggests that the relationship between legitimacy and accountability is key in cases of DAPC and that it is subject to the dynamic relationship between police, state and society.

## Legitimacy and Accountability

Events such the 1984/5 miner's strike and the 1981 Brixton Riots effectively led to certain communities' relationship with the police experiencing a breakdown in legitimacy (Leishman and Mason 2003). The Stephen Lawrence case raised more general concerns about the broader role of police, particularly about interaction with BME groups (Jesilow and Meyer 2001). Similarly, the deaths of Ian Tomlinson[1] and Jean Charles de Menezes[2] generated public unease about the legitimate right of police to use force (Greer and McLaughlin 2012). Conversely, the role of police at Hillsborough[3] highlighted concerns about their ability to preserve life (Scraton et al. 1995). To some degree, these events challenge the symbolic construction of legitimate policing in the eyes of the public. Writing about cases of DAPC, Benn and Worpole (1986: 41) observe: 'It is the consistency with which officers have remained unprosecuted even after clear crimes have been committed that produces the deepest cynicism about the police amongst many people.' This observation from the 1980s seems topical today and suggests that although there may have been change on the issue of DAPC, the societal perception is that little has changed in terms of police being prosecuted. From another perspective, Belur's (2009, 2010) research suggests that a societal majority tacitly accepts that, although unfortunate, 'accidents' will happen if the police utilise their mandate to use force. This underlines the importance of legitimacy to police actions—the use of force may be socially accepted by society provided that its exercise appears to be legitimate, echoing Terpstra and Trommel's (2009) notion of pragmatic legitimacy.

Legitimacy may also be enhanced by police engaging with errors and aiming to deal effectively with misconduct or poor performance. Similarly, it might be the case that as police attempt to live up to increased public expectations, the level of scrutiny of their actions increases (Chermak and Weiss 2005). Cronin and Reicher (2009) assert that to some extent, police practice is shaped by the need to produce legitimacy to audiences that are able to sanction the police, which leads to a question about who and where these audiences might be, as was discussed in the Introduction and is further analysed in Chap. 6. Attempting to overtly manage the construction of legitimacy may result in the public becoming suspicious

---

[1] Died after being struck with a police baton and pushed to the ground in London by an MPS officer during the London G20 protests in 2009. Determined to have been 'unlawfully killed' by a coroner's court jury in 2011.

[2] Died after being shot dead by undercover police in London in the aftermath of the 7/7 terrorist attacks. The MPS reached an £100,000 legal settlement with Mr de Menezes' family and offered an 'unreserved apology' for his 'tragic' death (Dodd 2009).

[3] Failure by police to control the crowd at a football match in Sheffield in 1989 led to ninety-six people dying and subsequent attempts by police to cover up what actually happened.

and distrustful of the police due to the obtrusive nature of such a construct (Terpstra and Trommel 2009). The discussion above needs to be balanced by noting that the majority of the public do not have direct experience of police activity (Morgan and Newburn 1997; Bittner 1975). Consequently, this underlines the symbolic nature of much of the discussion around the production of legitimacy and consensus amongst society about the police and their role. Legitimacy is fundamentally important to the police function and intimately linked to the way in which accountability is constructed in cases of DAPC. Legitimacy is not only a relational concept, but also a symbolic and practical construct with regards to police, state and society.

## Symbolic and Practical Representations of Policing

The police are a symbolic representation of the state and consequently a visible manifestation of its relationship with citizens (Loader and Walker 2001). They are keenly aware of their symbolic value to society, particularly in terms of order maintenance and peace keeping (Morgan 1992). This type of symbolic function bolsters public confidence and in turn produces legitimacy. Policing is both a matter of symbolism and substance, and to some degree one reinforces the other (Mawby 2002). Both 'factual' and 'fictional' representations of the police confer legitimacy on them being an organisation that is necessary and generally effective (Reiner 2010). The construction of legitimacy involves both substantive and symbolic elements, as outlined above. The latter tends to receive greater focus than the former due to the importance invested in the police by society as a symbolic institution (Terpstra and Trommel 2009). A lack of effectiveness may not necessarily affect the symbolic value of police to society in terms of fulfilling a useful purpose, as the 'factual' and 'fictional' representations do not necessarily co-exist in the public's perception of the police (Reiner 2000).

One manifestation of this is the symbolic representation that police are subject to the same laws as citizens. This is critiqued by Smith (2001) who asserts that this may be the case in theory, but on the basis of empirical research, police are significantly less likely to be prosecuted than citizens, particularly in cases where citizens die. One focus of social media movements such as #blacklivesmatter and 'Hands Up United' is the repeated failure of US police officers to be prosecuted in cases of DAPC. Thus one might say that police symbolism works both ways: for campaigners in cases of DAPC, the failure to prosecute has become highly symbolic of the asymmetry of power in the relationship between police, state and society. It is clear that the relationship between symbolic and practical policing affects how relational forms of legitimacy and accountability are constructed, and this is manifest in the increasingly complex structures of regulation that police are subject to.

Policing works within an increasingly diverse arrangement of structures to manage and regulate activity and promote best practice. In the first instance, the practical application of policy and statute is ensured by the PSD (Professional Standards Department) within each force, supported by the supervision of line managers (Waddington 1999). HMIC (Her Majesty's Inspectorate of Constabulary) and the IPCC represent external organisations that provide accountability in policing, formulating guidelines and policies that aim to promote best practice. Regarding cases of DAPC one example is the IPCC's 'Learning the Lessons' series[4] that focuses on reducing the number of such deaths by improving best practice based on findings from previous cases. HMIC's (2013) report 'A Criminal Use of Police Cells?' on the use of police cells as a place of safety for those detained under s136 of the Mental Health Act 1983 is an example of guidelines that aim to promulgate best practice in relation to a marginalised group.

ACPO (Association of Chief Police Officers)[5] and the National Policing Improvement Agency (NPIA)[6] are examples of organisations within the 'policing family' that formulate policy and guidance about events and developments within the policing environment. A key example of this is the 'Guidance on the Safer Detention and Handling of Persons in Police

---

[4] It should be noted that this series was originally begun as a Home Office initiative in collaboration with the Police Complaints Authority (PCA) in 1998 (see, for example Leigh et al. 1998).

[5] This agency was replaced by the National Police Chiefs Council (NPCC) in April 2015.

[6] This agency was replaced by the College of Policing (CP) in January 2013.

Custody' produced by ACPO in conjunction with the NPIA, the first edition appearing in 2006 with a second, updated edition published in 2012. This document is particularly relevant in accountability construction in cases of DAPC as demonstrated in Chaps. 4 and 5. It provides frameworks and directions as to how detainees should be treated and emphasises the importance of duty of care, particularly the preservation of life, an issue noted by the jury verdict in the death of Sean Rigg. Policy developments from the IPCC, ACPO and HMIC illustrate that the environment within which accountability is constructed in cases of DAPC is evolving, and driven in part by the requirements of Article 2 of the ECHR.

Policing is notable for its hierarchy and rigid structures of management and supervision. The division of the 'rank and file' from management leads to a system whereby policies and procedures are determined by senior managers and external agencies in response to statutory regulation, but their application is enacted by more junior officers who must exercise discretion in order to do so. In this sense, 'buy in' from junior officers in the formulation of policies and guidelines is key to them being followed in practice (Cronin and Reicher 2009; Uildriks and van Mastrigt 1991). In order to promote and maintain the production of legitimacy and consensus, policing in practice must have a relationship with policy and law. It is one thing for more policies and guidelines to be published on the issue of DAPC, but quite another for those policies and guidelines to be enacted by officers on the ground, as was evident in the events leading to the death of Sean Rigg.

## Discretion: A Relational Concept

Discretion is a key feature in the practical application of policing. It is typically exercised by those at more junior levels of the organisation (Newburn 2008). There is widespread agreement amongst academic authors that discretion in police work is both inevitable and essential (see, for example Poyser 2004; Wortley 2003; Westmarland 2001). Discretion is also noted as being widely linked to discrimination regarding which social group or individual becomes subject to it (Ellis 2010). This appears to be partly related to the situationally variable use of discretion highlighted by Terril and Mastrofski (2002) and Rojek et al. (2012). It depends, amongst other issues, on certain places, times and individuals—what might be commonplace police practice in one location, with a certain group at a certain time, might be quite different given alternative situational variables. In cases of DAPC this can relate to police using force or not.

Each officer is granted discretion on the basis that they will legitimately exercise their right to use it in given circumstances. Not all infractions can be dealt with due to time constraints and also the ambiguity of police role and functions. At the most basic level, an officer's use of discretion with a member of public covers the gamut from inaction, to giving a verbal reprimand, caution, arrest, through to the use of lethal force. These are subjective decisions made by individual officers and can be notionally held to account in retrospect. Discretion plays a significant part in determining police action or inaction in cases of DAPC as is established in Chaps. 4 and 5. It tends to be exercised in incidents that occur out of sight of passers-by and are largely unsupervised. This illustrates the paradox of discretion—it is a key function of policing, yet can also be problematic due to its inherent informality and lack of oversight.

Discretion is a useful starting point for understanding instances of police misconduct (McLaughlin 2007). Simmons (2012) proposes that misconduct stems from organisational cultures, and therefore attempts to minimise misconduct should focus on changing cultures as distinct from focusing on structural or organisational change, a view shared by Maguire (1991). Furthermore, he asserts (2012: 9) that police culture tolerates misconduct in a number of ways: by failing to monitor and discipline 'problem' officers; by officers maintaining a 'code of silence'; and because of a belief in the underlying necessity of force. This creates an 'us and them' mentality when put into the context of police interactions with marginalised groups in society that has been noted by many authors (see, for example Westmarland 2013; McLaughlin 1991). The gap between policy and practice can be exemplified by cultural issues in policing potentially causing a drift away from what the public deems to be legitimate, accountable or desirable in the realm of police activity. Conversely, technological advances mean that police discretion is subject to greater public surveillance than has previously been the case, an issue illustrated by the case of Ian Tomlinson (Goldsmith 2010; Price 2011). A more recent development is the increasing use of police body cameras to monitor encounters with citizens. The limited research currently available suggests that their use both reduces the use of police force and reduces citizens' use of force against police (see, for example Birch 2016; Ariel et al. 2015).

Bullock and Johnson's (2012) research on the impact of the HRA 1998 (itself a reaction to the obligation imposed on the state by the ECHR) on policing discovered that, somewhat counter-intuitively, officers used principles embedded in the Act to enable a greater degree of discretion in practice. The competing mix of principles, guidelines and policies that exist within the diversity of roles occupied by the police affords officers a good deal of discretion when practically applying their powers. Several commentators (see, for example: Uildriks and van Mastrigt 1991; Waddington 1999; Reiner 2010) have noted that officers at the 'sharp end' may act in ways tacitly accepted by senior officers while simultaneously being publicly condemned by those same officers. If discretion is exercised injudiciously, it might be a useful tool for senior ranks to distance themselves from actions taken at an operational level and dealing with issues on the basis of them being individual misdemeanours as distinct to them being more representative of systemic or cultural issues. The importance of investigating the wider issue of DAPC in relation to organisational systems as distinct from individual cases has already been noted and is further discussed throughout this book. Furthermore, the disparity between policy and practice demonstrates a potential accountability gap in cases of DAPC that does not sit comfortably with concepts such as legitimacy, consensus, transparency and the use of force.

It is possible to state that police are effectively accountable to no one due to the degree of discretion they are able to exercise (Waddington 1999). This raises a question about how effective policies, statute and guidelines can be in cases of DAPC. Rationally, one can be held accountable only for acts or omissions that come to light. As the basis of police work is that a significant part of it relates to interactions between a small number of individuals that are often unsupervised, Waddington's point appears sound. It is supported by Martin and Scott Bray (2013) who question whether police *could* be held to account. If a key function of policing is order maintenance, then it follows that exercising discretion is a logical corollary of this function. The ability to hold this function to account is therefore fundamentally important when considering officers' ability to use force rather than maintain order in any given situation, particularly if officers claim that the use of force was necessary to maintain order. Echoing the earlier discussion about relationships between policy and principles in police work, Reiner (2000: 72) believes the ability to hold officers to account may be less important than ensuring: 'working procedures and norms which embody universal respect for the rights even of weak or unpopular minorities, which the rhetoric of legality purports to represent'. This underlines the limitations of policy and law to police work and highlights the importance of occupational culture in affecting how police go about their work. It would seem that attempts to influence how discretion is used would need to incorporate a cultural shift within police work, and a wide range of authors (see for example Chan and Dixon 2007; Cronin and Reicher 2009; Gilsinan 2012) have noted that changing occupational culture is notoriously complex and riven with potential pitfalls. The exercise of discretion is inextricably linked with an officer's ability to legitimately use force, and it is to this topic that we now turn.

## Use of Force

The authority to use force within the state is principally entrusted to the police (Bittner 1975). The inappropriate use of 'excessive force' has been an ongoing concern in many countries, despite the existence of internal and external accountability structures that notionally restrain its use (Prenzler et al. 2013). Routine police work involves the threat of force coupled with techniques to avoid using it, but the threat remains, nonetheless. If police encounter opposition, force can be deployed (Reiner 2013). Police authority is typically exercised through physical presence or psychological advantage (McLaughlin 2007). Indeed, Westmarland (2001) observes that force in police work is used relatively infrequently.

Nonetheless, police do use force in certain contexts, and this can result in injury or death to citizens. Restrictions on using force are set out in common law, and in theory are equally applicable to citizens and police officers (Smith 2001). When force is deployed, it should be 'proportionate', 'necessary', and 'reasonable' to the context in which it is used (ACPO 2012). Concepts such as 'proportionate', 'necessary' and 'reasonable' are notable for being ambiguous and subjective. This dovetails with the inherent discretion and ambiguity of policing roles. Kelling (1987) observes that the justification for police interventions in volatile situations can be uncertain and contested, a point recently illustrated by the death of Mark Duggan.[7]

The unique capacity of the police to legitimately use force means that public agencies tend to fall back on the police if they believe coercion might be necessary. When social workers, and physical or mental health practitioners feel that they do not legitimately have the capacity to use force, their last resort is to 'call the cops' (Bittner 1975: 43). This means that, to some extent, the police may be considered an 'agency of last resort'. Society expects police to use force if necessary and consequently seem less likely to be critical of the police if they resort to it, as is illustrated in Chap. 4 (see, for example Belur 2009; Smith 2009). On the other hand, if the use of force appears to be disproportionate, unreasonable, and excessive, public opprobrium may result and damage legitimacy (see, for example Greer and McLaughlin 2012; Hirschfield and Simon 2010). This demonstrates the subjective and relational nature of legitimacy: the use of force may be constructed as being positive or negative when life is extinguished, thus illustrating the complex and relational aspects of accountability construction in these cases. These observations underscore the limitations of policy, guidelines and structures in minimising the use of force and also the fundamental relevance of discretion to the occupational reality of policing. Numerous authors (see, for example McLaughlin 2007; Smith 2001; Reiner 2000) assert that if the police are to be the primary agency legitimately capable of exerting force on citizens, then it is of the utmost importance that they are held accountable through democratic, transparent systems and procedures in order to ensure that legitimacy and consensus are maintained.

---

[7] Shot dead by MPS officers in London in 2011. Widely believed to have precipitated the London riots that followed (Dodd 2014).

# Marginalised Groups

Marginalised groups that come into contact with the police, particularly in cases of DAPC, are typically characterised as individuals from BME groups; with mental health issues; or with dependency issues (IPCC 2012). The police focus on the former group has been the subject of a significant body of academic literature (see, for example Rowe 2007; McLaughlin 1991). It is not my intention here to examine this in detail, other than to note that BME communities are disproportionately over-represented in cases of DAPC. With regards to the other two groups, it appears from this research that police increasingly come into contact with these groups due to other agencies' failings (see, for example Coles and Shaw 2012; Kutcher et al. 2009; Fulton 2008). The agencies involved are typically part of NHS provision in England and Wales. In this sense, police might be considered the 'agency of last resort' in reacting to marginalised individuals when other agencies are absent. It might also be argued that the police are an agency of first resort in the absence of other agencies, and that this may become increasingly prevalent in an age of austerity, as will be discussed directly. This highlights both the diversity of police roles and functions and their dynamic relationship with society and other state agencies, as was illustrated in the death of Sean Rigg.

Marginalised groups represent an exponentially growing portion of society due to increasing pluralism (Reiner 2000). Growing inequalities in society are marked by increasing numbers of immigrants and expanding areas of poverty, particularly in urban areas (Morgan and Newburn 1997). These observations support the assertion that marginalised groups have effectively become citizens who do not enjoy a full set of rights when interacting with police (Waddington 1999). Reiner (2000: 79) calls this a process of 'de-incorporation'. It may also be the case that legitimacy and accountability are maintained within the majority of society at the expense of those marginalised groups who are disproportionately affected by police violence (Hirschfield and Simon 2010; Uildriks and van Mastrigt 1991). Thus the relationship police have with society depends to some extent upon which section of society they deal with and in what context.

Concerns over the use of excessive force by the police were driven in part by the number of high-profile cases of DAPC, particularly involving individuals from BME groups, which occurred in the years around the death of Stephen Lawrence (see, for example Savage 2007b; Morgan and Newburn 1997). More recently, the deaths of Ian Tomlinson, Azelle Rodney[8] and Sean Rigg have kept issues of accountability, excessive use of force and marginalised groups firmly in the public eye. Evidence states that in 2011, 38 per cent of cases of DAPC were from BME backgrounds,[9] and that 'almost half' of those who died had mental health issues[10] (HAC 2013: 3). These observations support Scraton's (2002) view that such deaths might be better considered the result of structural factors rather than being constructed as individual tragedies. These structural factors include the tendency to be in contact with public service organisations other than the police, and also in combination with the police, as was discussed above. This raises the relevance of multi-agency working, and how this might be relevant in cases of DAPC in terms of working practices, and learning lessons.

## Multi-agency Working and Austerity

As many of the people who die in cases of DAPC have mental health or substance-dependency issues, it is unsurprising that they should come into contact with healthcare services in addition to the police. If public services are to play a part in creating a society in which the right to life is enabled, as envisaged by Article 2 of the ECHR, then clearly public services working in isolation is not ideal, particularly when considering vulnerable members of society. The extent, therefore, to which public services can cooperate and coordinate their service delivery should be part of the key to reducing the number of deaths after police contact. As

---

[8] Died after being shot six times by MPS undercover armed police in 2005. Found to have been 'unlawfully killed' by judicial inquiry in 2013.

[9] This compares to census figures from 2011 which state that the BME population of England and Wales was 14 per cent (ONS 2012).

[10] This compares to estimates from MIND that 25 per cent of the population of the UK have mental health issues (MIND 2012).

the death of Sean Rigg illustrated, better communications between his mental health team, the community mental health hostel provider, the CAD operators and police could all have led to his death being avoided.

The issue of multi-agency working has been the subject of much academic research (see, for example Charman 2014; Shane 2013; Skinns 2011). A common theme is that while it is essential to provide joined-up public services to an increasingly plural and complex society, this is difficult to achieve in practice. The reasons for this are manifold, but the key issues are addressed here. First, each of the public services involved has different aims and purposes, meaning that whereas police may see a case in terms of law enforcement, the NHS may see the same case as being one of care provision (Skinns 2011). Second, these organisations are large, complex bureaucracies that tend to be characterised by hierarchical structures. Such organisations are notable for having trouble communicating within their structures, let alone communicating with other public sector organisations (Charman 2014). Third, and related to the previous points, these organisations function principally as regional services, albeit they exist at a national level. This means that if they are to cooperate this needs to be negotiated and agreed at a regional level between the relevant services (de Viggiani et al. 2010). In England and Wales, there are forty-three police forces, 155 NHS trusts, fifty-six mental health trusts and ten ambulance trusts (NHS Confederation 2015). This means that some police forces have agreements (usually termed protocols) with healthcare trusts about operational practice, and others do not (see, for example Payne-James et al. 2010). In practice this means, for example, that in parts of the country officers who wish to take drunk detainees to a hospital accident and emergency department may do so, but in other parts of the country they are dissuaded from doing so because no protocol exists between the local force and NHS trust (see, for example Deehan et al. 2002).

The discussion above must also be put into the context of cuts in spending on public services during the government's austerity drive since 2010. This has seen police officer numbers fall by approximately 17,000 in the period 2010–15, and a projected further cut in policing staff of 22,000 by 2020 (Dodd 2015); in mental health services, acute bed places were reduced by 2,100 in the period 2011–15 (Cooper 2015a); and a speech by the Chancellor demanding that the NHS find £22bn savings by 2020 illustrates how services will continue to be affected (Cooper 2015b). These cuts have been made in addition to significant cuts to local authority budgets that have affected the provision of welfare based services such as social work, housing provision, homeless outreach programmes and programmes aimed at those dependent on substances. These developments create an environment whereby marginalised groups are expanding while provision to support them is contracting. In particular, the increase in mental health-related conditions during an economic recession is well documented (see, for example Marmot et al. 2013; Mattheys 2015). In a simple sense, public providers are expected to 'do more, with less'. This has led the current commissioner of the MPS to state that the only way for public services to provide effective services in the future is to merge provision (Dodd 2014).

The effects of these cuts on the issue of DAPC is as yet uncertain, but it seems reasonable to assert that the police will increasingly become the agency of last resort due to an increasingly circumscribed provision of healthcare services when demand for those services is rising. The importance of relationships to understanding issues related to cases of DAPC is examined throughout this book, and is highlighted in this section on multi-agency working. The diversity of role and function in policing is further complicated by their interaction with other public services, serving to underline the relationality of provision, particularly in relation to healthcare and welfare in cases of DAPC. Interdependence is woven into these relationships, as is also the case in the role and function of organisations in the police regulatory sphere. Thus the diversity of role and function, the importance of relationships, and the relationality of practice are also manifest in the sphere of regulatory accountability that aims to hold police accountable, as is discussed below.

## Accountability: Dynamic Relationships

At the most basic level, Zedner (2006) believes that asking who *ought* to control the police is key to any question on police accountability. The police are subject to a 'proliferation of regulatory agencies' who might hold them to account (Savage 2007a: 315). The relevance of the PSD, the IPCC, ACPO, the NPIA and HMIC has been previously established. Police are also subject to the civil, criminal and coronial court system in England and Wales. Civil prosecutions of police officers are more common than criminal prosecutions, partly because they are more likely to succeed, thus highlighting the relational importance of the legal forum to the type of accountability applied (Smith 2004). Furthermore, since 2012 police are accountable to democratically elected Police and Crime Commissioners (PCCs) (Reiner 2013). Moreover, as Reid (2005) notes, each chief constable is ultimately accountable to the Home Secretary. Accountability is also provided by Parliament through its daily business and the increasingly vocal HAC (House of Commons Home Affairs Select Committee).

In a more diffuse sense, police may be held accountable by the media (see Greer and McLaughlin 2012; Goldsmith 2010), pressure groups (see Savage et al. 2007) and finally, the public who ultimately confer legitimacy on the police and can therefore notionally withdraw it (Seneviratne 2002). The diversity of groups seeking accountability means a very broad section of interests are able to call upon the police to demonstrate their accountability depending on a number of contingencies. This has two consequences: first, the police are aware of the need for their actions to be perceived as accountable (Cronin and Reicher 2009). Second, the various groupings have interests that do not necessarily overlap and depend upon particular agendas. These competing discourses influence the complex nature of accountability construction in cases of DAPC and illustrate the relational aspect of accountability. Police accountability is constructed in a context of interdependence with numerous other public services, regulatory organisations and not least, the public.

Accountability may exist in the first instance with the police protecting the public and ensuring their safety (Sen 2010); it may relate to the upholding of procedural obligations imposed upon the police in terms of legal or policy requirements (Klockars et al. 2006); and/or it could be viewed from organisational or financial perspectives (Edwards 2005). Symbolically, police not only need to be held accountable, but they need to be seen to be held accountable in order to promote legitimacy (Warburton 2004). The discussion on accountability mirrors the earlier discussion of legitimacy in terms of it being established as a relational construct. Subjectivity and ambiguity are inherent in the concepts of legitimacy and accountability. Public demands for increased police accountability may have more to do with public sensitivity and changes to normative values in society than any escalation in police misconduct (Reiner 2000). To some degree this is borne out by the relatively stable number of cases of DAPC over the last ten years (see Fig. 2.1).

The ambiguity of the police role is reflected in their mode of account-ability, which is equivocal. For much of their history, the police self-policed their domain, but calls grew from a panoply of interested parties demanding greater transparency and independence in how police are held accountable (Savage 2007a). As such the police are no different to other large public institutions such as the NHS or the Prison Service in being affected by trends driven by increasingly managerialist agendas. That said, Waddington (1999) notes that despite the MPS being lauded as a model for responsive policing the world over, it remains one of the least

| Year | Deaths |
| --- | --- |
| 2004/5 | 153 |
| 2005/6 | 161 |
| 2006/7 | 133 |
| 2007/8 | 126 |
| 2008/9 | 149 |
| 2009/10 | 140 |
| 2010/11 | 147 |
| 2011/12 | 122 |
| 2012/13 | 130 |
| 2013/14 | 136 |
| 2014/15 | 142 |
| Total | 1539 |

Fig. 2.1  Deaths after police contact per year 2004–15

accountable police agencies when viewed against comparable national or international policing agencies. This suggests that accountability might have less to do with legitimate policing than first meets the eye and perhaps more to do with the symbolic representation of accountability.

The current system of police accountability is viewed by Stone (2007) as 'a network of accountability'. It is clear that no single agency or organisation holds police accountable for their actions. Indeed, it is uncertain whether a single agency or organisation could, or even whether this might be ideal. Police accountability is increasingly delivered through a system of checks and balances spread across several agencies and organisations (Van Sluis et al. 2009; Puddister and Riddel 2012). This underlines the relational nature of accountability provision and raises questions about how different organisations construct accountability and how they relate to each other in the processes of accountability construction (see, for example Skinns 2011). Whether the process of accountability construction in cases of DAPC in England and Wales could be termed a 'system' or 'network' is examined in more detail in Chap. 7.

Chan (1999: 253) views policing and accountability less optimistically than Stone (2007), preferring to interpret the concept of accountability as *evaluation*, which is not synonymous with accountability. As such, any inability to meet certain prescribed standards may not be problematic because the primary importance of evaluation is an ability to: 'satisfy "audiences" by providing an acceptable excuse or justification, a credible denial, or an apology'. Viewed from this perspective, systems of accountability exist to placate potentially censorious voices, not necessarily promote high standards of professionalism or lawfulness. Furthermore, Chan and Dixon (2007) found that a managerialist approach leads to a focus on quantitative analysis of issues as distinct from cultural issues that might exist in the production of those statistics, an issue that appears to be particularly relevant in cases of DAPC as is discussed in Chaps. 4 and 5. It might be explained by managerialist traits within (but not limited to) the police that tend to focus more on policies, audit trails and representational strategies as distinct from practical, operational functions that police perform (Stone 2007; Chan 1999). This may further enhance the argument towards symbolic structures being more relevant in justifying the legitimacy and accountability of the police use of force rather than the actual efficacy of these structures. What is clear is that by the early twenty-first century societal and state expectations of police accountability had evolved to include concepts such as 'independence', 'accountability' and 'transparency' (Harrison and Cuneen 2000).

Literature on police complaints procedures (see, for example Waddington 1999) notes a focus on individual officers and cases as distinct from organisational or systemic factors. There is a tendency to view incidents such as cases of DAPC as bad practice or mismanagement by individual officers from the outset as distinct to being potentially criminal acts, or as having their foundations in organisational cultures (Shane 2013; Gottschalk 2009; Shaw and Coles 2007). The practice of investigating cases of DAPC on an individual basis can lead to a lack of oversight of systemic issues affecting accountability and the use of police force (Smith 2009; Waddington 1999). Smith (2001: 375) points out that all cases being dealt with as complaints prior to any decision to pursue criminal prosecutions epitomises the asymmetrical power structures involved because: 'the police officer arguably enjoys a privileged position relative to the citizen from the outset'. In a later article (2009), he argues that this state of affairs co-exists with the development of international human rights laws that place the onus on the state to overtly demonstrate its respect for the right to life of each individual citizen, as is discussed in the following chapter. Clearly there are numerous tensions apparent in relationships between both the roles of the police and between organisations related to police oversight on the issue of DAPC.

## Accountability in Cases of Death after Police Contact

While there is a significant body of academic literature on the police role and function, their use of force, and how police accountability might be produced in theory and practice, there is relatively little written on the issue of DAPC (Sim 2004). One exception is Savage (2008) who notes that cases of DAPC are highly symbolic as they are bound up with other factors such as transparency, the quality of justice and effectiveness of accountability structures. Savage (2008) aside, much of what is written tends to focus on media representations of DAPC (see, for example Hirschfield and Simon 2010; Greer and McLaughlin 2012); or to focus on the broader issue of regulators holding police accountable (see, for example Savage et al. 2009; Smith 2013). However, numerous official reports and research papers exist on the issue of DAPC from diverse sources such as the IPCC (and its predecessor, the PCA), ACPO, NPIA or HMIC; from Parliament, for example via the HAC or the Independent Advisory Panel (IAP) on deaths in custody; from medical bodies such as the British Medical Association (BMA) and the Faculty of Forensic and Legal Medicine (FFLM); and from NGOs (Non-Governmental Organisations) such as *Inquest*.

Deaths in police custody were not counted at a national level in England and Wales until 1981. This followed a recommendation from the first HAC (1980) report into deaths in police custody (Rogers and Lewis 2007). This is in stark contrast to the situation in the United States where legislation was passed enabling the collation of such data in 2000 (Fyfe 2002). In 2015 the *Washington Post*, in conjunction with the UK newspaper the *Guardian* began to collate data from media sources that charted the number of deaths after police contact in the USA, thus illustrating that such data is not being collated nationally in the USA. This data is updated daily on the website 'The Counted'. In November 2015 the figure had already exceeded 1,000 deaths since the start of that year. In October 2015, James Comey, director of the FBI, called the lack of national US police data on police shooting 'embarrassing' and 'ridiculous' (Davis and Lowery 2015). Nor is the lack of data on DAPC limited to the USA, with Bruce-Jones (2015) noting a failure to compile such data in Germany. Figure 2.1 sets out the annual number of DAPC cases in England and Wales during the period 2004–15 (IPCC 2014).

Police, like most large organisations, tend to activate critical thinking subsequent to acts that occur (Gilsinan 2012). In this sense, one might note that not only are the police a reactive agency on behalf of the public, but also a reactive agency when considering their own actions (Chan and Dixon 2007). This leads to a situation whereby it is more common to piece together events and seek justification for them in the aftermath of an incident than to promote an environment that seeks to minimise the occurrence of such events in the first place, much as Chan (1999) envisaged by re-imagining 'accountability' as 'evaluation'. It is therefore logical to investigate how accountability *is* constructed in cases of DAPC and consider what this suggests about the nature of accountability production and construction in cases of DAPC regarding the relationship between the police, state and society in England and Wales.

Article 2 of the ECHR has been a key driver in how accountability construction has altered in cases of DAPC. Article 2 partly resulted in a parliamentary Joint Commission on Human Rights (JCHR) report in 2004 focusing on the issue of deaths in all types of state custody. This proposed that a joint party committee should be set up to monitor the issue and suggested that an independent review be set up to design such a committee. This eventually became the Independent Advisory Panel (IAP) on deaths in custody. As part of this process the Fulton review reported in 2008 and set out the key issues on deaths in custody. It noted that deaths in custody were 'uniquely serious'; that those who died were owed a 'special duty of care'; that factors involved in such cases were complex; that similarly these cases were notable for more than one organisation being involved in the death; and that 'deaths could be prevented … if there were more effective ways of learning lessons across sectors' (Fulton 2008: 13.1). These issues encapsulate much of the focus of this book. For the time being, however, the focus will rest on the 'duty of care' and 'learning lessons' aspects in relation to Fulton's findings. Article 2 of the ECHR makes clear that the state should create an environment where life is enabled, rather than merely seeking to prevent death. While there is an increasing focus from the state on the issue of DAPC there appears to be little change in terms of a reduction in the number of people who die. It is difficult to escape the conclusion that much of the effort expended on this issue has been focused on the production of policies and directives as distinct from addressing the structural and cultural issues that may result in deaths occurring.

Writing about the criminal justice system, Doyle (2010) and Shane (2013) take their cue from Reason's (1990) work on error and fatal accidents in the fields of surgery and aeronautics. Their primary focus is on changing culture within policing to more closely resemble these professional fields. Doyle (2010: 130) notes that both medicine and aeronautics have cultures that encourage openness when dealing with errors, but that reporting error in the criminal justice system is unlikely due to the culture of 'it's best not to say anything where possible'. In this analysis, 'near misses'[11] in other fields are treated as opportunities to learn lessons that can be applied to future practice, whereas in the criminal justice system: '[a] near miss generates grim sighs of relief, but little incentive for instigating an analysis' (Doyle 2010: 135). Shane (2013: 3) argues that a 'culture of safety' might grow from this approach. He notes that when deaths occur they cannot usually be attributed to an individual person and thus must be considered within the organisational contexts in which the death occurred. Razack (2015) notes that a culture of care tends not to be a primary consideration in police custody, and that this needs to change to reduce the number of cases of DAPC. All of this suggests that the investigation of such deaths should consider the cultures within which they occur, much as envisaged by the requirements of Article 2 of the ECHR, as is discussed in the following chapter.

Shane (2013) asserts that the management role of the police should focus on reducing error and promoting a culture of safety. From this perspective, he believes that it is not merely a question of reviewing what an individual did, but what conditions produced the actions or omissions that led to a death. Both Doyle (2010) and Shane (2013) believe that policing culture must change from the 'bottom up' and incorporate continuous quality improvement rather than focus on retrospective process driven inspection. This is some distance from current police practice and also regulatory practice about policing, but practitioner literature overlaps with these ideas. Coles and Shaw (2012) talk about 'accountable learning'; and Downham and Lingham (2009) discuss the importance of 'organisational learning'. Both focus on the relevance of Article 2 of the ECHR in ensuring a thorough investigation is undertaken into all deaths in custody. The importance of preserving life has long been acknowledged by police, but it is now a matter of legal necessity due to the state's obligation to Article 2 of the ECHR. Clearly, the issue of accountability construction in cases of DAPC is evolving and being driven by numerous dynamic imperatives. This book aims to understand how and why these changes occur and what they say about accountability construction in cases of DAPC.

---

[11] An IPCC ten-year review into cases of DAPC noted approximately 1,000 'near misses' in the period 1998–2008 (Hannan et al. 2010).

## Conclusion

Police aim to fulfil a wide range of roles and functions and this leads to ambiguity over their general purpose to society. This is exacerbated by complications in the real and symbolic nature of policing to society as was evidenced in the principle of their role existing as a 'law of opposites'. The equivocal nature of their role is further muddied by the use of officer discretion, the use of which means that police in reality may be accountable to no one. While the police rely on society viewing their activities as legitimate in order to achieve societal consensus, both legitimacy and consensus have been shown to be relational concepts and thus dependent upon a complex number of contingencies.

The issues above come to a head in cases of DAPC. Officer discretion, for example, can affect whether police approach individuals focusing on enforcement or welfare, as was seen in the death of Sean Rigg. This in turn can affect whether officers decide to use force or preserve life in the first instance. These issues have a real effect on marginalised groups in England and Wales because they are proportionately more likely to die after coming into contact with police than any other group in society. A significant majority of people who die in cases of DAPC have mental health issues or substance dependency; this means they have often been in contact with healthcare providers in addition to the police, as was also seen in the death of Sean Rigg. This creates further complexities in these deaths due to questions over the capacity of police to deal with such individuals, both from a point of view of skills and knowledge, but also from the point of view of austerity and cuts to public services.

All of this leads to cases of DAPC being characterised by complexity, multi-causality and also being of symbolic relevance to the state and society. Thus accountability in these cases is both important to society and the state but also often likely to be contentious due to the complex interactions involved in such deaths. It has been established that accountability, like legitimacy and consensus, is a relational construct. The following chapter looks in more detail at how accountability is constructed in cases of DAPC by the two regulatory bodies that investigate and report on such deaths. It highlights a number of similar issues to this chapter, unsurprisingly perhaps, given that regulators must to some degree reflect aspects of those who are subject to regulation. Similar issues include the ambiguous roles and functions of the regulators, the symbolic and practical nature of regulation, the key issue of legitimacy being a relational construct, and the centrality of discretion to the processes of regulation. Not only is accountability a relational construct, but the way in which accountability is constructed is shown to be relational and dependent upon a wide variety of contexts and contingencies.

# References

ACPO. (2012). *Guidance on the safer detention and handling of persons in police custody* (2nd ed.). Available at: https://www.gov.uk/government/uploads/system/uploads/attachment_data/file/117555/safer-detention-guidance-2012.pdf. Accessed 5 Jan 2014.

Ariel, B., Farrar, W., & Sutherland, A. (2015). The effect of police body-worn cameras on use of force and citizens' complaints against police: A randomised trial. *Journal of Quantitative Criminology, 31*, 509–535.

Belur, J. (2009). Police use of deadly force: Police perceptions of a culture of approval. *Journal of Contemporary Criminal Justice, 25*(2), 237–252.

Belur, J. (2010). Why do the police use deadly force? Explaining police encounters in Mumbai. *British Journal of Criminology, 50*(2), 320–341.

Benn, M., & Worpole, K. (1986). *Death in the city*. London: Canary Press.

Birch, P. (2016). The panopticon effect: The surveillance of police officers. *Journal of Criminological Research, Policy and Practice, 2*(1), 28–39.

Bittner, E. (1975). *The functions of the police in modern society: A review of background factors, current practices and possible role models*. New York: Aronson.

Bruce-Jones, E. (2015). German policing at the intersection: Race, gender, migrant status and mental health. *Race and Class, 56*(3), 36–49.

Bullock, K., & Johnson, P. (2012). The impact of the Human Rights Act 1998 on policing in England and Wales. *British Journal of Criminology, 52*(3), 630–650.

Chan, J. (1999). Governing police practice: Limits of the new accountability. *British Journal of Sociology, 50*(2), 251–270.

Chan, J., & Dixon, D. (2007). The politics of police reform: Ten years after the Royal Commission into the New South Wales Police Service. *Criminology and Criminal Justice, 7*(4), 443–468.

Charman, S. (2014). Blue light communities: Cultural interoperability and shared learning between ambulance staff and police officers in emergency response. *Policing and Society, 24*(1), 102–119.

Chermak, S., & Weiss, A. (2005). Maintaining legitimacy using external communication strategies: An analysis of police-media relations. *Journal of Criminal Justice, 33*(5), 501–512.

Coles, D., & Shaw, H. (2012). *Learning from death in custody inquests: A new framework for action and accountability.* London: Russell Press.

Cooper, B. (2015a). 'British mental health is in crisis.' *New Statesman.* Available at: http://www.newstatesman.com/politics/health/2015/08/british-mental-health-crisis. Accessed 8 Oct 2015.

Cooper, C. (2015b). Budget 2015: George Osborne promises £8bn more annual funding for NHS by 2020. *The Independent.* Available at: http://www.independent.co.uk/life-style/health-and-families/health-news/bud/get-2015-live-emergency-uk-8bn-more-annual-funding-for-nhs-by-2020-10375397.html. Accessed 8 Oct 2015.

Cronin, P., & Reicher, S. (2009). Accountability and group dynamics. *European Journal of Social Psychology, 39*(2), 237–254.

Davis, A., & Lowery, C. (2015). FBI director calls lack of data on police shootings 'ridiculous' and 'embarrassing'. *Washington Post.* Available at: https://www.washingtonpost.com/national/fbi-director-calls-lack-of-data-on-police-shootings-ridiculous-embarrassing/2015/10/07/c0ebaf7a-6d16-11e5-b31c-d80d62b53e28_story.html. Accessed 13 Oct 2015.

De Viggiani, N., Kushner, S., Last, K., Powell, J., & Davies, J. (2010). *Police custody healthcare: An evaluation of an NHS commissioned pilot to deliver a police custody health service in a partnership between Dorset Primary Care Trust and Dorset Police.* University of West of Bristol. Available at: http://eprints.uwe.ac.uk/8253/1/PC_Evaluation_final.pdf. Accessed 10 Dec 2013.

Deehan, A., Marshall, E., & Saville, E. (2002). *Drunks and disorder: Processing intoxicated arrestees in two city-centre custody suites* (Police research series: paper 150). London: Home Office.

Dodd, V. (2009). Jean Charles de Menezes' family settles for £100,000 Met payout. *The Guardian.* Available at: http://www.theguardian.com/uk/2009/nov/23/jean-charles-de-menezes-settlement. Accessed 2 Dec 2015.

Dodd, V. (2014). Planned cuts to the police will endanger the public, says UK's top police chief. *The Guardian.* Available at: http://www.theguardian.com/uk-news/2014/dec/14/police-cuts-public-safety-bernard-hogan-howe. Accessed 8 Oct 2015.

Dodd, V. (2015). Police force could lose 22,000 jobs under new spending cuts. *The Guardian*. Available at: http://www.theguardian.com/uk-news/2015/aug/31/police-force-new-spending-cuts-22000-jobs. Accessed 8 Oct 2015.

Downham, G., & Lingham, R. (2009). Learning lessons: Using inquiries for change. *Journal of Mental Health Law, 18*(1), 57–69.

Doyle, J. (2010). Learning from error in American criminal justice. *Journal of Criminal Law and Criminology, 100*(1), 109–149.

Edwards, C. (2005). *Changing police theories for 21st century societies*. Sydney: Federation Press.

Ellis, D. (2010). Stop and search: Disproportionality, discretion and generalisations. *Police Journal, 83*(3), 1–18.

Fulton, R. (2008). Review of the forum for preventing deaths in custody: Report of the independent reviewer.

Fyfe, J. (2002). Too many missing cases: Holes in our knowledge about police use of force. *Justice Research and Policy, 4*, 87–102.

Gilsinan, J. (2012). The numbers dilemma: The chimera of modern police accountability systems. *Saint Louis University Public Law Review, 32*, 93–108.

Goldsmith, A. (2010). Policing's new visibility. *British Journal of Criminology, 50*(5), 914–934.

Gottschalk, P. (2009). Policing police crime: The case of criminals in the Norwegian police. *International Journal of Police Science and Management, 11*(4), 429–441.

Greer, C., & McLaughlin, E. (2012). This is not justice: Ian Tomlinson, institutional failure and the press politics of outrage. *British Journal of Criminology, 52*(2), 274–293.

Hannan, M., Hearnden, I., Grace, K., & Bucke, T (2010). *Deaths in or following police custody: An examination of the cases 1998/99–2008/09* (IPCC research series paper: 17). London: IPCC.

Harrison, J., & Cuneen, M. (2000). *An independent police complaints commission*. London: Liberty.

Hinds, L., & Fleming, J. (2006). Crime victimisation and political legitimacy: The importance of beliefs and experience. *Proceedings of the Australasian Political Studies Association conference, 25–27 September 2006*. Newcastle, New South Wales.

Hirschfield, P., & Simon, D. (2010). Legitimating police violence—Newspaper narratives of deadly force. *Theoretical Criminology, 14*(2), 155–182.

HMIC. (2013). *A criminal use of police cells?* Available at: http://www.hmic.gov.uk/media/a-criminal-use-of-police-cells-20130620.pdf. Accessed 14 July 2013.

House of Commons Home Affairs Committee. (1980). *Deaths in police custody: Together with the proceedings of the Committee, and the minutes of evidence and appendices.* London: HMSO.

House of Commons Home Affairs Committee. (2013). *Independent police complaints commission.* London: TSO.

IPCC. (2012). *Deaths during or following police contact: Statistics for England and Wales 2011/12.* Available at: http://www.ipcc.gov.uk/en/Pages/reports_pol-custody.aspx. Accessed 7 Nov 2012.

IPCC. (2014). *Review of the IPCC's work in investigating deaths: Final report.* Available at: http://www.ipcc.gov.uk/sites/default/files/Documents/deaths_review/Review_of_the_IPCCs_work_in_investigating_deaths_2014.pdf. Accessed 17 Mar 2014.

Jackson, J., Bradford, B., Stanko, B., & Hohl, K. (2013). *Just authority? Trust in the police in England and Wales.* Abingdon: Routledge.

Jesilow, P., & Meyer, J. (2001). The effect of police misconduct on public attitudes. *Journal of Crime and Justice, 24,* 109–121.

Kelling, G. (1987). Acquiring a taste for order: The community and the police. *Crime and Delinquency, 33*(1), 90–102.

Klockars, C., Ivkovic, S., & Haberfield, M. (2006). *Enhancing police integrity.* New York: Springer.

Kutcher, S., Bowes, M., Sanfold, F., Teehan, M., Ayer, S., Ross, J., Smith, L., & Thornhill, S. (2009). *Report of the panel of mental health and medical experts review of ED.* Available at: http://novascotia.ca/just/Public_Safety/_docs/Excited%20Delirium%20Report.pdf. Accessed 30 Sept 2013.

Leigh, A., Johnson, G., & Ingram, A. (1998). *Deaths in custody: Learning the lessons* (Police research series paper 26). London: Crown.

Leishman, F., & Mason, P. (2003). *Policing and the media. Facts, fictions and factions.* Cullompton: Willan.

Loader, I., & Walker, N. (2001). Policing as a public good: Reconstructing the connections between policing and the state. *Theoretical Criminology, 5*(1), 9–35.

Maguire, M. (1991). Complaints against the police: The British experience. In A. Goldsmith (Ed.), *Complaints against the police: The trend to external review* (pp. 178–209). Oxford: Clarendon Press.

Mark, R. (1977). *Policing a perplexed society.* London: Allen and Unwin.

Marmot, M., Bloomer, E., & Goldblatt, P. (2013). The role of social determinants in tackling health objectives in a context of economic crisis. *Public Health Reviews, 35*(1), 1–24.

Martin, G., & Scott Bray, R. (2013). Discolouring democracy? Policing, sensitive evidence, and contentious deaths in the United Kingdom. *Journal of Law and Society, 40*(4), 624–656.

Mattheys, K. (2015). The coalition, austerity and mental health. *Disability and Society, 30*(3), 475–478.

Mawby, R. (2002). *Policing images: Policing, communication and legitimacy*. Cullompton: Willan.

McLaughlin, E. (1991). Police accountability and black people: Into the 1990s. In E. Cashmore & E. McLaughlin (Eds.), *Out of order: Policing black people* (pp. 109–133). London: Routledge.

McLaughlin, E. (2007). *The new policing*. London: Sage.

MIND. (2012). *Mental health facts and statistics*. Available at: http://www.mind.org.uk/information-support/types-of-mental-health-problems/statistics-and-facts-about-mental-health/. Accessed 29 July 2013.

Morgan, R. (1992). *Talking about policing*. London: Macmillan.

Morgan, R., & Newburn, T. (1997). *The future of policing*. Oxford: Oxford University Press.

Newburn, T. (2008). *Handbook of policing* (2nd ed.). Cullompton: Willan.

NHS Confederation. (2015). *Key statistics on the NHS*. Available at: http://www.nhsconfed.org/resources/key-statistics-on-the-nhs. Accessed 8 Oct 2015.

ONS. (2012). *2011 Census for England and Wales*. Available at: http://www.ons.gov.uk/ons/guide-method/census/2011/index.html. Accessed 29 July 2013.

Palmiotto, M., & Unnithan, P. (2011). *Policing and society: A global approach*. New York: Delmar Cengage Learning.

Payne-James, J., Green, P., Green, N., McLachlan, G., Munro, M., & Moore, T. (2010). Healthcare issue of detainees in police custody in London, UK. *Journal of Forensic and Legal Medicine, 17*(1), 11–17.

Ponsaers, P. (2015). Is legitimacy police property? In G. Meško & J. Tankebe (Eds.), *Trust and legitimacy in criminal justice: European perspectives* (pp. 93–110). London: Springer.

Poyser, S. (2004). The role of police discretion in Britain and an analysis of proposals for reform. *Police Journal, 77*(1), 5–17.

Prenzler, T., Porter, L., & Alpert, G. (2013). Reducing police use of force: Case studies and prospects. *Aggression and Violent Behaviour, 18*(2), 343–356.

Price, G. (2011). The visual documentation of public protest: G20, London, 2009. *Crime Media Culture, 7*(1), 99–101.

Puddister, K., & Riddell, T. (2012). The RCMP's 'Mr Big' sting operation: A case study in police independence, accountability and oversight. *Canadian Public Administration, 55*(3), 385–409.

Punch, M. (2009). *Police corruption: Deviance, accountability and reform in policing*. Cullompton: Willan.

Razack, S. (2015). *Dying from improvement: Inquests and inquiries into indigenous deaths in custody*. Toronto: University of Toronto Press.

Reason, J. (1990) *Human Error*. Cambridge. Cambridge University Press.

Redshaw, J., Sanders, F., & Mawby, R. (1995). *Core policing, ancillary tasks and alternative providers: Views from the ground*. Exeter: Devon and Cornwall Constabulary.

Reid, K. (2005). The home secretary and improved accountability of the police? *Journal of Criminal Law, 69*, 232–255.

Reiner, R. (2000). *The politics of the police* (3rd ed.). Oxford: Oxford University Press.

Reiner, R. (2010). *The politics of the police* (4th ed.). Oxford: Oxford University Press.

Reiner, R. (2013). Who governs? Democracy, plutocracy, science and prophecy in policing. *Criminology and Criminal Justice, 13*(2), 161–180.

Rogers, C., & Lewis, R. (Eds.). (2007). *An introduction to police work*. Cullompton: Willan.

Rojek, J., Alpert, G., & Smith, H. (2012). Examining officer and citizen accounts of police use-of-force incidents. *Crime and Delinquency, 58*(2), 301–327.

Rowe, M. (2007). Policing and racism in the limelight—The politics and context of the Lawrence report. In M. Rowe (Ed.), *Policing beyond Macpherson: Issues in policing, race and society* (pp. Xi–xxiv). Cullompton: Willan.

Savage, S. (2007a). Give and take: The bifurcation of police reform in Britain. *Australian and New Zealand Journal of Criminology, 40*(3), 313–334.

Savage, S. (2007b). *Police reform: Forces for change*. Oxford: OUP.

Savage, S., Grieve, J., & Poyser, S. (2007). Putting wrongs to right: Campaigns against miscarriages of justice. *Criminology and Criminal Justice, 7*(1), 83–105.

Savage, S (2008) 'Deaths in Police Custody.' In Newburn, T. and Neyroud, P. (eds) *Dictionary of Policing*. Cullompton. Willan. 384–385.

Savage, S., Grieve, J., & Poyser, S. (2009). Stephen Lawrence as a miscarriage of justice. In N. Hall, J. Grieve, & S. Savage (Eds.), *Policing and the legacy of Lawrence* (pp. 25–40). Cullompton: Willan.

Scraton, P. (2002). Lost lives, hidden voices: 'Truth' and controversial deaths. *Race Class, 44*(1), 107–118.

Scraton, P., Jemphrey, A., & Coleman, S. (1995). *No last rights: The denial of justice and the promotion of myth in the aftermath of the Hillsborough disaster*. Liverpool: Liverpool City Council.

Sen, S. (2010). *Enforcing police accountability through civilian oversight*. London: Sage.

Seneviratne, M. (2002). Ombudsmen and police complaints. *Journal of Social Welfare and Family Law, 24*(2), 195–203.

Shane, J. (2013). *Learning from error in policing: A case study in organisational accident theory*. Heidelberg: Springer.

Shaw, H., & Coles, D. (2007). *Unlocking the truth: Families' experiences of the investigation of deaths in custody*. London: Inquest.

Sim, J (2004) 'The victimised state and the mystification of social harm.' 113–132. In Hillyard, P, Pantazis, C, Tombs, S and Gordon, D (eds) Beyond Criminology: Taking Harm Seriously. London: Pluto.

Simmons, K. C. (2012). Stakeholder participation in the selection and recruitment of police: Democracy in action. *Saint Louis University Public Law Review, 32*(7), 7–32.

Skinns, L. (2011). *Police custody: Governance, legitimacy and reform in the criminal justice process*. Abingdon: Willan.

Skogan, W., & Frydl, K. (2004). *Fairness and effectiveness in policing: The evidence*. Washington: National Academies Press.

Smith, G. (2001). Police complaints and criminal prosecutions. *Modern Law Review, 64*(3), 372–392.

Smith, G. (2004). Rethinking police complaints. *British Journal of Criminology, 44*(1), 15–33.

Smith, G. (2009). Why don't more people complain against the police? *European Journal of Criminology, 6*(3), 249–266.

Smith, G. (2013). Oversight of the police and residual complaints dilemmas: Independence, effectiveness and accountability in the United Kingdom. *Police Practice and Research: An International Journal, 14*(2), 92–103.

Stone, C. (2007). Training police accountability in theory and practice: From Philadelphia to Abuja and Sao Paolo. *Theoretical Criminology, 11*(2), 245–259.

Surrette, R. (2007). *Media, crime and criminal justice: Image and realities* (3rd ed.). Belmont: Wadsworth.

Terpstra, J., & Trommel, W. (2009). Police, managerialisation and presentational strategies. *Policing: An International Journal of Police Strategies and Management, 32*(1), 128–143.

Terrill, W., & Mastrofski, S. (2002). Situational and officer based determinants of police coercion. *Justice Quarterly, 19*(2), 215–248.

Tyler, T., & Fagan, J. (2008). Legitimacy and cooperation: Why do people help the police fight crime in their communities? *Ohio State Journal of Criminal Law, 6,* 231–275.

Uildriks, N., & van Mastrigt, H. (1991). *Policing police violence*. Aberdeen: Aberdeen University Press.

Van Sluis, A., Ringeling, A., & Frevel, B. (2009). Evolving patterns in the police systems of North Rhine-Westphalia, the Netherlands and England & Wales. *German Policy Studies, 5*(2), 145–168.

Waddington, P. A. J. (1999). *Policing citizens.* London: UCL Press.

Warburton, D. (2004). Drawing the thin blue line: The reality of who controls the police. *Police Journal, 77*(2), 135–144.

Westmarland, L. (2001). Blowing the whistle on police violence: Gender, ethnography and ethics. *British Journal of Criminology, 41*(3), 523–535.

Westmarland, L. (2012). *Gender and policing: Sex, power and police culture.* London: Routledge.

Westmarland, L. (2013). "Snitches get stiches": US homicide detectives' ethics and morals in action. *Policing and Society, 23*(3), 311–327.

Wortley, R. (2003). Measuring police attitudes towards discretion. *Criminal Justice and Behaviour, 30*(5), 538–558.

Zedner, L. (2006). Policing before the police. *British Journal of Criminology, 46*(1), 78–96.

# 3

# Regulating Death after Police Contact

## Introduction

Having set out key issues in policing and accountability in cases of DAPC in the previous chapter, this chapter will consider the role of the two principal organisations responsible for investigating these cases. It argues that cases of DAPC are regulated in a manner which is relatively arbitrary. The system of regulation for these cases appears to be non-systematic, discretionary and often reliant upon non-standardised practices. The type of regulation produced depends largely on the institution that produces it. The relationships a regulatory institution has with other regulators, the state and society are also shown to be important in determining the type of accountability constructed in these cases. Issues such as independence, transparency and legitimacy are all demonstrated to be relational and ambiguous concepts in this domain, perhaps reflecting the fact that the sphere of policing and regulation is suffused by relationality and ambiguity. The chapter argues that regulation exists in both a symbolic and practical way in cases of DAPC.

The first half of the chapter discusses the role of the coroner's court in constructing accountability in these cases. It assesses the origins, history

D. Baker, *Deaths After Police Contact*,
DOI 10.1057/978-1-137-58967-5_3

and relevance of the coroner's court in cases of DAPC and how these might be contextualised in terms of its relationship with the state and society. The way in which coronial roles, functions and structure might affect the investigation of such cases is considered, particularly regarding the use of discretion. The role of the coroner and jury is established as being both symbolic and practical, much as was the case with the role of policing in the previous chapter. Furthermore, the chapter examines processes and procedures in the coronial system that influence how cases are investigated and findings subsequently recorded. The coronial system is essentially regional and lacks central oversight, leading to a somewhat arbitrary application of processes and outcomes. This section of the chapter touches on issues such as non-standardised practices, ambiguity of purpose and the relatively autonomous methods used by coroners. Finally, it considers the role of the ECHR in effecting change in coronial processes relating to cases of DAPC.

In addition to discussing the coronial system, the chapter examines the role of the IPCC in these cases. This section of the chapter discusses the IPCC's origins and purpose and considers the relationship between the IPCC, state, police and society and how this relationship has evolved since its inception in 2004. It examines the IPCC's need to demonstrate independence, legitimacy and transparency in these cases. The processes and procedures employed by the IPCC and how these relate to its structures are considered. The concept of independence—fundamental to its existence as a legitimate organisation—is examined in practical and symbolic terms in an attempt to assess the legitimacy of the IPCC in terms of expectations from the state and society when investigating cases of DAPC.

The regulation of cases of DAPC is relatively non-systematic—not only between the coronial system and IPCC, as was illustrated in the death of Sean Rigg, but also *within* each organisation. Article 2 of the ECHR is a key component driving the evolution of accountability construction in both organisations. The processes, practices and mechanisms for recording accountability in these cases have evolved in the twenty-first century and this reflects a shift in the discourse of accountability construction in cases of DAPC. The chapter demonstrates how this affects the regulation of cases of DAPC and thus the type of accountability that is constructed in cases of DAPC.

# The Coronial System: Atypical and Ambiguous

'It is the duty of the coroner as the public official responsible for the conduct of inquests ... to ensure that the relevant facts are fully, fairly and fearlessly investigated. He is bound to recognise the acute concern rightly aroused where deaths occur in custody. He must ensure that the relevant facts are exposed to public scrutiny particularly if there is evidence of foul play, abuse or inhumanity.' (Bingham M.R., in House of Lords 1995)

Deaths that occur while an individual is in the care of the state should be investigated before a jury in the coronial system (Ministry of Justice 2012). Bingham's quotation (above) underlines the gravity and import of these cases to the state and society. An independent role in publicly scrutinising suspicious deaths and attempting to learn lessons that prevent future deaths is central to the coroner's *raison d'être*. The coroner's role demonstrates legitimate and transparent processes to society. Minimising future harms to citizens is key to Article 2 of the ECHR and consequently the regulation of cases of DAPC, as is discussed presently. In this sense, inquests undertaken by coroners are both symbolic and practical in constructing accountability in cases of DAPC.

The coroner typically conducts investigations in public. Investigation takes the form of an inquest, and is based on fact-finding about the death. Coroners or juries are not able to ascribe guilt or blame. Their role is to establish who died, when and where they died, and how they died. The question of 'how' an individual died is ambiguous due to interpretation of the word 'how' regarding the death. It can be understood as the individual act that precipitated the death, or as a result of wider systemic processes. It is the 'how' that authors writing in this sphere (see, for example Dorries 2004; Matthews 2002) note as a key question in terms of interpretation. Prior to the enactment of the HRA (Human Rights Act) 1998, 'how' was considered to be 'by what means' they came to meet their death, whereas it is now interpreted as 'in what circumstances' (Matthews 2014: 123). The immediate effect of this on coronial practice has been to broaden the scope of the inquest and consider a wider range of issues that might have led to the death of an individual, as was demonstrated in the verdict returned in the Sean Rigg case.

Coroners provide a transparent and legitimate independent inquiry into cases of DAPC. As such, they have a significant role to play in protecting society from avoidable death and holding state agencies to account for such deaths (Levine 1999). The system is unique within the wider system of justice in England and Wales in that there is no defendant and no accused (Matthews 2002). The system is, in theory, inquisitorial as distinct from adversarial (Tarling 1998). Adversarialism is based on legal proceedings whereby one party attempts to secure a favourable verdict at the expense of the other party. In coronial proceedings there are no parties to 'take sides'. Consequently, the emphasis is on fact finding as distinct from blame finding (Beckett 1999).

## Processes and Procedures: Ambiguity and Discretion

The coronial system is typically the only forum where cases of DAPC are heard in public. The retention of the jury system has historical links to the coroner's court, providing a legitimate and transparent response to the community where deaths of an unusual or suspicious nature occur (Dorries 2004). Inquests can consider any issue which may have been causal in the death, meaning that they examine the circumstances leading to the death in a holistic sense. Once the evidence is heard, the jury delivers a verdict based on the inquiry into the facts of the death. Typically, this is known as a 'short-form' verdict in that it reflects a number of categories available to them. There is insufficient space to list all of these types here but they range from suicide, misadventure, and open, through to unlawful killing. Coroners are not restricted to using short-form verdicts, but in practice they are used in the majority of cases (Luce 2003). The general principle guiding the recording of a verdict[1] is that a conclusion should be reached whereby the principal facts relevant to the death are stated (Matthews 2002).

There are currently ninety-nine coronial districts in England and Wales (Ministry of Justice 2014). The number has decreased markedly since the

---

[1] Now termed 'conclusions' (Chief Coroner 2015).

1980s, partly because local authorities sought to reduce costs as coroners retired their positions, and partly as a result of the Ministry of Justice attempting to streamline a notoriously regional service. It is regional largely due to its roots in community-based justice, but also because it has evolved over 900 years with little central oversight (Luce 2003). Coronial districts are not necessarily contiguous with the local authority, NHS authority or the area of police authority. The organisation of coronial districts appears to be without regard for specific requirements such as case load or capability and illustrates the relatively non-systematic nature of regulation in this sphere. In some local authorities there may be a number of coroners, in others there may be one. Coroners and their staff are widely held to be under resourced (Smith 2003).

The highly regionalised demarcation of the system can lead to coroners becoming protective of their autonomy (Davis et al. 2002). For example, the place the deceased meets their death dictates which coroner the death is reported to[2] and may also dictate the type of knowledge and expertise that the coroner possesses. Consequently, the ability of the coroner to conduct a rigorous inquest in a case of DAPC may have more to do with geographical jurisdiction than experience, training or statutory requirements. The majority of coroners in England and Wales rarely conduct an inquest into a case of DAPC (Dorries 2004).

Further underlining the non-systematic theme, the coronial system offers little recourse for complaint to those who are dissatisfied with their experience of it (Luce 2003). There is no complaints body and limited central oversight of cases or jurisdictions. One fundamental recourse is via judicial review to the High Court to have an inquest quashed and reheard. This tends to be prohibitively expensive and, as a consequence, rarely used. In the period 2001–10 there were an average of 1.6 cases per year quashed on judicial review (Ministry of Justice 2010). The relatively arbitrary nature of the coronial system is noted by Smith (2003: 158): 'Because there is no appeal structure and applications for judicial review are relatively rare, coroners are effectively free to develop their own responses to the legislative provision.' The appointment of a Chief

---

[2] Following guidance from the Chief Coroner (2013: 18.127) this can now be overridden in 'exceptional circumstances'.

Coroner, Judge Peter Thornton, in September 2012 was intended to provide greater leadership, structure, a more standardised set of procedures, and to promote best practice in the coronial system. Guidance has since been produced by the Chief Coroner on a wide range of issues regarding policy and practice (see, for example Chief Coroner 2015; Chief Coroner's Office 2013). It is too early at this point to assess the impact of the Chief Coroner on cases of DAPC.

To a great extent, the role and purpose of inquests lack clarity (Davis et al. 2002). Practitioners and family members commonly remark on the inherent ambiguities present in the inquest system (Shaw and Coles 2007). Family members feel that although the inquest is supposedly inquisitorial, often the reality is that it resembles a highly charged adversarial arena. Families often approach the inquest at a time of intense grief and tend to be bewildered by the process (Hallam et al. 1999). There is widely considered to be a lack of information about coronial processes and this can lead to unrealistic expectations on behalf of the family as to what the inquest is, and accordingly what it might achieve. Families tend to approach the inquest, knowing it to be in a courtroom, with a presiding 'judge', as an opportunity to 'get justice' (Matthews 2007).

As previously outlined, the inquest should determine who died, how they died, and when and where they died. The scope of the 'how' question can be ambiguous, highlighting the relationship between fact finding and investigating liability. It may bring into consideration wider systemic issues relevant to the death that might prevent future loss of life. Examples of this could be the way in which particular state organisations train their staff (for example regarding restraint), or how they formulate particular policies (for example regarding the use of tasers). 'How' an individual came to meet their end might be as simple as 'died as a result of being struck with a baton'. However, the appropriate use of the baton in the context of police training and policy may also be considered, and/or the type of baton used by police in England and Wales. As such, the 'how' question might cover individual and/or collective acts, and/or omissions. Thus the 'how' question sometimes becomes the 'why' question in inquests dealing with cases of DAPC, in that it considers wider issues about state organisations as distinct from actions or omissions from individual agents of the state (Dorries 2004). Evidently, in the Sean Rigg case, the 'how' question enabled the jury to focus on issues such as the failures of SLaM and CAD operators rather than merely the events that occurred during the police contact with Sean.

Although the attribution of blame and liability does not fall within the ambit of the inquest, it is virtually inevitable that within the parameters of the inquisition there will be an examination of issues touching on the *possibility* of blame and liability (Levine 1999). It is this ambiguity of stated intention when contrasted with actual practice that typifies ambiguity and discretion within the coronial sphere. Discretion is a recurring theme within the coronial system. Luce's (2003: 71) comprehensive review of the coronial system states: 'The phrase we have heard more than any other during the Review is "the coroner is a law unto himself [*sic*]"'.

Under the 2009 Coroners and Justice Act (s1, (2)) an inquest is compulsory if 'the deceased died while in custody or otherwise in state detention' (Parliament 2009). This Act is the fundamental statutory instrument for coroners in England and Wales having replaced the 1988 Coroners Act. They are further guided in practice by a framework termed 'Coroners Rules' dating from 2013. These replaced the 1984 Coroners Rules that functioned in tandem with the 1988 Coroners Act. These rules are updated by Home Office circulars[3] and the Chief Coroner to reflect current developments in case law and precedent in coroners' courts. Thus coronial practice is guided by statute but also by precedent. Coroners Rules reflect the discretionary and non-systematised nature of proceedings as they effectively represent a set of guidelines as distinct from a 'hard and fast' framework. There are significant differences of interpretation by coroners at inquests with factors as diverse as family involvement, post-mortem procedure, verdict framing and jury direction all having demonstrably divergent interpretations dependent on coronial jurisdiction (Smith 2003). These differences are the result of structural issues as distinct to individual idiosyncrasies (Luce 2003). Such issues indicate a lack of consistency in training and appointment, an ambiguous procedural framework and a lack of clear objectives. To these, Smith (2003: 57) adds a lack of leadership and regulation, noting that when compared to the rest of the judiciary, coroners are: 'to a very large extent … left to their own devices'.

---

[3] The Chief Coroner now publishes 'law sheets' that appear to replace Home Office Circulars (Chief Coroner 2015).

## The European Convention on Human Rights: An Evolution of Accountability

The most significant changes to the operation of the coronial system in cases of DAPC have been effected by the ECHR. It has affected the coronial system in three distinct ways: first, through the inquest process; second, because of the type of verdict recorded; and third, due to the increased use of coroners' reports post-inquest. The ECHR has major ramifications to the procedural duty of the state when investigating deaths relating to its agents (Wadham 2004). It constitutes a 'living instrument' in that it should dynamically reflect changes within society. The ECHR does not merely protect the rights of citizens, but actively seeks to enable an environment where rights are upheld (Thomas et al. 2008). The key component of the ECHR germane to cases of DAPC is Article 2: the right to life. This is seen as being a fundamental right from which all other rights necessarily follow.

Article 2 of the ECHR acknowledges that deaths will occur as a result of interaction with state agents. Consequently, deaths incurred after contact with these agents should be investigated with a rigour and thoroughness that demonstrates the state actively sought to enable citizens' right to life. The ECHR requires the state to be transparent in disclosing documents and making witnesses available to whichever forum will hear such cases (Matthews 2011). The HRA 1998 is the UK's statutory response to the ECHR. Since its enactment in October 2000 coroners' practices must be interpreted in a manner compatible with the ECHR (Davis et al. 2002). The state's response to deaths involving its agents is manifest in the coronial system in what are termed 'Article 2 inquests'. Article 2 inquests are investigated more rigorously than any other type and as a result are more complex, contested and more likely to be subject to appeal via judicial review (Matthews 2011). The significance of the ECHR has been to impose 'an evidential burden' on the state to provide an explanation of such a death that is satisfactory and convincing. However, until late 2013 (Chief Coroner's Office 2013) there was no explicit direction from the state on how coroners were to undertake these type of inquests, once again underlining the themes of ambiguity and non-statutory practice apparent in the coronial sphere.

A significant development in Article 2 inquests is the growth of what are termed 'narrative verdicts'. These replace the typically used short-form verdicts and set out a narrative description of the key 'facts found' in the inquest. Such verdicts do not have a standardised format and can vary significantly in style, content and length (Matthews 2011). Numerous judgements have been made in judicial reviews noting the relevance and appropriateness of narrative verdicts fulfilling the state's response to Article 2 of the ECHR, most notably in the landmark case of Middleton (Widdicombe 2012). Colin Middleton died in Bristol prison in 1999. The first inquest into his death was quashed due to an insufficiently rigorous enquiry. In the second, the coroner did not grant the jury the option of 'neglect' as a verdict. The jury chose instead to record their findings in narrative format, stating (in part) that the Prison Service had failed in its duty of care to the deceased. This might be seen as validation of what Farrell and Givelber (2010: 1549) term the 'liberation hypothesis'. This states that when cases are highly contested, juries may feel liberated from the demands of the law and: 'give expression to extralegal views in arriving at verdicts'. In a decision that appeared to endorse the independence, legitimacy and transparency bestowed by jury inquests, the House of Lords upheld both the verdict and the method in which it was recorded, creating a precedent for narrative verdicts to be used in future inquests (Inquest 2004). Without such a precedent, the jury in the Sean Rigg inquest would not have been able to record such a lengthy and detailed verdict.

Consequently, narrative verdicts function as a statement of findings rather than a label as is the case in short-form verdicts (Dorries 2004). Luce (2003) believed such verdicts satisfied public interest and noted that the narrative should involve systemic issues if relevant to the specific case. The increasing use of narrative verdicts is illustrated in Fig. 3.1. Their use illustrates a number of themes apparent in the coronial system. First, their use in principle is not codified, but is consistent with the discretion afforded the coroner and jury. Second, their use in practice differs depending on coronial districts. Third, at a national level they are recorded under the heading of 'other verdict' (see, for example Hill and Cook 2011). This means that their meaning is ambiguous in terms of statistical representation, and their content is effectively unknown to those who have not had direct access to the content of each narrative verdict. What is clear is that they represent an evolution in accountability construction in the coronial system since the turn of the century. Chapter 4 examines the use of narrative verdicts in detail and highlights how accountability construction is evolving in cases of DAPC. The role of narrative verdicts in highlighting an increasing variety of actions and omissions from numerous state agencies in these cases, as evidenced in the Sean Rigg case, will become increasingly clear.

Narrative verdicts enable juries to consider circumstantial factors if they are able to demonstrate a 'sensible direct relationship' between those factors and the death (Matthews 2011). If systemic weaknesses are noted, then under Article 2 the preventability of death may be focused upon as distinct from issues purely relating to the cause of death, and this tends to include other organisations in addition to the police being identified as being related to the death. Thomas et al. (2008) believe this could lead to a process termed 'accountable learning', similar to the ideas outlined in Chap. 2 (see Doyle 2010; Shane 2013; Shaw and Coles 2007; Downing and Lingham 2009) whereby organisations amend policies, procedures and practice based on findings from death investigations. However, whilst narrative verdicts are public documents in as much as they are read aloud in court, they are not collated as public records within any governmental agency. To some degree, this highlights the regionalised nature of the coronial service. There is also an irony in the fact that the system intended to hold organisations to account for preventable death is itself widely criticised for being insufficiently accountable (Luce 2003; Smith 2003).

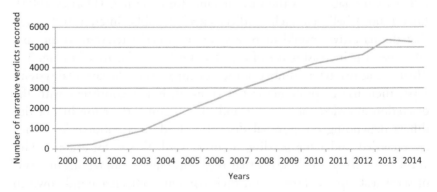

**Fig. 3.1**  Narrative verdicts per year 2000–14 (all deaths in England and Wales)

In addition to Article 2 inquests and narrative verdicts, the third major development under ECHR requirements is the increasing use of the coroner's 'rule 43' report.[4] Coroners are entitled[5] to write to relevant agencies in the aftermath of an inquest with recommendations suggesting potential alterations in training or practice which might reduce future fatalities. Coroners consider this to be a key aspect of their function in the promotion of public safety, prevention of future fatalities and regulation of agencies (Davis et al. 2002). Nevertheless, it is important to note that although the coroner may write a report to an agency, the agency is under no obligation to act on the recommendations. Indeed, research by Claridge et al. (2008) found that the majority of healthcare agencies that received these reports did not know what they were, or how they should respond to them. There is an expectation that agencies receiving such a report should reply to the coroner within fifty-six days (Thomas et al. 2008). It is unclear what would occur should such a reply not be forthcoming.

In conclusion, the coronial system is atypical within the legal system in England and Wales and consequently its processes are atypical. Due to non-standardised and often non-statutory processes it is better imagined as a regional rather than a national service. Inquests are characterised by ambiguity and discretion, and their processes can be somewhat arbitrary. That said, in cases of DAPC, it appears that the coroner fulfils a number of important requirements in the regulation of state agencies. Inquests in these cases are heard in public before juries. This provides a sense of legitimacy and transparency that is key in contentious cases. The coroner, as an autonomous judicial officer, has a duty to rigorously examine these cases to evaluate whether foul play or wrongdoing has occurred, to hold the state to account if this has occurred, and to make recommendations where necessary that attempt to prevent future similar deaths. It is, however, important to note that the coronial system is unable to ascribe blame, it can only record findings, and it cannot enforce the recommendations it makes. Thus although on the one hand the coronial system

---

[4] Now termed 'report to prevent future deaths'.

[5] According to guidelines developed by the Chief Coroner (2013: 23.172) they now have a duty to compile such a report if they believe it may prevent future deaths.

might appear to be legitimate and relevant in regulating these cases, on the other it might not, further underlining the relational aspects of legitimacy and accountability in these cases.

The ECHR has placed a renewed focus on these processes and enabled a broader and more thorough type of investigation via the Article 2 inquest. It encourages the consideration of systemic and organisational factors that may have been causal in the death. This has produced an opportunity for juries to publicly record findings in the form of narrative verdicts. These developments suggest that, to some degree, a new mode of regulation is unfolding in these cases. Greater oversight, however, does not necessarily equal fewer cases of DAPC or lessons being learned as a result of such oversight. This issue is picked up in the second part of this chapter which considers the role of the other organisation charged with regulating cases of DAPC since 2004: the IPCC.

## The IPCC: A Purpose-Designed Regulator

As was shown in the case of Sean Rigg earlier in this book, the IPCC has suffered a crisis of legitimacy during the relatively short time it has existed. Criticisms have focused on its perceived lack of independence, its lack of analytical investigative processes, and its lack of power to enforce recommendations and sanction police. That such a crisis has occurred in what is a relatively new, purpose designed, and statutorily enabled regulator raises a considerable number of questions about policing, the state and accountability. This section of the chapter discusses how this state of affairs has come to be by examining the IPCC as both a symbolic and practical organisation. It considers independence as a relational construct and how this affects the IPCC's legitimacy on both a practical and symbolic level. In order to provide context, the discussion begins with the principles underpinning the foundation of the IPCC and how it is currently organised and functions.

Police complaints organisations have existed in England and Wales since 1976 with the inception of the Police Complaints Board (PCB). The PCB was replaced in 1986 by the PCA (Police Complaints Authority) primarily due to criticisms that the PCB was under-resourced, staffed by ex-police officers and insufficiently independent to ensure public trust in its operations (Waters and Brown 2000). The PCA was similarly criticised, and a series of contentious cases of DAPC in the mid-1990s in combination with findings from the Macpherson report led to the government instigating a process that eventually led to the creation of the IPCC in 2004 (Savage 2013a). A core principle in the formation of the IPCC was the promotion of public trust in the police complaints system and this reflects the discussion in the previous chapter about the principles of consensual, legitimate policing in England and Wales (Harrison and Cuneen 2000). These developments underscore the importance of a working relationship between police, state and society and how this relationship is dynamic and subject to changes in events and expectations.

The IPCC was established as part of the 2002 Police Reform Act. Central to its creation was the principle of independence, and as corollaries the concepts of legitimacy and transparency in its working practices. According to its statement of purpose, the IPCC exists to increase public confidence in the police and investigate the most serious complaints made against the police (HAC 2013). The discussion below principally focuses on its role in investigating and reporting on cases of DAPC. It considers the processes and procedures that the IPCC follows; the structures such processes exist within; the centrality of public confidence and legitimacy to its mission; and the real and symbolic relevance of independence to its existence.

The IPCC works within what is termed a 'two-tier system' of regulation whereby it investigates the more serious complaints made against police whilst the relevant force's PSD investigates those deemed to be less serious. It is widely accepted that a two-tier system investigating issues regarding police accountability is increasingly typical and represents value for money (see Punch 2009; Prenzler 2009). However, it is not the only system available, in Northern Ireland the police ombudsman investigates all complaints (Smith 2013). Moreover, Goldsmith (1991) notes that the key to a two-tier system functioning efficiently is an effective balance between the two systems and that this involves a constant readjustment of the balancing act depending on context. It was evident in the case of Sean Rigg that there was little evidence of balance in the regulatory relationship. Relationality is thus demonstrated through the two-tier principle of accountability, and also because of the relationships these tiers have with other organisations in the regulatory sphere. The balance between these relationships is examined in more detail in Chap. 6.

The organisation has three potential modes of investigation when responding to complaints: supervised, managed and independent. Managed cases occur where the PSD of the force investigates the complaint, passes the paperwork to the IPCC and this is either validated or returned for further investigation. Supervised cases are directed and controlled by IPCC investigators but investigated by officers from the PSD. Thus, both managed and supervised cases are effectively investigated by the relevant PSD, meaning that they belong to the 'first tier' of investigation (Savage 2013a). Independent cases are undertaken by IPCC investigators under the supervision of an IPCC commissioner and effectively represent the 'second tier' of investigation, which appears to represent the most legitimate approach to society (ACPO 2012). In 2008–09, independent investigations accounted for 0.3 per cent of cases that the IPCC undertook (HAC 2010). In the cases of DAPC I examined, one-third were not investigated by the IPCC (personal correspondence 2015). In these cases, the PSD investigated the death. This calls into question how the decision was made about which organisation should conduct the investigation, in addition to posing a question as to who made such a decision. Announcing a significant budget increase for the IPCC in 2014, the policing minister, Mike Penning, stated this would enable the IPCC to conduct 'significantly more independent investigations' (BBC 2014).

IPCC investigators have similar statutory powers to police officers in as much as they can make arrests and search premises. IPCC commissioners are appointed directly by the Home Secretary and charged with upholding public confidence in the system. They are 'the embodiment of independence itself' (Savage 2013a: 100). Cases of DAPC should be automatically referred to the IPCC by the force in which the death occurs. In this sense, the IPCC are reliant in the first instance on police informing them of such a case. However, in the case of Ian Tomlinson, for example, the referral occurred eight days after his death. It is clear then, that IPCC processes when responding to cases of DAPC are equivocal, ambiguous and marked by discretion.

The organisation has the capacity to recommend disciplinary action against a police officer, but it cannot compel action to be taken, nor does it believe it is desirable to do so (IPCC 2014). An investigation by the National Audit Office (NAO) in 2008 found no centralised records to track the application of recommendations made by the IPCC, with different IPCC regions following 'wildly varying approaches' (NAO 2008: 7) highlighting arbitrary practices. This is remarkably similar to the diversity of practice in the coronial system. Consequently, Smith (2009) notes that, in reality, the complaints system continues to operate as a function of police management in that they ultimately decide if an officer is to be disciplined. This is exacerbated by the fact that the vast majority of police complaints are investigated by the force PSD. Thus the IPCC is seen to be more of a symbolic organisation than a practical one.

As part of promulgating best practice in policing, the IPCC publishes bulletins such as the 'Learning the Lessons' series referred to in Chap. 2 (see, for example IPCC 2012). These focus on reducing deaths and serious injury after police contact and are constructed using an approach whereby stakeholders such as the NPIA, HMIC and ACPO collaborate to inform each other's practice. It highlights recurring issues in these cases such as mental health, drugs and drunkenness in custody, and the way in which these conditions can be best managed in those contexts. It is notable that the coronial service is not part of this process, underlining the ambiguous relationship between the two regulators in these cases, as was noted in the Sean Rigg case, and also placing a significant question mark over the effectiveness of lesson learning in cases of DAPC.

# Accountability: Relationships and Contexts

The initial enthusiasm which greeted the IPCC in 2004 soured relatively quickly, and this was to some degree foreseen by Reiner's (1991) research on chief constables. He found the majority of chief officers believed that developments in systems of accountability were driven by either cosmetic, partisan or public relations imperatives; that change was motivated by symbolic rather than practical considerations. Most senior officers who favoured a shift to independent oversight did so because they felt it would enhance police legitimacy in the eyes of the public, *not* because they believed such a system would be more effective. Indeed his research participants believed that the PSD in each force would be more effective than any police complaints organisation, underlining the significance of symbolism to police accountability.

External oversight of policing has become a focus of policy makers worldwide. Smith (2013: 92) believes that cycles of reform interspersed with scandals 'have contributed to a growing police complaints discourse'. To some extent, this discourse has been driven by factors such as the ECHR which underline the importance of independence to the process of investigation. Savage's (2013a: 95) research led him to assert that the independence of investigations in this sphere has reached 'near totemic status', again emphasising the symbolic importance of independence. The concept of independence is vital to the production of legitimacy and accountability in these cases. Prior to the formation of the IPCC there were repeated demands from various parties that an independent body should be responsible for holding police accountable (Wadham 2004). The dominion of coroners, pathologists and regulators is notable for independence being evident in their work. Thus the symbolic meaning of independence takes on particular importance. In Savage's (2013a) research into three national police complaints bodies, he discovered that investigators believed a truly independent investigation was not practically possible due to a reliance, at the very least, on police cooperation with the investigation. This underlines both the dynamic relationship between police, society and state when considering independence, and between symbolic and practical forms of police accountability.

The existence of independent organisations within the regulatory domain of policing promotes an air of legitimacy and accountability. The system of independent bodies includes the coronial system and the IPCC. Yet the processes promoting this system of independent monitoring are in reality lacking fully independent or accountable properties. The coronial system, as previously discussed, is renowned for possessing arcane and opaque procedures. Reid (2005) is not alone (see, for example Maguire 1991) in suggesting that bodies ensuring police accountability prefer to stress compliance above formal sanction and to encourage a high standard of professionalism in distinction to criminal prosecution. In this sense, the IPCC and coronial system are similar. Neither can formally sanction the police, but they can make recommendations about future practice, guidelines and training. Furthermore, they can refer police to the Crown Prosecution Service (CPS) based on findings gleaned during their investigations. Consequently, independence from the police might equate to a lack of power to sanction them.

Independence as a relational concept can be assessed from a variety of perspectives: operational, procedural and functional. A critical discussion of the concept is outlined below in order to unpick what these terms mean in the context of regulating cases of DAPC. Gilsinan (2012) uses the term 'isomorphic' to describe police accountability systems. This means that elements within a system might have different ancestry but essentially retain the same appearance as their predecessors. This accurately describes the history of police complaints organisations in England and Wales since their inception in 1976. Although three organisations have assumed this role under different statutory instruments, the criticism of specific aspects of each has remained relatively constant (see, for example NAO 2008; HAC 2013). A key criticism levelled at the IPCC, like its forebears, is over-reliance on ex-police officers as investigators. A review by the HAC in 2010 found that 89 per cent of senior investigators and 30 per cent of investigators were ex-police officers. This is exacerbated by the fact that the great majority of complaints are investigated by serving police officers as part of PSD cases (HAC 2010). The IPCC also relies heavily on senior officers and experts as consultants from bodies such as ACPO on specific technical or procedural issues (HAC 2013). These issues question the claim of the IPCC to be operationally and procedurally independent of the police. The concepts of independence, legitimacy and transparency are clearly relational and ambiguous in regulatory practice in cases of DAPC.

The symbolic principle of independent investigation runs up against the practical reality that the specialised skills required for investigation are most likely possessed by police officers (Savage 2013b). BME groups, in particular, lack confidence in police complaints bodies due to the perception that they are still 'the police investigating the police'. Giving evidence to the HAC, Marcia Rigg, commenting on the IPCC investigation into the death of her brother, stated a commonly held view: 'Everything is sent out to ex-police, and families have no confidence in this' (HAC 2010: Ev2). In evidence given to the HAC (2010), the Police Action Lawyers Group (PALG) felt the IPCC had a culture that viewed officers as witnesses as distinct from potential suspects and that this stemmed from it mistaking neutrality for independence. This highlights relationality in both the concept of independence, and the forum in which accountability is constructed. The PALG also raised the issue of the failure to interview police officers under caution, as noted by Casale et al. (2013). Another concern is that officers are able to confer prior to giving statements to IPCC investigators in many contentious cases (Griffin and Moran 2010).

Both Smith (2013) and Savage (2013a, b) stress the notion of 'capture' whereby independent investigators effectively become captured by the organisation they are charged with overseeing. Investigators may become susceptible to adopting a police mind-set due to their proximity to officers and the need to maintain a working relationship with them, what Savage (2013a: 104) terms 'cultural empathy'. The observations in the discussion above cast doubt on the functional independence of the IPCC. These doubts over the IPCC's operational, procedural and functional independence can be viewed in light of Terpstra and Trommel's (2009) work on the police, as discussed in the previous chapter, about cognitive and procedural legitimacy. From this perspective, the public could question whether the IPCC are a meaningful or relevant organisation (cognitively legitimate); and also whether they use socially accepted means to achieve their goals (procedurally legitimate).

In contrast, a coroner, as an autonomous judicial officer with comparable status to a High Court judge would seem less susceptible to the possibility of capture. However, concern has been voiced over the relationship the coroner has with the local authority that employs them and the possible ramifications this might have (Scraton et al. 1995). The difference between the respective modes of investigation is that one is in public with a jury and the other is conducted in private. This might afford the coronial system greater cognitive and procedural legitimacy when investigating cases of DAPC. Either way, neither organisation could be said to be completely independent of the police.

A multi-faceted interpretation of independence is outlined by Smith (2009) who adopts categories identified by the European Court of Human

Rights. He posits there are numerous indicators of independence regarding agencies regulating the police. First, that adequate resources exist within the organisation to function independently of the police. Second, that their operations are demonstrably transparent, and decision making structures are open to public scrutiny. Third, that the complainant has access to advice, representation and assistance. Finally, that the complainant has the right to challenge procedures or outcomes. Considering the earlier discussion of IPCC shortcomings, it is unproblematic to assert that the IPCC fails to meet these criteria when investigating cases of DAPC (Smith 2009). Coroners, however, appear to meet the first two criteria discussed above, but not the third and fourth. It is clear that legitimacy and transparency are relational and ambiguous concepts in the regulation of these cases, and that the type of accountability constructed depends upon the regulatory context in which it is produced.

## Systems and Structures: Relationality and Interdependence

Similar to the coronial system, geographic areas affect the expedition of IPCC processes. However, in the IPCC's case, five regions are charged with covering forty-three police forces, which can lead to significant challenges in securing the scene of death. This refers to the much vaunted 'golden hour' after the event where the crime scene is secured and evidence gathered (ACPO 2006). The IPCC's lack of resources and excessive volume of work was cited as the reason that on average an independent investigation took 269 days to conclude by the then chair of the organisation (Nick Hardwick) when giving evidence to the HAC (2010). The length of time for the investigation to conclude and the failure to secure evidence were evident in the Sean Rigg case, and this affected the legitimacy of the IPCC investigation. In this sense, little has changed since the late 1990s when Goldsmith and Lewis (2000) noted that a major problem in non-police investigations was the length of the time taken relative to similar police investigations. The IPCC's lack of resources was starkly illustrated by the HAC (2013) who observed that their entire budget was smaller than the DPS for the MPS. There are striking similarities here with the coronial system which has long been held to be under-resourced (see, for example Luce 2003; Smith 2003).

Rather than focus on one regulatory agency, Stone (2007) prefers to focus on the practical piecing together of systems of accountability that, he asserts, have and will continue to reduce police use of force. He believes that balancing accountability between agencies is more important than the efficacy of any one in particular, noting the prevalence of two-tier systems of accountability. Reiner (2000) believes that in order to promote greater accountability, there needs to be a more transparent system of accountability whereby internal police procedures mesh with the procedures of external regulators, a perspective recently embraced by an IPCC review (2014) and espoused by the Home Secretary, Theresa May (Home Office 2015). It is clear that an interdependent system of regulation has replaced the notion that a particular agency is most likely to hold police accountable. This further emphasises the notion that relationality is key in the construction of accountability in these cases, and that the balance between organisations in the regulatory sphere is key to understanding how accountability is constructed.

Interdependency and cooperation are important factors in regulating cases of DAPC. As such, the relationships between and within these organisations are worth investigating due to the possible tensions that such interdependence may produce. With regards to organisational structures, whilst the IPCC and HMIC are national organisations, police and coroners' courts are demonstrably not. Whilst ACPO and the NPIA produce guidelines on best practice and the IPCC promotes its 'Learning the Lessons' series at a national level, it rather overlooks the fact that there are forty-three police forces in England and Wales. This leads to tensions when these organisations begin to interact, as they inevitably must do in cases of DAPC. The local ethos of police in England and Wales sits uneasily with the increasingly centralised machinery of regulation (Savage and de Maillard 2012). Reiner (2000: 193) observes: 'Rejecting a *de jure* national police force, we have ended up with the substance of one, but without the structure of accountability for it ... You cannot have accountability for something that is not supposed to be there.' An assessment of the ideological landscape during a significant part of this period might explain these developments. 'New Labour's' administration reshaped conceptions of the rule of law and its role and purpose to citizens and state. The growth of organisations providing independent oversight is, to some degree, characteristic of the trend to valuing management responsibilities over lawfulness, and community relationships over universal rights (McLaughlin 2007). The lodestone of independence that the IPCC represents may therefore be indicative of symbolic political and ideological developments in accountability between citizens and state agencies. This may say more about efficiency and managerialism than about holding the police to account for their actions, as is discussed in more detail in Chap. 7.

## Conclusion

This chapter has demonstrated that the 'system' that constructs accountability in cases of DAPC is essentially non-systematic. It is marked by ambiguous processes and concepts, and subject to relatively arbitrary practices often characterised by discretion. The type of regulation that is produced is largely dependent on the institutional context in which accountability is constructed. Both regulators are characterised by concepts of independence, legitimacy and transparency, and these concepts are in turn shown to be relational and ambiguous in terms of practical and symbolic meaning.

The coronial system and the IPCC have different origins. The former is the longest established part of the justice system in England and Wales. As such, it has evolved through a number of guises that reflect its status within the legal system and its relationship between state and society. To some extent this has been an organic, evolutionary process. It is unsurprising that such a process might produce a decentralised, non-standardised and discretionary approach to investigating cases of DAPC. On the other hand, the IPCC is a twenty-first century invention. It was purpose designed, not least by statutory instrument, to address criticisms levelled at its predecessors by promoting public trust in policing whilst holding police accountable. That it is afflicted with the same problems as the coronial system suggests that regulation of the police is both a long standing and complex issue. Furthermore, while the coronial system focuses exclusively on deaths (not only cases of DAPC), the IPCC is principally part of the police complaints system. Indeed, this is underlined by the ex-chair of the IPCC criticising the amount of time spent investigating cases of DAPC as he did not consider it the core focus of the organisation (HAC 2010).

Both systems have audiences they must satisfy, and to some degree this affects their processes and practices. Both organisations aim to hold other organisations to account. Due to the remit of the coronial system, this is not limited to the police, whereas in the IPCC's case it is. Another commonality is the aim of learning lessons from deaths so that future deaths might be prevented. Furthermore, both organisations focus more on the investigation of individual cases as distinct from analysing and evaluating patterns between cases and issues. The IPCC appears to be somewhat more proactive in the latter regard with annual reports on DAPC and a number of research papers on the subject (see, for example Hannan et al. 2010). This perhaps reflects the national character of the IPCC in comparison with the more regionalised coronial system, although there are signs that coronial reporting procedures are becoming more centralised, albeit in a limited way with the introduction of the Chief Coroner (see, for example Ministry of Justice 2014). Neither coroners' courts nor the IPCC can sanction police or demand that their policies be altered in light of acts or omissions uncovered in the course of their investigations. Both, however, can demonstrate to the public that acts or omissions *have* been uncovered and require police to consider their recommendations. Finally, it has been established that both organisations have significant structural impediments, a commonality being lack of resources.

Both organisations exist as symbolic as well as practical entities. This creates a sense of ambiguity about the role and purpose of the coronial system and the IPCC when constructing accountability in these cases. Consequently, ambiguity creates tension in their respective relationships with the state and society in addition to the uncertain relationship they share with each other. These relationships are dynamic and evolving, often driven by events or circumstances that subsequently affect policies and practices in accountability construction. A fundamental driver since the turn of the century is Article 2 of the ECHR. Key concepts such as legitimacy, accountability and independence are intimately linked to

Article 2 and have been shown to be relational in the regulation of cases of DAPC. Having established the key issues in investigating these cases as they relate to the two principal regulators, the following two chapters go into more detail by considering the types of recording mechanism they use in these cases and what this says about the type of accountability that is constructed in cases of DAPC in England and Wales.

# References

ACPO. (2006). *Murder investigation manual.* Available at: http://www.acpo. police.uk/documents/crime/2006/2006CBAMIM.pdf. Accessed 16 Feb 2014.

ACPO. (2012). *Guidance on the safer detention and handling of persons in police custody* (2nd ed.). Available at: https://www.gov.uk/government/uploads/system/uploads/attachment_data/file/117555/safer-detention-guidance-2012. pdf. Accessed 5 Jan 2014.

BBC News. (2014, February 7). Police watchdog may 'double' staff to investigate complaints. Available at: http://www.bbc.co.uk/news/uk-politics-26084624. Accessed 8 Apr 2014.

Beckett, C. (1999). Deaths in custody and the inquest system. *Critical Social Policy, 19*(2), 271–280.

Casale, S., Corfe, M., & Lewis, J. (2013). *Report of the independent external review of the IPCC investigation into the death of Sean Rigg.* Available at: http://www. ipcc.gov.uk/news/Pages/pr_170513_Riggreview.aspx. Accessed 21 May 2013.

Chief Coroner. (2015). *Report of the Chief Coroner to the Lord Chancellor.* Second Annual Report: 2014–2015. Available at: https://www.judiciary.gov.uk/wp-content/uploads/2014/07/ann-report-chief-coroner-to-the-lord-chancellor-2014-5.pdf. Accessed 12 Oct 2015.

Chief Coroner's Office. (2013). *The Chief Coroner's guide to the Coroners and Justice Act 2009.* Available at: http://www.judiciary.gov.uk/wp-content/uploads/JCO/Documents/coroners/guidance/chief-coroners-guide-to-act-sept2013.pdf. Accessed 20 Dec 2013.

Claridge, T., Cook, G., & Hale, R. (2008). Organisational learning and patient safety in the NHS: An exploration of the organisational learning that occurs following a coroner's report under Rule 43. *Clinical Risk, 14*, 8–13.

Davis, G., Lindsey, R., Seabourne, G., & Griffiths-Baker, J. (2002). *Experiencing inquests. Home office research study,* 241. Home Office Research, Development and Statistics Directorate.

Dorries, C. (2004). *Coroners' courts: A guide to law and practice* (2nd ed.). Oxford: Oxford University Press.

Downham, G., & Lingham, R. (2009). Learning lessons: Using inquiries for change. *Journal of Mental Health Law, 18*(1), 57–69.

Doyle, J. (2010). Learning from error in American criminal justice. *Journal of Criminal Law and Criminology, 100*(1), 109–149.

Farrell, A., & Givelber, D. (2010). Liberation reconsidered: Understanding why judges and juries disagree about guilt. *Journal of Criminal Law and Criminology, 100*(4), 1549–1586.

Gilsinan, J. (2012). The numbers dilemma: The chimera of modern police accountability systems. *Saint Louis University Public Law Review, 32*, 93–108.

Goldsmith, A., & Lewis, C. (2000). *Civilian oversight of policing.* Oxford: Hart.

Goldsmith, A. J. (ed) (1991). *Complaints Against the Police: The Trend to External Review.* New York. Oxford University Press.

Griffin, S., & Moran, J. (2010). Accountability for deaths attributable to the gross negligent act or omission of a police force: The impact of the corporate manslaughter and corporate homicide act 2007. *Journal of Criminal Law, 74*(4), 358–381.

Hallam, E., Hockey, J., & Howarth, G. (1999). *Beyond the body: Death and social identity.* London: Routledge.

Hannan, M., Hearnden, I., Grace, K., & Bucke, T. (2010). *Deaths in or following police custody: An examination of the cases 1998/99–2008/09* (IPCC research series paper: 17). London: IPCC.

Harrison, J., & Cuneen, M. (2000). *An independent police complaints commission.* London: Liberty.

Hill, C., & Cook, L. (2011). Narrative verdicts and their impact on mortality statistics in England and Wales. *Health Statistics Quarterly, 49*(1), 1–20.

Home Office. (2015). *Improving police integrity: Reforming the police complaints and disciplinary systems.* London: HMSO.

House of Commons Home Affairs Committee. (2010). *The work of the independent police complaints commission.* London: TSO.

House of Commons Home Affairs Committee. (2013). *Independent police complaints commission.* London: TSO.

House of Lords. (1995). *Judgements—Regina v. Her Majesty's Coroner for North Humberside ex parte Jamieson [1995] QB1.*

Inquest. (2004). *Major breakthrough for inquest law: Sacker and Middleton— House of Lords ruling returned.* Available at: http://inquest.gn.apc.org/pdf/2004/Verdict_11_03_04.pdf. Accessed 8 Jan 2013.

IPCC. (2012). *Learning the lessons. Bulletin 16: Custody.* Available at: Accessed 16 Dec 2013.

IPCC. (2014). *Review of the IPCC's work in investigating deaths: Final report.* Available at: http://www.ipcc.gov.uk/sites/default/files/Documents/deaths_review/Review_of_the_IPCCs_work_in_investigating_deaths_2014.pdf. Accessed 17 Mar 2014.

Levine, M. (1999). *Levine on Coroners' Courts.* London: Sweet and Maxwell.

Luce, T. (2003). *Death certification and investigation in England, Wales and Northern Ireland: The report of a fundamental review.* London: The Stationery Office.

Maguire, M. (1991). Complaints against the police: The British experience. In A. Goldsmith (Ed.), *Complaints against the police: The trend to external review* (pp. 178–209). Oxford: Clarendon Press.

Matthews, P. (2002). *Jervis on the office and duties of coroners: With forms and precedents 12th edn.* London: Sweet and Maxwell.

Matthews, P. (2007). Show me the money: The new death investigation system. *Medico-Legal Journal, 75*(4), 123–138.

Matthews, P. (2011). *Jervis on the office and duties of coroners: With forms and precedents. Fourth cumulative supplement to the twelfth edition.* London: Sweet and Maxwell.

Matthews, P. (2014). *Jervis on the office and duties of coroners; with forms and precedents. Thirteenth edition.* London: Sweet and Maxwell.

McLaughlin, E. (2007). *The new policing.* London: Sage.

Ministry of Justice. (2010). *Summary of reports and responses under rule 43 of the coroners' rules*: September 2010.

Ministry of Justice. (2012). *Guide to coroners and inquests; And charter for coroner services.* London: TSO.

Ministry of Justice. (2014). *Coroners statistics 2014 England and Wales.* Available at: https://www.gov.uk/government/uploads/system/uploads/attachment_data/file/427720/coroners-statistics-2014.pdf. Accessed 2 Dec 2015.

National Audit Office. (2008). *The independent police complaints commission.* London: TSO.

Parliament. (2009). *Coroners and Justice Act.* Available at: http://www.legislation.gov.uk/ukpga/2009/25/section/1. Accessed 10 Aug 2015.

Prenzler, T. (2009). *Ethics and accountability in criminal justice.* Brisbane: Australian Academic Press.

Punch, M. (2009). *Police corruption: Deviance, accountability and reform in policing.* Cullompton: Willan.

Reid, K. (2005). The home secretary and improved accountability of the police? *Journal of Criminal Law, 69,* 232–255.

Reiner, R. (1991). Multiple realities, divided worlds—Chief constables perspectives on the police complaints system. In A. J. Goldsmith (Ed.), *Complaints against the police: The trend to external review* (pp. 211–231). Oxford: Clarendon Press.

Reiner, R. (2000). *The politics of the police* (3rd ed.). Oxford: Oxford University Press.

Savage, S. (2013a). Thinking independence: Calling the police to account through the independent investigation of police complaints. *British Journal of Criminology, 53*(1), 94–112.

Savage, S. (2013b). Seeking 'civilianness': Police complaints and the civilian control model of oversight. *British Journal of Criminology, 53*(5), 886–904.

Savage, S., & de Maillard, J. (2012). Comparing performance: The development of police performance management in France and Britain. *Policing and Society, 22*(4), 363–383.

Scraton, P., Jemphrey, A., & Coleman, S. (1995). *No last rights: The denial of justice and the promotion of myth in the aftermath of the Hillsborough disaster.* Liverpool: Liverpool City Council.

Shane, J. (2013). *Learning from error in policing: A case study in organisational accident theory.* Heidelberg: Springer.

Shaw, H., & Coles, D. (2007). *Unlocking the truth: Families' experiences of the investigation of deaths in custody.* London: Inquest.

Smith, J. (2003). *The shipman inquiry (third report): Death certification and the investigation of deaths by Coroners.* London: The Stationery Office.

Smith, G. (2009). Why don't more people complain against the police? *European Journal of Criminology, 6*(3), 249–266.

Smith, G. (2013). Oversight of the police and residual complaints dilemmas: Independence, effectiveness and accountability in the United Kingdom. *Police Practice and Research: An International Journal, 14*(2), 92–103.

Stone, C. (2007). Training police accountability in theory and practice: From Philadelphia to Abuja and Sao Paolo. *Theoretical Criminology, 11*(2), 245–259.

Tarling, R. (1998). *Coroner service survey. Home Office research study 181.* London: Home Office.

Terpstra, J., & Trommel, W. (2009). Police, managerialisation and presentational strategies. *Policing: An International Journal of Police Strategies and Management, 32*(1), 128–143.

Thomas, L., Straw, A., & Friedman, D. (2008). *Inquests: A practitioner's guide* (2nd ed.). London: Legal Action Group.

Wadham, J. (2004). Investigations into deaths in police custody and the independent police complaints commission. *European Human Rights Law Review, 4,* 353–361.

Waters, I., & Brown, K. (2000). Police complaints and the complainants' experience. *British Journal of Criminology, 40*(4), 617–638.

Widdicombe, K. (2012). How … the deceased came by his death. In I. McDougall (Ed.), *Cases that changed our lives* (pp. 175–181). London: Lexis Nexis.

# 4

# Constructing Verdicts in the Coronial System

## Introduction

It has been established that the coronial system has relatively ambiguous aims and processes, and is essentially regional. The ambiguity stems from, and is driven by discretion, and the regional nature of the system emphasises both ambiguity and discretion. These issues are particularly apparent in the way that narrative verdicts are recorded in the coronial system in cases of DAPC. The wide variety of format, style and content in narrative verdict construction emphasises the non-systematic and relational nature of accountability construction in the coronial system. The chapter uses sixty-eight narrative verdicts to examine how juries use specific measurements to assess actions and inactions related to state organisations in these cases. This highlights the fundamental importance of how and why parameters are constructed in the first place in order for juries to be able to use them.

It is argued that the term 'death after police contact' should be re-assessed in light of findings in the dataset that half of these cases involve agencies other than the police. Typically in these cases juries are more likely to be critical of non-police agencies than they are of the police. This has implications for the way we view these cases, and suggests we overly

© The Editor(s) (if applicable) and The Author(s) 2016
D. Baker, *Deaths After Police Contact*,
DOI 10.1057/978-1-137-58967-5_4

focus on the police when considering these deaths. The reality is that these deaths often occur as a result of insufficient care from other public services, making them more of a healthcare or welfare issue than one related to the enforcement of criminal justice. The issue of measurement is discussed regarding comments made in the majority of narrative verdicts about actions or omissions identified in these cases. Benchmarking and auditing have become increasingly important in holding police account-able in these cases. This is because organisations must demonstrate they adhere to the requirements of Article 2 of the ECHR by producing poli-cies that their employees should follow when faced with crisis situations. Measurement through benchmarking is specifically examined in relation to policy and procedure, communication, risk assessment and training. The chapter considers how criteria and guidelines are produced by agen-cies in this sphere and are subsequently measured and evaluated by juries in these cases. The chapter demonstrates that these criteria are assessed with regard to all organisations relating to cases of DAPC, making the coroner's inquest the only forum in which all relevant organisations are theoretically called to account. These issues illustrate the fact that as the construction of accountability evolves, the accountability it constructs in cases of DAPC becomes increasingly dispersed and relational, and conse-quently more difficult to learn lessons from because the coronial system is essentially regionalised.

The jury focus on measurement has highlighted the relevance of omis-sion, suggesting that inaction might be as relevant as action in cases of DAPC. Article 2 of the ECHR is particularly relevant in enabling juries to highlight omission due to its requirement that the state actively pro-motes an environment whereby the right to life is enabled—hence what state agents do *not* do may have become as important as what they *do*. On the other hand, narrative verdicts also underscore the key issue that the use of force is central to many of these cases. In this chapter, the issue is examined under the headings of 'restraint' and 'shooting'. These provide a stark counterpoint to the discussion of omission in narrative verdicts. Euphemisation is evident in the way that the jury rationalises and distances police from the use of physical violence. Indeed, the word 'violence' does not appear in the dataset, instead it is typically termed 'restraint', and less frequently 'force'. It is argued that this fits within the use of rational benchmarking criteria discussed above. This facilitates the use of more euphemistic terms and legitimises the use of violence as a necessary and proportionate response in particular contexts given specific sets of contingencies.

Shooting represents the ultimate use of force. In these cases juries do not use euphemisation, preferring to clearly state that firearms are used to inflict terminal injuries and recording this as the cause of death. Most cases of DAPC are notable for having deaths which are multi-causal (see, for example Prior 1985). In the relatively infrequent number of cases in which shooting occurs it is presented by juries as the most straight-forward type of death in which accountability is constructed. This is because such cases: are represented as being uni-causal, as distinct from multi-causal; typically involve one agency as distinct from multiple agencies; and are held to be instances where tighter control and supervision is demonstrated by police. This results in relatively uncritical verdicts being recorded. Whereas most of the issues examined in this book are typified by ambiguity and relationality, shooting appears to be an exception. This may be a reflection of the symbolic function of the police in being able to legitimately use lethal force in certain contexts.

Findings within the narrative verdict dataset illustrate the complexity and diversity of these cases of the individuals that die; the agencies they come into contact with; the way in which actions and omissions are evaluated in light of specific contexts; and the type of structure, agency and style used to record the narratives. The chapter examines the processes by which accountability is constructed in cases of DAPC and also analyses patterns and trends in the production of documents that are fundamental to understanding accountability construction in these cases. While half of these deaths might be better conceived of as health or welfare issues, and related to omission or inaction, the other half are more definitely related to what we typically conceive of as cases of DAPC in that police are the primary agency involved and force is used. Cases of DAPC are complex and marked by multi-causality. This chapter demonstrates that narrative verdicts capture such complexity and multi-causality in the attempt to construct accountability when a person dies after contact with police. The wider question of whether lessons are learned for the future as a result of such verdicts is considered in more detail in the subsequent two chapters. For now, we begin by considering the diverse formats, styles and contents within the narrative verdict dataset that typify the non-systematic and discretionary aspects of accountability construction in the coronial system.

## Format, Style and Content

Inquests typically begin a significant amount of time after the death of the individual. In the Sean Rigg case, for example, the inquest began forty-eight months after his death. The limited practitioner literature that exists on Article 2 jury inquests indicates that typically two to four years elapses between death and the inquest, but it can be in excess of six years (Thomas et al. 2008; Shaw and Coles 2007). The dataset confirms this: in three-quarters of cases two years or more has elapsed between the death of the individual and their inquest being heard. In nearly half of the cases, three years or more has elapsed. While there is no available data on how long murder cases take to come to court, it is unproblematic to state that such cases are typically heard more quickly than cases of DAPC. The most immediate observation about narrative verdicts is that they are strikingly diverse in the format used and the manner of recording details, reflecting decentralised and non-standardised practices in the coronial system. Evidently not only is there a dispersal of accountability across organisations in the wider sphere of police regulation, but there is a dispersal of accountability within the coronial system about the way accountability is constructed in these cases. Thus the type of accountability constructed is relational and dependent upon multiple contexts, not least regarding where they are recorded and who they are recorded by. Narrative verdicts represent an evolving form of accountability construction in cases of DAPC and consequently legal ambiguity over their format, style and content might be expected. The great majority of people who die in cases of DAPC are male (see, for example Leigh et al. 1998; Hannan et al. 2010; IAP 2015). This is replicated in the narrative verdict dataset; out of sixty-eight cases considered, only three are female.

The majority of narrative verdicts surveyed are of a pure narrative type in the sense that they are written entirely as free-form prose. This adheres to the general principle of using narrative verdicts in Article 2 inquests—to record the most relevant facts, as the jury sees it, about each death (Matthews 2011). This type of narrative verdict reflects the discretion of the jury, as although they are directed by the coroner, they have the ultimate decision as to what should be recorded (Levine 1999). Within this group of narrative verdicts the diversity in length of verdict is striking. Some are three or four sentences in length. Others are in excess of 100 sentences in length, some being typewritten while others are handwritten.

In other cases questionnaire verdicts are produced by the coroner for the jury to record answers to predetermined questions about the case set before them. They account for approximately one-fifth of the dataset. The number of questions posed within this portion of the dataset varies from five to forty-two. Similarly, the type of answers available to the jury vary from the relatively closed 'yes, no, do not know', to more expansive multi-choice options. Within this category are a number of verdicts where juries have recorded comments in handwriting on the questionnaire, exhibiting a sense of jury agency on the structure imposed by the coroner. The final category is narrative plus questionnaire. Within this group, there is a similar diversity of recording style. Some questionnaires pose questions which invite answers in prose. Some have 'yes, no, do not know' answers combined with an additional section of narrative written in prose.

The inquisition sheet on which the details of the death are recorded is similarly non-standardised in these cases. There are variances in the type of form used, the specific boxes filled in within that form, or of incomplete details about the date of birth, or the place where the inquest was heard. There is irregularity in the types of formats used to record narrative verdicts and also in the inquisition sheet used to record such findings. The diversity of verdict construction added to the atypical nature of the coronial system emphasises how different this legal forum is when compared to the civil and criminal court systems in England and Wales. It puts into question the value the state puts on the process of accountability construction in cases of DAPC, and this is considered in more detail in subsequent chapters. Having established the diverse formats, styles and lengths of narrative verdicts we now consider their content in terms of issues highlighted in cases of DAPC.

## Deaths after Police Contact?

Approximately half of the narrative verdicts surveyed involve agencies other than the police. This occurs either with other agencies present at, or near the time of death; or about failures or oversights of agencies that result in police ultimately becoming involved with the individual who died. Cases of DAPC are notable for lacking singular causes attributable to an individual's death (see, for example, ACPO 2012; Matthews 2011; Hannan et al. 2010; Marsh et al. 2009). Thus it is unsurprising that more than one agency is involved in circumstances surrounding such deaths. Terpstra and Trommel's (2009) concept of cognitive legitimacy might explain this aspect of accountability construction. From this perspective, legitimacy is produced that is relevant and meaningful to society. As a significant proportion of these cases include agencies other than the police, if the jury were to ignore this when constructing accountability they would produce findings of questionable relevance to society. In this sense, the role of the lay-person in constructing accountability in these cases reflects a holistic construction that considers lesson learning with a view to future life preservation. On the other hand, the regional nature of the coronial system and the diversity of narrative verdict recording suggests that lesson learning is less likely as a result.

The term 'DAPC' is thus somewhat of a misnomer. The explicit representation is that these deaths occur after police contact, which suggests that the event is relatively unambiguous. This needs to be qualified on two counts. First, that in a considerable number of cases, the death occurs after contact with more than one agency. Second, that in a number of instances, the death occurs as a result of police being called to an event which subsequently appears to have been caused by the acts or omissions of one or other agency, as occurred in the death of Sean Rigg. Both of these observations suggest that the event is likely to be more complex than it is currently constructed as being. It suggests that not only should police legitimacy be examined in these cases, but the legitimacy of other public services should as well. Numerous official reports have highlighted the multi-agency issue in cases of DAPC (see, for example: Casale et al. 2013; Adebowale 2013; Hannan et al. 2010; BMA 2009; Fulton 2008).

Official reports into this area invariably highlight the issue of marginalised groups and their interactions with police, as noted in Chap. 2.

It has been established that a significant majority of cases can be linked to any one (or any combination) of alcohol, drugs or mental health. In the dataset these cases account for two-thirds of the total deaths, which compares with the IPCC ten-year review of cases of DAPC of 77 per cent (Hannan et al. 2010). The finding highlights the perennial question of whether the police are the appropriate organisation to deal with vulnerable individuals who often have complex needs (see, for example BMA 2009; Shaw and Coles 2007). This emphasises whether the issue of DAPC might be better considered to be a health or welfare issue rather than one of enforcement and control. A consistent theme in the dataset is for juries to be critical of non-police services regarding deaths, underlining fact that accountability is relatively dispersed and relational. For example, in a questionnaire verdict:

Case 28: Question 1a: 'Was calling the police a reasonable option to adopt given the presentation of [the deceased] on [date]?'
Answer 'No'
Question 3 'Was sufficient information, including risk information, passed from hospital staff to the arresting officer at the time of the arrest?'
Answer 'No.'

Thus hospital staff are criticised while police are portrayed as being inappropriately engaged and inadequately informed. Another case highlights failings of NHS and Mental Health teams in a way that appears to question the legitimacy of the service similar to the case above:

Case 20: There was no proper understanding on the part of the Trust or the clinicians of the way in which the Care Programme Approach should have been implemented. There was no formal training in the Care Programme Approach or in the completion of forms. This was a singular failing.'

This is in sharp contrast with a passage that records police interaction with the deceased:

Case 20: 'The two officers dealt with him in a kindly and humane way and there were no steps that they could have taken other than those that they did, given their assessment of the situation.'

Another is more openly critical of civilian Custody Assistants working within the custody suite:

Case 41: 'Although they couldn't see him breathing, and in spite of having adequate medical training, as well as possessing the authority to enter [the deceased's] cell, the Custody Assistants decided to return to the custody suite and inform the Custody Officer.'

If other agencies are present in these cases it appears the jury are more predisposed to be critical of those agencies rather than the police. When no other agencies are involved, juries appear more likely to be critical of police acts or omissions, for example:

Case 35: 'The briefing was inadequate due to the gross failure of the intelligence systems in place at the time.'

When juries are critical of police, it is typically in the abstract sense of police organisation, systems, procedures or training, rather than of individual officers. That said, it must be noted that this may be because while, for example, only one FME (Forensic Medical Examiner), or two paramedics may be present, there are often numerous police officers and this might diffuse the perceived responsibility somewhat. Conversely, while agencies' systems, processes and training might be focused on, the deceased is considered as an individual 'case'. The dispersal of responsibility in these cases highlights a common thread in official discourse (Fulton 2008).

Official reports into this subject are remarkably consistent on the issue of multi-agency involvement in cases of DAPC and apparent inability to learn from trends and patterns due to lack of analysis. In a piece commissioned by the PCA in 1998: 'Deaths in Police Custody: Learning the Lessons', Leigh et al. highlighted issues relating to the care of detainees regarding drugs, alcohol and mental health and questioned whether police custody was the appropriate environment for such individuals. This underlines the ambiguous role of the police as discussed in Chap. 2 about their role in the preservation of life when balanced with the need to enforce law and order. Leigh et al.'s (1998) research presaged the 'Learning the Lessons' series produced quarterly by the IPCC that aims to improve best practice and consequently minimise the number of DAPC cases (IPCC 2013). Issues highlighted by Leigh et al. (1998) are reiterated in the IPCC 10-year review into cases of DAPC (Hannan et al. 2010). Furthermore, they are emphasised in policy guidance such as ACPO's (2012) second edition of 'Safer Detention and Handling of Persons in Police Custody'. Finally, they are underlined in reports such as the Casale (2013) review into the death of Sean Rigg, and Adebowale's *Independent Commission on Mental Health and Policing* (2013). Clearly such issues are structurally deep-seated, persistent and long standing. Despite numerous official reports and commissions consistently highlighting these issues there has been little improvement in this area. This suggests not only problems with lesson learning but also problems with multi-agency working with vulnerable individuals as discussed in Chap. 2. Findings from the dataset bear this out, as is discussed presently. While official reports focus primarily on the quantitative recording of data, narrative verdicts are typically examples of qualitative data. It would appear that the public, jury-based Article 2 inquest is a way of ensuring that legitimate accountability is constructed in cases of DAPC. The following section discusses the relevance of official agencies in the production of guidelines and policies that provide juries with measurement criteria when considering acts or omissions in cases of DAPC.

## Measurement

Acts or omissions linked to the death of an individual represent a significant aspect of the dataset. Communication, policy and procedure, training and risk assessment are noted either individually or in any combination in more than half of the cases. A key change effected by Article 2 with regards to narrative verdicts was the ability of juries to consider wider issues about 'how the individual met their death' as distinct from the act that led to the death (Widdicombe 2012). Given this, it is unsurprising that juries have focused on communication, policy and procedure, training and risk assessment as issues. Communication is highlighted in one-third of cases as an issue relating to the death of an individual, for example:

Case 7: 'A contributory factor in [the deceased's] death was the lack of communication between all services as to his condition.'

Approximately one-third of deaths focus on policy or procedure, for example:

Case 48: 'During this time the Custody Sergeant did not institute the half hourly checks upon [the deceased] but instead left the regime as the standard hourly checks. As it transpired even these hourly checks did not take place properly.'

Training is noted as an issue in one quarter of deaths, for example:

Case 12: 'Training was in place for custody staff but seems to have been ineffective in ensuring that all staff knew and understood policy and procedures.'

Similarly, risk assessment is noted in a quarter of cases, for example:

Case 55: 'The DDO[1] had access [sic] the risk assessment and should have carried out rousing checks. Thiss [sic] was a gross failure by the DDO.'

Risk assessment is prominent in the ACPO (2012: 23–25) guidelines on safer detention, which state that it should be conducted both prior to arrest and upon arrival at the custody suite. However, an investigation into healthcare in custody suites by de Viggiani et al. (2010: 8) found that the process of risk assessments was of debatable worth due to their uneven application. This raises the question of whether accountability is a matter of checking for function or procedure, or is considered in terms of effectiveness. Ericson and Haggerty (1997: 87) believe that: 'Rationalities of risk are designed to reduce uncertainty to the point where the actor feels confident in taking action.' It must, however, be remembered that inaction is also a significant issue in construction of narrative verdicts, and this is discussed presently.

---

[1] Duty Detention Officer.

Analysis of the dataset reveals that evaluation and assessments of actions or omissions on the part of individuals involved with the death are made by referring to policies and guidelines that benchmark best practice. Chan's (1999) view is that police accountability is intrinsically linked to evaluation: judging actions or omissions requires measurement against prescribed standards. Shane (2013: 9) notes that 'policies are the organisation's first line of defence to unsafe acts'. In this sense, Williams' (2014: 127) view that information: 'provides a version of events which can be consulted as a guide to further action' appears apposite. This chimes with Smith's (2009) assertion that while regulation is prospective in that it seeks to prescribe future actions, accountability is retrospective as it constructs a version of reality after the fact. The temporal nature of accountability construction is examined in more detail in Chap. 7.

Due to the diverse number of organisations involved, and the diversity of complex cases across the dataset, the findings produced are increasingly complex, leading to a construction of accountability that produces findings that are more ambiguous. One requirement of Article 2 of the ECHR is that state organisations are required to demonstrate they have policies, practices and training in place to guide their employees in how they should act in critical situations. Consequently, as the impact of Article 2 on cases of DAPC has become more pronounced, the number of guidance documents on this issue has burgeoned, illustrating both the dispersal of accountability and Chan's (1999) concept of evaluation regarding the construction of accountability in these cases. Examples of guidance and policy documents include those produced by ACPO (2012), the IPCC's 'Learning the Lessons' series, FFLM (2010a, b, 2007), BMA (2009), and HMIC (2013). The coroner's court is the single forum in which the actions or omissions of multiple agencies can be evaluated and recorded in cases of DAPC. It may be the case that the principal audiences that consume accountability production are: first the coronial system; and, second, the other agencies involved in the production of guidelines who may re-assess their policies based on inquest findings. The issue of multiple audiences in the construction of accountability is further discussed in Chap. 6 as it relates to an expanding discourse of accountability in cases of DAPC. Similarly, the expansion of documentation is considered in more detail in Chap. 6 about discursive changes within the sphere of accountability production.

Actions or omissions are assessed in light of institutional frameworks that provide policies and procedures, or training for dealing with potentially critical situations. Article 2 inquests have expanded the scope of which factors should be considered, and consequently recorded, in cases of DAPC. This has enabled a broader commentary to be constructed taking into account organisational issues leading to the death. One consequence of this is that the actions or omissions of police may be criticised because of structures put in place to manage the use of officers' discretion, rather than merely focusing on what an officer did or did not do. A second consequence is that these verdicts might confer more legitimacy to the construction of accountability because they allow lay-persons to apply their own assessments and evaluations of acts or omissions when put into the context of the structures that should guide officers. Both of these consequences have enabled the production of a verdict that is significantly more detailed and wide-ranging in scope than the previously used short-form verdicts. This marks a significant evolution in the discourse of accountability construction in cases of DAPC. The major question, as yet unanswered, is whether this evolution leads to a reduction in the number of deaths or whether it fulfils the obligation to Article 2 of the ECHR, and whether these two issues are mutually exclusive. This question is evaluated in greater detail in Chap. 7., For now, we focus on the increasingly highlighted issue of inaction in cases of DAPC.

## Omission

Omissions or inaction on the part of organisations involved in these deaths are noted by juries in nearly half of the cases surveyed. Academic literature on cases of DAPC tends to focus on issues of police misconduct or use of force (for example; see Pinizzotto et al. 2012; Greer and McLaughlin 2012; Belur 2010; Hirschfield and Simon 2010; Fyfe 1998). However, Savage (2007) does note the issue of failure of police to act as being increasingly relevant in miscarriages of justice. In particular he notes failures to act on information, or to pass information on to other agencies, and there are numerous examples that reinforce this in the data-set. It appears that a significant issue is the inaction of individuals from a number of agencies who come into contact with the deceased, much as was the case in the death of Sean Rigg. Similar to the misnomer regarding death after police contact, the issue of contact should be viewed more equivocally. Omission is a form of commission, by not doing something, the individual or group choose to do something else (even if that 'something' is nothing). By stating that omission occurs, the jury might avoid using the word 'neglect' due to the connotations this has with liability. This finding is further analysed under the heading 'specific ambiguity' presently. The ability of juries to identify omission relates to measurement and benchmarking. This is sometimes stated in abstract:

Case 9: 'Had the appropriate precautions and actions been taken death may have been prevented.'

Conversely it is sometimes stated in emphatically concrete terms:

Case 37: 'We unanimously agree that on the balance of probabilities, the omissions of the ambulance crew contributed to the cause of [the deceased's] death.'

Similarly, the significance of omission could be seen as a reflection of the Article 2 requirement that the right to life is not merely to be protected, but promoted by the state actively seeking to enable the right to life (Thomas et al. 2008). It has become incumbent on state agencies to demonstrate they have policies, procedures, training and risk assessments in place to ensure this. The following examples illustrate a specific measurement identified by the jury as being lacking, and that omission leads to a 'lost opportunity' to preserve life:

Case 18: 'Annex H was not adhered to at any time or Code C.[2] Therefore we believe that many opportunities were lost to check on [the deceased's] condition.'

---

[2] References to codes of practice in the 1984 Police and Criminal Evidence Act.

> Case 55: 'The [ambulance] crew did not take the opportunity available to them to carry out basic assessments at [place] custody suite and/or send [the deceased] to hospital. This represents a gross failure.'

Omission relates to measurement in that in order for something to be identified as being lacking, there must be existing criteria that state specific actions should occur. Omission is typically recorded due to life not being preserved as a result of inaction in the dataset. This may be on the part of police or other organisations, but it once again raises the issue of ambiguity in how these cases are represented. 'Contact' implies action, but as accountability construction evolves it appears that factors recorded as being causal in cases where people die after police contact increasingly relate to inaction. Writing about indigenous deaths in police custody in Canada, Razack (2015: 112) notes: 'indifference kills'.

# Failure

Fail as a stem to 'failing', 'failed' or 'failure' is recorded in one-third of the verdicts. 'Fail' may be defined as being unsuccessful, of falling short of expectations, or being less than required. In this sense, all relate to a discrepancy. 'Fail' is a relatively emphatic word for a jury to select. In order to record it, they must be able to measure a target that should, or could have been achieved, in order to identify a discrepancy. The identification of such a discrepancy falls short of ascribing liability, but does highlight acts or omissions that may have contributed to the death of an individual. Failures highlighted within the dataset relate variously to groups or individuals, usually about systems or procedures that have not been adhered to. The examples below refer to multi-agency failure, police failure and the failure of mental health teams:

> Case 4: 'We the jury found from beginning to end that the whole system has failed [the deceased]'

> Case 16: 'The failure by Police to follow hourly checks provided an unsatisfactory level of supervision.'

Case 20: '[the deceased] should have been dealt with under what is known as the enhanced level of care. The failure to recognize the need for this was a direct consequence of a failure to hold professional review meetings and of failings to communicate adequately, and sometimes at all, between individuals.'

Failure is being increasingly recorded in narrative verdicts in cases of DAPC. It occurs across a greater proportion of narrative verdicts, but also with greater frequency within narrative verdicts. It typically relates to omissions on the part of organisations involved in the death. A further development is the increasingly frequent use of the term 'gross failure'; for example in the case below 'gross failure' is recorded nine times:

Case 55: '[the deceased] should have been sent to hospital after he had been searched and risk assessed ... due to the fact that [*sic*] was intoxicated, incapable of meaningful communication, had received a head injury, was incapable of movement without assistance ... This was a gross failure on the part of the custody sargeant [*sic*].'

It is likely that juries have begun to select a word that is unambiguous, can usefully highlight omission but also does not necessarily ascribe liability. The growth of guidelines and policies within the discursive sphere of accountability construction has provided juries greater scope with which to assess whether a failure or omission has occurred. As discussed earlier, the issues of failure, inaction and omission point to such deaths perhaps being better considered as a matter for healthcare or welfare agencies. We now turn to what is considered to be more typical in cases of DAPC—the use of force and the police as an agency of enforcement.

## 'Restraint'

There are levels of euphemisation about the use of state sanctioned force that legitimates its usage. The word 'violence' does not occur in any example in the dataset. The *Oxford English Dictionary* (*OED*) (Pearsall 2002: 1600) definition of violence is: 'behaviour involving physical force intended to hurt, damage, or kill'. Therefore force is a synonym for violence, so it should not be entirely unreasonable to use it as such in public documents. If the word violence were used in its stead, this would imply intention on behalf of the user, which would mean that officers might be liable for prosecution in a criminal court. Hence it would seem that force is a more acceptable word from a legal as well as a euphemistic perspective. 'Force' in the *OED* (ibid: 553) has multiple definitions, the most relevant of which in this context is: 'coercion backed by the use or threat of violence'. Similarly, then, there is a link between force and violence. The primary difference between the two words is that of intent of use.

Particularly notable is the use of the word 'restraint', which is used more frequently than force in narrative verdicts. 'Restrain' is defined by the *OED* (ibid: 1221) as: 'Prevent from doing something, keep within limits; deprive of freedom of movement or personal liberty'. This would appear to fit with the principles under which police should employ force—'within limits'. From this perspective, restraint is situated at the milder end of the spectrum with 'violence' at the more extreme end and 'force' in between. The *OED* (ibid: 1221) definition of 'restraint' is: 'Dispassionate or moderate behaviour; self-control'. This fits within the principle of acting within limits, but also rationalises the use of force in a more palatable way than definitions of force or violence do. It implies that were a passionate or immoderate person exerting it, its use might not remain within limits. Viewed from this perspective, police do not only restrain individuals, but they exercise restraint while so doing. 'Restraint' is a relatively *passive* way to describe the use of force.

The process described above appears to represent a tacit acceptance within the discourse of accountability construction that police have a monopoly on the use of force, largely supported by the academic literature (see, for example Bittner 1975; Waddington 1999; Reiner 2010). This appears to reflect Terpstra and Trommel's (2009) concept of pragmatic legitimacy in that social audiences (in this case, juries) make rational, self-interested calculations. In this sense, some of these deaths may be viewed as 'collateral damage'. Euphemisation might be a way of distancing the jury, the constructers of narrative verdicts, from this tacit acceptance. If the use of force is to be legitimised, one way to ameliorate its use is to give it a different name. Hirschfield and Simon's (2010) analysis of 'media narratives of deadly force' in the USA identified the concept of euphemisation as being key to rationalising officers' actions in the media and consequently constructing legitimacy.

Hirschfield and Simon's (2010) antonym to euphemism is dysphemism: the use of harsh or derogatory words in the place of more neutral words. Conversely, this can be used to consider accountability production from the perspective of the deceased. Whereas euphemism replaces neutral words with more ameliatory examples that soften the meaning of those words, dysphemism replaces them with more pejorative examples. For example, references to the deceased being 'infested'. Similarly, examples referring to the deceased 'moaning', 'groaning', and 'growling'. These examples appear to situate the deceased as potentially being both pathological (Scraton 2002) and having atavistic undertones. Thus euphemisation might be seen to legitimise police actions while dysphemisation effectively dehumanises and pathologises the recipient of such actions within accountability construction (see also Razack 2015).

Restraint is noted in one-third of the narrative verdicts. This compares with the IPCC ten-year review that identified 26 per cent of cases relating to restraint (Hannan et al. 2010). Restraint is most commonly used in cases relating to mental health issues and/or drugs. The link between mental health and police restraint is long established and highlights two key issues: first, that research into police attitudes on individuals who have mental health issues typically demonstrates that police tend to view this section of the population as being potentially violent due to a somewhat stigmatised representation (Ruiz and Miller 2004). Consequently, police may be more likely to use force as a first, rather than last resort (Terrill 2005). Second, it has been established that police training on the issue of mental health is at best patchy (Adebowale 2013; Morabito 2007). However, police are often the only agency available able to deal with an individual with mental health issues, illustrating their position as the agency of last resort as was established in the discussion of Sean Rigg's death. Another persistent issue is the lack of an available space at the nearest appropriate mental health institution leading to police cells being used as a 'place of safety' (HMIC 2013; Andoh 2009).

In the case below, multiple instances of restraint at the deceased's home follow a failed attempt to conduct a mental health assessment. The positional aspect of the restraint is repeatedly commented on in addition to the length of time for which restraint occurs. It also records the comment:

> Case 7: 'Further police units arrived at the scene and took over forcibly restraining [the deceased] in the prone position.'

An example of restraint being used not in response to mental health issues, but still emphasising the jury's belief that it is necessary is listed below:

> Case 36: 'The officers did not recognise these risk factors in accordance with their training, because the officers were entirely focussed on controlling and restraining [the deceased]. The officers did not act in accordance with the Standard Operating Procedure in getting [the deceased] into a safe position as soon as possible after control was achieved.'

It is notable that in both cases police are not explicitly criticised for using force, rather the narrative is constructed to justify the use of force, albeit that in the latter example this is subject to qualified criticism. In this sense, the use of police force is usually seen to be legitimate by juries, perhaps underlining their support for the police as an essentially reactive organisation and reflecting the relative criticism of healthcare agencies. It may be that juries see the police function as enforcement and consequently support the use of force, whereas they view the function of healthcare organisations as essentially life preservation and are thus more critical of them.

Stories require characters. The assignment of roles to characters in narrative is key to interpreting how they behave in particular circumstances and why certain types of events unfold in the way they do, and this appears to be particularly the case in deaths where force has been used. In the dataset, the recording of specific human characteristics uniformly relate to the individual who has died. In this sense, the deceased may be seen as the 'lead actor' in the construction of the narrative. Typically, when characteristics are recorded, they are recorded early in the verdict as a way of establishing the individual within the narrative.

When physical characteristics are recorded in the initial stages of narrative construction they appear to situate the individual within a context that requires action to address the situation in which police find themselves. It is notable, for example that the recording of physical characteristics rarely relates to omissions. In the scenarios described in this section of the chapter, police are called to deal with an individual constructed as being either potentially dangerous, diseased or unpredictable. When such a narrative is constructed, it is perhaps unsurprising that police resort to using force. Such a reaction tends to be constructed as rational, necessary and measured. Hyden's (1997) research on reports by social workers and psychiatric nurses unequivocally stated narratives were a way of structuring events and behaviours in such a way as to justify the intervention of authority. It would appear much the same occurs in the way accountability is constructed in police interventions when force is used.

The tendency to focus on physical characteristics and/or the actions of the deceased, and the construction of certain conditions appears to fit with organisational research into cases of DAPC. In the PCA's major review of these cases, Leigh et al. (1998) grouped causes of death into three categories. First, those resulting from the deceased's own actions (estimated to be 63 per cent of cases). Second, those resulting from the deceased's medical condition (29 per cent of cases). Finally, those resulting from the actions of other individuals (8 per cent of cases). Examples from cases of DAPC where force was used include the following two cases, both of which are the opening line of the narrative verdict.

Case 1: '[the deceased] was 172cm tall considered medically obese (weighing approximately 20 stone), and exhibited considerable strength when restrained at [home address redacted].'

Case 7: '[the deceased] was a 28 year old male suffering from schizophrenia and diabetes. He was 6ft tall and obese.'

Thus it appears that constructing conditions for the deceased is one way of rationally explaining the use of force against them. In this sense, euphemism can be used to distance the jury from the use of violence, dysphemism can serve to pathologise the individual who is the recipient of violence, and the construction of conditions can justify the use of violence by police as a necessary response to a dangerous and potentially unpredictable individual. It must, however, be noted that euphemism is not used in all cases where force is used, a notable exception is shooting, which is discussed below.

## Shooting

There are relatively few cases of death by shooting in the dataset, and this appears to reflect the literature that states fewer than two people on average are shot dead by the police annually in England and Wales (Punch 2011; Squires and Kennison 2010). While multi-causality is characteristic of most cases of DAPC, in cases of shooting the cause of death is clear. It appears this clarity is less likely to produce criticism of the police by juries. These cases also tend not to involve other organisations at the time of death, removing the complexity of multi-agency contact from the death. As was established earlier in this chapter, juries are more likely to be critical of other organisations if they are actors involved in the narrative.

The issue of clarity is also manifest in the time elapsed between the death and the inquest. All inquests into shooting cases in the dataset were concluded within thirty-five months of the death. In contrast, nearly half of the cases in the dataset took in excess of thirty-six months to conclude. This suggests that cases of deaths by shooting have more explicable causes, are less likely to involve multi-agency contact, and are consequently more straightforward to expedite at inquest. The issue of the deceased provoking the shooting occurs in two of the six cases. This appears to highlight a trend discussed above about constructing conditions when describing the deceased in narrative verdicts. It suggests that when force is used, some narratives are constructed on the basis that the deceased to some degree initiates actions leading to their own death. In the case of police shooting, the academic literature contains limited references that suggest the possibility of individuals provoking their own death (see, for example Lord 2014).

Whereas juries may be critical of the use of restraint, there are no instances where they are critical of the use of firearms. On the contrary, the narrative constructs shootings as variously: 'appropriate'; as the result of 'risk assessment'; as 'necessary and reasonable'; and 'authorised'. It is clear, then, that although there is euphemisation around the use of force, the ultimate manifestation of force is dealt with unequivocally in narrative verdicts. It is constructed as being relatively uncomplicated and unproblematic when compared to other cases of DAPC. The level of control and planning that is a feature of armed police operations is typically not present in other narrative verdicts where force is used. Shane (2013) notes that as risk increases, the use of police discretion decreases. As was previously established, the use of benchmarking criteria is key to juries being able to assess actions and omissions. In cases of shooting, these criteria are clearer due to the level of supervision and control exercised by police. Therefore it is both more straightforward for juries to make decisions on the efficacy of actions and omissions of police and more problematic for juries to be critical of these actions or omissions. Two examples serve to illustrate how unequivocal and precise the construction of accountability is in cases of shooting:

> Case 24: 'The decision to deploy armed officers to challenge [the deceased] was an appropriate course of action. [The deceased] was challenged by two armed police officers who then fired nine shots from a carbine and one from a pistol. We are satisfied on the balance of probabilities that all of these shots were justified.'

> Case 47: 'Authorised firearms officers deployed to contain [the deceased]. These attempts failed. [The deceased] was shot 4 times by an authorised firearms officer … [the deceased] was lawfully killed.'

The type of force used by police appears to draw two different responses from juries. The more extreme use of force is explicitly legitimated, albeit this may be because it is subject to more supervision and control than any other type of force. The use of restraint is typically legitimated albeit in a way that is qualified in a number of narrative verdicts. The earlier focus in this chapter on juries tending to be critical of healthcare agencies sits in contrast to this discussion where juries appear to largely legitimate police use of force. This suggests juries are prepared to view the police role and function in cases of DAPC as principally one of law enforcers, reflecting the discussion in Chap. 2 that they are first and foremost 'police' officers and not 'peace' officers (Reiner 2000). Clearly, accountability construction in narrative verdicts is contingent upon multiple contexts, actors, organisations and structures, and this is further emphasised in the discussion below on the issue of what I term 'specific ambiguity'.

## 'Specific Ambiguity'

Juries may be constrained by the use of questionnaire verdicts although these might also be subject to exhibitions of agency by the jury in terms of striking out questions, recording majority verdicts adjacent to specific questions, or adding comments that were not requested. They are also constrained by the institutional requirements of the coronial system; for example, liability may not be ascribed to actions or omissions. This, however, has not prevented the construction of highly critical narrative verdicts supporting the view that inquests have a tendency to stray beyond their stated objectives (Davis et al. 2002). The more critical verdicts have an ability to hedge with words and formulate sentences that are more emphatic than others, similar to the term 'modality' from discourse analysis (Melia 2003). Below is a rising scale of critical statements, beginning with the relatively cautious:

> Case 9: 'Had the appropriate precautions and actions been taken death may have been prevented.'

> Case 20: 'These failings represented a significant loss of opportunity to properly care for and protect [the deceased]'.

Through to the more emphatic:

> Case 7: 'In all probability, if [the deceased's] position had been changed and oxygen administered, his chance of survival would have greatly increased.

Case 28: Question: 'Are there any further issues which you consider more than minimally contributed towards the death of [the deceased], and if so what are they?'

Answer:

'Lack of management support and a lack of confidence in management, reflecting in low morale. Therefore the level of care was insufficient.

NHS staff allowed personal issues to affect their judgement & performance.

Inadequate nursing records & failure to utilise them.'

To the overtly emphatic:

Case 37: 'We unanimously agree that on the balance of probabilities, the omissions of the ambulance crew contributed to [the deceased's] death.'

It was noted earlier in the chapter that juries were more likely to be overtly critical of non-police agencies, and the final two examples (above) illustrate this.

One objective of an inquest is to uncover facts about how the individual came to meet their death. In terms of definitions, the words 'blame' and 'liability' are synonymous with being responsible. The latter specifically relates to legal responsibility. In terms of narrative construction, the onus is placed on juries and coroners to develop a lexicon that can identify acts or omissions without ascribing liability or blame. Thus there are a number of phrases that sound unusual in conventional language, for example the repeated use of 'more than minimally contributed to' (used in one-quarter of cases) about actions or omissions leading to a death. Furthermore, there are examples of statements which are hedged to a point where they need to be read more than once to fully appreciate their meaning, for example:

Case 37: 'We do not find on the balance of probabilities deficiencies in the ambulance crew's training caused or contributed to the cause of [the deceased's] death.'

In this sense, the practice of hedging, caused by a number of structural constraints in the production of narrative verdicts leads to what I term 'specific ambiguity'. Statements are specific in the sense that consideration has been given to the formulation of sentences or statements. They are not typically expositions that would occur in lay-persons' discourse. The use of language in law is characterised by arcane vocabulary and sentence formulation that demands a specialised lexicon (Woods 2006). Woods (2006: 94) goes on to note that statements: 'frequently result in forms of language which are unusually and even outlandishly explicit, but which can be remarkably vague and open to subjective interpretation or semantic debate'. The formulations are considered, measured and specific to the discursive forum in which they are produced.

The use of narrative produces more specific detail in the construction of accountability in cases of DAPC, primarily due to the discursive practice of narrative formation. Yet this co-exists with the discursive institutional practices within which narrative is constructed. This complex relationship between content and structure can produce ambiguity. Fairclough (1992: 83) notes that: 'Coherence is often treated as a property of texts, but is better regarded as a property of interpretations.' Thus discrete sections of the text might be coherent, but the entirety of it might not. This leads us to question whether the recording of greater amounts of detail in these cases is producing more documents, or producing more accountability, as is analysed in more detail in Chap. 7. The apparent lack of lesson learning in cases of DAPC suggests that the former is more likely, albeit that this also happens due to a lack of national oversight of these verdicts as distinct from the content recorded in each verdict.

## Conclusion

Narrative verdicts have come about as a result of precedents driven by Article 2 of the ECHR. They have enabled a more detailed picture to be painted in cases of DAPC. In particular they have made it possible for juries to note systemic and organisational issues about these deaths rather than merely focusing on the actions or omissions of individuals. It should be noted that these changes have been wrought as a result of changes external to the state, in the form of the European Court of Human Rights, that obliges the state to demonstrate it meets a certain set of criteria, much as Chan (1999) imagined in her view of 'evaluation' as distinct from accountability. That these criteria are met is one thing, that narrative verdicts have an effect on learning lessons that reduce future deaths is another.

While discretion, ambiguity of purpose and an essentially regional system enable diverse, multi-causal and complex verdicts to be recorded, they also affect the subsequent learning of lessons. Without a national system of oversight to identify trends and patterns in cases of DAPC these deaths tend to be seen as individual cases. Although coroners can make recommendations to organisations about changing policies or training, or emphasising the need for better communication, they have no power to enforce such recommendations. The system of verdict construction records increasingly more information that could be used to learn lessons that may prevent future deaths. But it is recorded within a system that is neither structured in a way that lessons can be learned, nor given power to enforce its findings or recommendations.

The chapter has identified key findings highlighted in narrative verdicts. The term 'death after police contact' is a misnomer, and the issue of omission in many deaths further emphasises this. Clearly many of these deaths occur as a result of failures in other public services and often as a result of inaction rather than contact. The term DAPC might thus be seen as a symbolic construct in that it is useful in highlighting these deaths to society, but not so helpful in terms of identifying how these deaths might be minimised in future. If society focuses primarily on what police did in these deaths, by implication it will overlook the role of other public services and what was *not done* in these cases. In both examples, the practical reality of many of these cases may not be grasped, and that affects the ability to learn lessons, as much as the non-systematised nature of accountability construction in the coronial system does. If many cases of DAPC could be re-imagined as healthcare or welfare focused, then this might have an effect on reducing the number of deaths in these cases, but if we cannot conceive of these deaths as anything other than 'death after police contact' it questions the relevance of many of the findings recorded in narrative verdicts.

The issue of measurement was shown to be key to evaluating actions and omissions. Measurement has enabled omission and failure to be identified, albeit that they are recorded in a way that is constrained by the institutional structures of the coronial system. These issues are also apparent in the following chapter on IPCC investigation reports which demonstrates that the type of measurement used and the specific forum used largely dictates the type of accountability that is constructed, once again underlining the relational nature of accountability construction in cases of DAPC in England and Wales. Similarly, the jury tendency to legitimate police use of force by way of rationalisation, euphemisation and the construction of conditions can also be seen in IPCC investigation reports. There are, though, significant differences in the way that IPCC investigation reports construct accountability and we now turn to evaluate the similarities and differences in the mode of investigation and reporting used by the IPCC in comparison to the coronial system.

# References

ACPO. (2012). *Guidance on the safer detention and handling of persons in police custody* (2nd ed.). Available at: https://www.gov.uk/government/uploads/system/uploads/attachment_data/file/117555/safer-detention-guidance-2012.pdf. Accessed 5 Jan 2014.

Adebowale, V. (2013). *Independent commission on mental health and policing.* Available at: http://news.bbc.co.uk/1/shared/bsp/hi/pdfs/10_05_13_report.pdf. Accessed 23 June 2013.

Andoh, B. (2009). The police and section 135 (1) of the Mental Health Act 1983. *Medicine, Science and the Law, 49*(2), 93–100.

Belur, J. (2010). Why do the police use deadly force? Explaining police encounters in Mumbai. *British Journal of Criminology, 50*(2), 320–341.

Bittner, E. (1975). *The functions of the police in modern society: A review of background factors, current practices and possible role models.* New York: Aronson.

British Medical Association. (2009). *Health care of detainees in police stations.* Available at: http://bma.org.uk/-/media/Files/PDFs/.../Ethics/healthdetainees0209.pdf. Accessed 6 Sept 2013.

Casale, S., Corfe, M., & Lewis, J. (2013). *Report of the independent external review of the IPCC investigation into the death of Sean Rigg.* Available at: http://www.ipcc.gov.uk/news/Pages/pr_170513_Riggreview.aspx. Accessed 21 May 2013.

Chan, J. (1999). Governing police practice: Limits of the new accountability. *British Journal of Sociology, 50*(2), 251–270.

Davis, G., Lindsey, R., Seabourne, G., & Griffiths-Baker, J. (2002). *Experiencing inquests. Home office research study,* 241. Home Office Research, Development and Statistics Directorate.

De Viggiani, N., Kushner, S., Last, K., Powell, J., & Davies, J. (2010). *Police custody healthcare: An evaluation of an NHS commissioned pilot to deliver a police custody health service in a partnership between Dorset Primary Care Trust and Dorset Police.* University of West of Bristol. Available at: http://eprints. uwe.ac.uk/8253/1/PC_Evaluation_final.pdf. Accessed 10 Dec 2013.

Ericson, R., & Haggerty, K. (1997). *Policing the risk society.* Oxford: Oxford University Press.

Faculty of Forensic and Legal Medicine. (2007). *Advice to custody officers, gaolers and detention officers.* Available at: https://fflm.ac.uk/upload/documents/ 1195227243.pdf. Accessed 22 Sept 2013.

Faculty of Forensic and Legal Medicine. (2010a). *Management of choking in police care and custody: Recommendation for police personnel.* Available at: http://fflm. ac.uk/upload/documents/1288873161.pdf. Accessed 6 Sept 2013.

Faculty of Forensic and Legal Medicine. (2010b). *Acute behavioural disorder: Guidelines on management in police custody.* Available at: http://www.fflm.ac. uk/wp-content/uploads/documentstore/1310745561.pdf. Accessed 6 Sept 2013.

Fairclough, N. (1992). *Discourse and social change.* Cambridge: Polity.

Fulton, R. (2008). Review of the forum for preventing deaths in custody: Report of the independent reviewer.

Fyfe, J. (1998). Police use of deadly force: Research and reform. *Justice Quarterly, 5,* 165–205.

Greer, C., & McLaughlin, E. (2012). This is not justice: Ian Tomlinson, institutional failure and the press politics of outrage. *British Journal of Criminology, 52*(2), 274–293.

Hannan, M., Hearnden, I., Grace, K., & Bucke, T (2010). *Deaths in or following police custody: An examination of the cases 1998/99–2008/09* (IPCC research series paper: 17). London: IPCC.

Hirschfield, P., & Simon, D. (2010). Legitimating police violence—Newspaper narratives of deadly force. *Theoretical Criminology, 14*(2), 155–182.

HMIC. (2013). *A criminal use of police cells?* Available at: http://www.hmic.gov. uk/media/a-criminal-use-of-police-cells-20130620.pdf. Accessed 14 July 2013.

Hyden, L.-C. (1997). The institutional narrative as drama. In B.-L. Gunnarson, P. Linell, & B. Nordberg (Eds.), *The construction of professional discourse* (pp. 245–264). Harlow: Longman.

IAP. (2015). *Deaths in state custody: An examination of the cases 2000 to 2014.* Available at: http://iapdeathsincustody.independent.gov.uk/wp-content/uploads/2015/12/IAP-Statistical-Analysis-of-recorded-deaths-in-state-custody-between-2000-and-2014.pdf. Accessed 6 Jan 2016.

IPCC. (2013). *Review of the IPCC's work in investigating deaths: Progress report.* Available at: http://www.ipcc.gov.uk/sites/default/files/Review%20of%20 the%20IPCCs%20work%20in%20investigating%20deaths%20-%20 Progress%20report.pdf. Accessed 10 Dec 2013.

Leigh, A., Johnson, G., & Ingram, A. (1998). *Deaths in custody: Learning the lessons* (Police research series paper 26). London: Crown.

Levine, M. (1999) *Levine on Coroners' Courts.* London: Sweet and Maxwell.

Lord, V. (2014). Police responses in officer-involved violent deaths: Comparison of suicide by cop and non-suicide by cop incidents. *Police Quarterly, 17*(1), 79–100.

Marsh, D., Duque, L., Pablo, J., Qin, Y., Adi, N., Hearn, W., Hyma, B., Karch, S., Druid, H., & Wetli, C. (2009). Brain biomarkers for identifying excited delirium as a cause of sudden death. *Forensic Science International, 190*(3), 13–19.

Matthews, P. (2011). *Jervis on the office and duties of coroners: With forms and precedents. Fourth cumulative supplement to the twelfth edition.* London: Sweet and Maxwell.

Melia, J. (2003). *Modality.* Chesham: Acumen.

Morabito, M. (2007). Horizons of context: Understanding the police decision to arrest people with mental illness. *Psychiatric Services, 58*(12), 1582–1587.

Pearsall, J. (Ed.). (2002). *Oxford English dictionary* (10th ed.). Oxford: Oxford University Press.

Pinizzotto, A., Davis, E., Bohrer, S., & Infanti, B. (2012). Law enforcement restraint in the use of deadly force within the context of 'the deadly mix'. *International Journal of Police Science and Management, 14*(4), 285–298.

Prior, L. (1985). Making sense of mortality. *Sociology of Health and Illness, 7*(2), 167–190.

Punch, M. (2011). *Shoot to kill: Police accountability, firearms and fatal force.* Portland: Policy Press.

Razack, S. (2015). *Dying from improvement: Inquests and inquiries into indigenous deaths in custody.* Toronto: University of Toronto Press.

Reiner, R. (2000). *The politics of the police* (3rd ed.). Oxford: Oxford University Press.

Reiner, R. (2010). *The politics of the police* (4th ed.). Oxford: Oxford University Press.

Ruiz, J., & Miller, C. (2004). An exploratory study of Pennsylvania police officers' perceptions of dangerousness and their ability to manage persons with mental illness. *Police Quarterly, 7*(3), 359–371.

Savage, S. (2007). Restoring justice: Campaigns against miscarriages of justice and the restorative justice process. *European Journal of Criminology, 4*(2), 195–216.

Scraton, P. (2002). Lost lives, hidden voices: 'Truth' and controversial deaths. *Race Class, 44*(1), 107–118.

Shane, J. (2013). *Learning from error in policing: A case study in organisational accident theory*. Heidelberg: Springer.

Shaw, H., & Coles, D. (2007). *Unlocking the truth: Families' experiences of the investigation of deaths in custody*. London: Inquest.

Smith, G. (2009). Citizen oversight of independent police services: Bifurcated accountability, regulation creep, and lesson learning. *Regulation and Governance, 3*(4), 421–441.

Squires, P., & Kennison, P. (2010). *Shooting to kill? Police firearms and armed response*. Chichester: Wiley-Blackwell.

Terpstra, J., & Trommel, W. (2009). Police, managerialisation and presentational strategies. *Policing: An International Journal of Police Strategies and Management, 32*(1), 128–143.

Terrill, W. (2005). Police use of force: A transactional approach. *Justice Quarterly, 22*(1), 107–138.

Thomas, L., Straw, A., & Friedman, D. (2008). *Inquests: A practitioner's guide* (2nd ed.). London: Legal Action Group.

Waddington, P. A. J. (1999). *Policing citizens*. London: UCL Press.

Widdicombe, K. (2012). How ... the deceased came by his death. In I. McDougall (Ed.), *Cases that changed our lives* (pp. 175–181). London: Lexis Nexis.

Williams, C. (2014). *Police control systems in Britain, 1775–1975: From parish constable to national computer*. Manchester: Manchester University Press.

Woods, N. (2006). *Describing discourse: A practical guide to discourse analysis*. London: Hodder Arnold.

# 5

# IPCC: Fit for Purpose?

## Introduction

The documents examined in this chapter are investigation reports produced by the IPCC into cases of DAPC. The chapter evaluates similarities and differences between the IPCC and coronial system in how they construct accountability in terms of processes used and findings produced. The relationality of independence has been established, as was the fact that this linked to other relational concepts such as accountability and transparency. The latter issue has been repeatedly criticised by families of those who have died, by campaign groups and most recently by the Home Office (2015) in its triennial review of the IPCC. This is borne out in my research. Of the narrative verdicts considered in the previous chapter, approximately one-third were available as investigation reports through the IPCC web portal. After a Freedom of Information request it became apparent that one-third of the deaths were not investigated by the IPCC but by PSDs within the police. The final third were eventually made available to me in a redacted form. Clearly this brings into question the openness and transparency of IPCC processes. It also

© The Editor(s) (if applicable) and The Author(s) 2016    **109**
D. Baker, *Deaths After Police Contact,*
DOI 10.1057/978-1-137-58967-5_5

brings into question how accountable the IPCC are in investigating cases of DAPC, not least because it did not investigate a third of the deaths in the dataset. Finally, it brings into question the IPCC role in promoting public confidence in the police: if the investigations into the majority of these deaths were not available, this would suggest a system of police regulation that was at best disorganised and at worst had something to hide. This is far from ideal when its goal is to promote public trust in policing throughout England and Wales. A more general point is to consider the issues listed above in questioning the cognitive and procedural legitimacy of the IPCC in terms of its relevance to society, police and the state. Evidently these concepts exist in both symbolic and practical form, with the discussion above demonstrating that the practical forms of openness and transparency are questionable in the context of the IPCC investigating cases of DAPC.

This chapter examines the diversity of format, style and themes that are apparent in IPCC investigation reports. There is an evident similarity with the diversity of narrative verdicts. In a relatively new, purpose-designed national organisation, this might be somewhat of a surprise, but it seems to illustrate the relatively arbitrary way in which these reports are produced. This suggests both a level of discretion in their production and a lack of oversight in the end product that appears to mirror the coronial system. On the other hand, there are clear differences between IPCC investigation reports and narrative verdicts in specific cases, an issue discussed under the heading further below section 'Notable Omissions and Selective Presentation' that highlights how those differences are manifest. Thus the relational nature of accountability construction in cases of DAPC can be seen to be manifest not only between both of the regulators in these cases, but also within each regulator.

In the case of Sean Rigg the IPCC investigation into his death was criticised for favouring explanation over critical investigation and analysis, and this is something which the chapter considers in more detail, particularly in relation to the Casale (2013) review into IPCC investigatory processes in these cases. The aftermath of Sean Rigg's death sparked a crisis of legitimacy for the IPCC in terms of how it investigated and reported on cases of DAPC. The latter part of the chapter focuses on how it navigated this crisis and how it sought to re-establish its legitimacy.

I argue that it has done so largely by adopting principles and processes from the coronial system. This illustrates discursive processes migrating from one regulatory mechanism to another. Thus the relationship between the two regulators, which has been shown to be ambiguous so far in this book, appears to be becoming more closely aligned, and Article 2 of the ECHR seems to be a significant factor driving this alignment. The issue of what this might mean in the wider sense of accountability in cases of DAPC is analysed and evaluated in the following chapter. For now, we turn to examine the diversity in format, style and themes apparent in IPCC investigation reports.

## IPCC Investigation Reports: Format, Style and Themes

The investigation reports are diverse in terms of structure and content. There is usually an introduction followed by a background to the case that contextualises relevant issues about the deceased. This is typically followed by a chronology of events leading to the death succeeded by a description of the IPCC investigation and its conclusions. Finally, a list of recommendations is set out together with a conclusion to the investigation. There are exceptions to this format, but this broadly describes the layout of the IPCC reports in this dataset. The variety of report types appear to reflect the variety of structures used to construct the report. It is not clear why in cases of DAPC there should be this diversity of approach from the IPCC. It was established in Chap. 3 that the diversity of narrative verdicts comes about primarily because of the non-standardised, regionalised and discretionary nature of the coronial system. In comparison, the IPCC is a national organisation, founded on statutory principles (Wadham 2004). Given that a key aspect of its role is to promote public trust in the police, one might expect that prescribed structures would be used in independent investigations to ensure transparency and legitimacy. The length of reports is notable in that they polarise towards being either under thirty pages or over seventy pages with relatively few in the middle ground. This aspect of accountability construction in IPCC reports is loosely structured similar to the coronial system.

Without exception, narrative verdicts are significantly shorter in length than IPCC reports. The main reason for this appears to be that IPCC reports tend to incorporate significant amounts of detail about the investigation, while narrative verdicts merely record findings. Recommendations are made in a significant majority of IPCC reports, and these, in principle at least, appear to be analogous with the coroner's rule 43 report discussed in Chap. 3 in making recommendations about practice, training, and policy that may prevent future deaths. The difference between the two documents is that the IPCC's is notionally public, the coroner's is not. Furthermore, it should be noted that while the coroner can send this report to any organisation they deem relevant, the IPCC makes recommendations only in respect of policing. The following discussion considers the most prominent themes from the available IPCC investigation reports, incorporating a number of issues discussed in the previous chapter, such as training, policy and risk assessment.

Training, adherence to policy, first aid and risk assessment appear in the majority of these reports, particularly those recorded subsequent to the first ACPO *Guidance on the Safer Detention and Handling of Persons in Police Custody* published in 2006 (ACPO 2006). This suggests the IPCC has given particular consideration to this document as a benchmark against which measurement can be made when investigating cases of DAPC. On the other hand, it must be acknowledged that not all post-2006 cases focus on training, policies or risk. Indeed, those that do rarely make reference to the ACPO guidance by name. This is surprising given that it is the key guidance document on minimising deaths in custody. It is produced by a working group of police and medical experts and gives in-depth guidance on key issues such as mental health, intoxication, drugs and restraint; furthermore it makes numerous references to the importance of Article 2 of the ECHR. The absence of it within IPCC investigation reports casts doubt on the type of framework the IPCC *does* use to assess police actions or omissions in these cases.

In approximately half the cases, the narrative verdict is either quoted in part, in full or referred to in the IPCC report. Furthermore, one-quarter of cases refer to Article 2 being taken into account within the context of the IPCC investigation. The use of the narrative verdict in half of these cases appears to acknowledge a memorandum of understanding signed between the IPCC and Coroners' Society of England and Wales in 2007 establishing best practice when reporting these cases (IPCC 2007). One-third of cases refer to police experts used as consultants on a number of technical issues such as firearms, CCTV and restraint in the construction of the IPCC report. This was an area of concern highlighted in Chap. 3 about the degree of legitimacy conferred on such an investigation due to its perceived lack of independence (HAC 2013).

The majority of these reports focus on police actions or omissions in events leading to a death. This should not necessarily be unexpected because two principal aims of the IPCC are to regulate police and promote best practice. Indeed, a consistent theme throughout the reports is to praise best practice where possible, albeit this appears perversely misplaced in some cases, notably the death of Sean Rigg where officers were praised for following best practice in transporting detainees. However, given that half of the narrative verdicts considered relate to police being involved with at least one other agency, it appears that the focus of IPCC reports precludes taking into account potentially relevant information when accountability is constructed in these cases. This was particularly apparent in the death of Sean Rigg and the accountability constructed after his death. If most cases of DAPC are the result of multi-causal factors, and half include other agencies, then any attempt to reduce future fatalities might be expected to adopt a more holistic approach to lesson learning. The discussion now shifts to an evaluation of factors shared by IPCC reports and narrative verdicts.

## Constructing Conditions, Constructing Characters

In the previous chapter the practice of constructing characteristics and conditions to fit narrative convention and structure was noted. The IPCC reports are similar in this respect. The majority of reports include a short section on 'background' which typically provides a character sketch of the person who died, for example:

Case 29: '[the deceased], a twenty nine year old single man, had a long standing problem with substance abuse. This had led to his involvement in the criminal justice system over a number of years.'

The discussion below compares and contrasts examples between the IPCC reports and narrative verdicts in the same cases regarding the construction of characteristics of the person who dies after police contact. In a case linked to cocaine use, the term 'excited delirium'[1] is used consistently throughout the IPCC report yet is not present in the correlate narrative verdict. In a case of police shooting, the 320-page IPCC report makes numerous references to the individual's binge drinking and episodes of depression. This is not referred to in the narrative verdict. In another case, the 162-page IPCC report foregrounds the investigation with a discussion of the deceased's 'history' which makes reference to mental health issues and previous attempts at self-harm and suicide. The narrative verdict makes reference to mental health issues but not to suicide attempts or self-harm, presumably on the basis that they were not considered relevant to the events leading to death. The reference to conditions experienced by the deceased in one report but not the other illustrates that accountability is constructed using processes and texts that are specific to the agency that constructs accountability.

This construction method establishes characters in the narrative at an early stage. It enables subsequent events to unfold in light of character being established, as was discussed in the previous chapter about the use of force. Therefore the mention of 'excited delirium' might be linked to later episodes in the IPCC report where the deceased 'writhes around' and is 'sweating and covered in blood'. This is not recorded in the correlate narrative verdict. In one investigation report, comments on binge drinking and depression could be linked to a nine-page section where multiple officer witness accounts focus on the deceased's irrational and apparently inexplicable behaviour. Finally, in a case where self-harm and suicide have been identified, this appears to link to the death of the individual by swallowing a packet of drugs in police custody. In these cases, the characteristics are those of the deceased.

There are, though, notable exceptions. IPCC reports into two cases focus not on the deceased individual whose character is constructed, but

---

[1] There is insufficient space to discuss this 'condition' here, but numerous medical papers have been produced on this issue in relation to police contact (see, for example Aiken et al. 2011; Kutcher et al. 2009; Marsh et al. 2009; Menaker et al. 2011).

on officers involved in the death. These cases are atypical for a number of reasons: first, they are cases where a single officer can be identified as being directly involved in the death, as distinct from a group of officers or other individuals. As has been established, uni-causality is relatively unusual in cases of DAPC. Second, the officers are named—it is notable that nowhere in narrative verdicts are officers named. Third, the officers are recorded as being subsequently disciplined. It is the third point that might be most relevant to the issue of constructing characteristics. In the previous paragraph, the cases established aspects of the deceased's character prior to establishing the events that led to their death. In the case of the two officers, their characteristics are established prior to establishing the events that led to them being disciplined. Thus in Case 31, the IPCC report records:

> Case 31: 'PC [redacted] has a history of complaints concerning his attitude.'

In the second case, the IPCC report highlights an issue of previous misconduct for which the officer was charged by the CPS only for the officer to retire on medical grounds and then re-join another force, subsequently transferring from that force back to his original force. In both cases, the officer was subsequently tried in a criminal court and dismissed from the respective police force. Thus there is a tendency to construct characteristics that subsequently legitimise events in IPCC reports. In this sense, there are similarities with the production of narrative verdicts. This should not be unexpected given that both documents are narrative constructs.

## Notable Omissions and Selective Presentation

In Case 36, restraint is acknowledged by the narrative verdict and IPCC report to be a factor relating to the death. The IPCC experts, one from the MPS and another from the NPIA focus on the use of restraint as being:

> Case 36: 'Ultimately a personal choice for officers dealing with an incident.'

Given this case occurred after the production of ACPO (2006) guidelines, it is a surprising observation from an expert and underlines the role of officer discretion when both using force and assessing the use of force. It contrasts markedly with the jury view:

> Case 36: 'The officers did not act in accordance with the Standard Operating Procedure in getting [the deceased] into a safe position as soon as possible after control was achieved. Had the risk factors been correctly identified and acted upon it is likely that [the deceased] would have survived.'

Similarly, while the narrative verdict records the use of CS gas and a baton strike, these are not mentioned in the IPCC report. The identification of 'Standard Operating Procedure' in the use of restraint is not mentioned in the IPCC report. Furthermore, the narrative verdict includes verbatim quotes recounted by witnesses, for example:

> Case 36: 'He was heard to say "you're killing me, I can't breathe".'

This is not reflected in the IPCC report. In this case the IPCC report appears to construct a different version of events when compared with the narrative verdict, much as it did in the case of Sean Rigg. This highlights Terpstra and Trommel's (2009) concepts of legitimacy discussed earlier in this book. In the narrative verdict, this case is represented in terms that are meaningful and relevant to society—it produces cognitive legitimacy. In the IPCC report it is produced using consequential legitimacy—according to rules and criteria particular to the organisation that constructs accountability. Clearly this raises the issue of how such rules and criteria are produced and this issue is examined in more detail in the following chapter.

In Case 40, a death by shooting, the IPCC report is constructed primarily on the basis that the police have acted 'lawfully' and 'appropriately' in their actions leading to the shooting. While the narrative verdict questionnaire is not explicitly critical of police actions, it does record more specific and rigorous questions and consequently elicits some different answers about police actions:

Case 40: Q10 'Do you consider it as more likely than not that the Police failed to give weight to other explanations for [the deceased's] failure to respond to their attempts to make contact with him?'
Answer: 'Yes.'
Q18 'Do you consider that it is established as more likely than not that the slow methodical search did not incorporate an adequate plan for what to do if [the deceased] was found?' Answer: 'Yes'.

The narrative questionnaire also records a number of pieces of information that were not passed to the tactical ('Silver') commander about the deceased—this is not discussed in the IPCC report. The questionnaire appears to be based on investigative questions analysing and evaluating the actions or omissions of police at each discrete stage leading to the shooting. The IPCC report appears more focused on explaining why police acted in a particular way as distinct from questioning why they did so. In this sense, there is a relational difference in accountability construction in the respective documents. To approach the event from an angle that considers whether actions are 'lawful' or 'appropriate' is quite different to an angle that considers whether lessons can be learned to prevent future deaths. Police action might be viewed as legitimate, but that does not necessarily make it desirable in a particular context (Bullock and Johnson 2012). Ultimately, it is not for the IPCC to decide whether something is 'lawful', that is the job of the CPS. Furthermore, 'appropriate' is a relative term that could produce a quite different result if assessed, for example, by a different force's PSD or coroner's jury—it is contingent upon the criteria used to determine what is 'appropriate', as was established in the case of Sean Rigg. There are, though, examples in the IPCC reports where it is acknowledged that although the letter of policy is adhered to, there is criticism of the effectiveness of following such a policy. For example, regarding rousing checks under code C of PACE 1984:

Case 41: 'Whilst the checks were numerically appropriate, there is no evidence of [redacted] monitoring the quality of the checks, or of [redacted] satisfying [redacted] about [the deceased's] well being.'

The measurement systems adopted in investigations to some degree dictate the type of finding produced. This occurs not just as a result of practices adopted by the relevant institutions, but also the interpretation of measurement within each institution. Hence while some juries question the cognitive legitimacy of certain policies or laws, others do not, and similarly for the IPCC, as can be seen above. Without a system that provides an overview of these reports, the findings remain isolated to individual cases and mean lesson learning is at best piecemeal, and at worst unlikely. Narrative verdicts and IPCC investigation reports gather significant amounts of rich detail that may assist the learning of lessons that prevent future deaths, but without a system or function that oversees this data, the utility of such data is questionable. A key series of questions thus becomes apparent: first, how has the system of accountability construction come to be like this? Second, why is the system of accountability construction configured in this way, given that both institutions are publicly funded bodies? Third, what can be done to improve the system? I hope that the book to this point has effectively given an answer to the first of these questions. The remaining two questions largely guide the discussion in the remaining chapters of this book.

## Explanation and Investigation

It is notable that while a variant of the word 'failure' is recorded in one-third of narrative verdicts, it is rarely used in the IPCC investigation reports. For example, in a death in police custody as a result of drunkenness, the narrative verdict records the word 'failure' repeatedly in a cumulative series of questions, for example:

> Case 45: Q16: 'If there were any failures did the [*sic*] contribute directly to [the deceased's] death—i.e in the absence of the failures he would not have died.'
> Answer: 'YES'.

However, the IPCC's report does not use the word failure. Rather, there is a focus on certain issues not occurring, or not being recorded. In the previous chapter, 'failure' recorded by the jury is directly linked to omissions being highlighted within the narrative verdict. Therefore, there appears to be some similarity with 'absences' being recorded in the IPCC report on Case 45. Thus issues not occurring or not being recorded are unfortunate mistakes as distinct from omissions that lead to an individual dying. Conversely, the narrative verdict explicitly states that a combination of factors contributed to the individual dying in custody.

In Chap. 3 of this book, Gilsinan (2012) and Chan and Dixon (2007) noted the inclination of police regulators to compile reports focusing on detail, sometimes to a deleterious extent. Case 38 provides a good example of this at a micro level:

> Case 38: 'The IPCC investigation ... collated 305 witness statements, collected 433 exhibits and obtained advice from a firearms advisor and forensic scientists.'

At a macro level, Case 38 represents the longest IPCC report at 320 pages (the shortest being five pages). In this case, the section titled 'chronology of events' covers 193 pages in precise detail, dealing with the events of one day. However, Case 24 was also an incident of fatal shooting and the former report covers eight pages compared to 320 pages in Case 38. The very significant difference in the length of the report used by the IPCC to investigate a fatal shooting, serves to underline the issues of diversity and non-standardisation within these investigation reports.

In another case, a death in custody subsequent to the deceased being arrested for being drunk and incapable, the detention officer, custody sergeant, and custody sergeant's line manager all claimed to be unaware of ACPO's 2006 guidelines despite the fact that they were produced two years previously and were considered the primary reference document outlining practices and policies about duty of care in custody suites. This suggests, *pace* the discussion in Chap. 2 that police have considerable discretion regarding their actions and this can lead to exceptions in practice. It also highlights the lack of sanction available to the IPCC. One might expect that being unaware of the key document that guides actions in a workplace is a priori sufficient reason to be criticised or possibly disciplined. That this does not occur critically questions the cognitive legitimacy of both the IPCC and the function of the ACPO guidelines—why have them if they can effectively be ignored? These issues echo the failure of officers in the Sean Rigg case to recognise that he had mental health issues. Had they recognised such issues, they would have been bound by policy to approach him in a different way, and, as the narrative verdict notes, he may still have been alive today.

There are two exceptions worthy of comment in the investigation reports. Case 31 is the only known example in the dataset of the CPS successfully prosecuting an officer based on an IPCC investigation.[2] It is not an independent investigation, it is a managed investigation conducted by the local force's PSD. Moreover, this report is an exception in that it contains a 'post-report update'. Finally, it is the case that was most rapidly expedited, taking eight months to complete. Although one case might be an exception, it is noteworthy that this is the single case that resulted in an officer being held to account in a criminal court for their actions. This was carried out not by the IPCC but by the relevant PSD. The officer was given a suspended prison sentence and subsequently dismissed from the force. This appears to reinforce Reiner's (1991) research finding that chief officers believed PSDs were more effective in dealing with misconduct, albeit that this is only one case. Undoubtedly, pressure groups would consider this to be a more legitimate investigation than the bulk of the IPCC investigation reports in the dataset. The unfortunate inference from this is that the PSD investigation and findings are more legitimate than those of the IPCC suggesting that IPCC investigations may be largely symbolic into cases of DAPC.

In summary, the public accessibility of IPCC investigation reports into cases of DAPC is questionable. Clearly this raises concerns about the legitimacy of the IPCC in terms of goals set out in its statement of purpose. The fact that one-third of the deaths in my research were not investigated by the IPCC further damages the IPCC in terms of it being a cognitively legitimate, publicly funded organisation. The reports that are publicly available, combined with those acquired by Freedom of Information requests are strikingly diverse in terms of structures used to produce the report, and consequently the length of the report. There appear to be

---

[2] The prosecutions in the Ian Tomlinson and Sean Rigg cases, for example, occurred as a result of evidence uncovered during inquests.

similarities between narrative verdicts and IPCC investigation reports on issues such as training, policy and risk assessment, and these reflect measurement criteria that assess acts or omissions in relation to such issues. Similar to narrative verdicts, the IPCC investigation reports have examples of constructing characteristics explaining subsequent acts or omissions that lead to events occurring. The issues of notable omission and selective presentation demonstrate differences between the two organisational processes that construct accountability, particularly regarding the use of force. Thus a different type of investigative method constructs a different type of accountability. The tendency of the IPCC to explain issues rather than critically investigate them was identified by comparing examples of difference within the two datasets, and was notable in the case of Sean Rigg as established earlier in this book. Exceptions were noted, underlining the non-standardised processes of investigation and reporting employed by the IPCC. These exceptions suggest that, similar to juries in inquests, there are examples of agency being used within the IPCC investigation that overcome the typical structure of the processes that investigate and report on cases of DAPC. The death of Sean Rigg and the subsequent investigation into his death sparked a legitimacy crisis for the IPCC. We now turn to consider how this affected the IPCC's role in investigating and reporting on cases of DAPC.

## Investigating the Death of Sean Rigg: Evaluating Accountability Construction

As established earlier, the case of Sean Rigg encapsulates many key issues in cases of DAPC. These relate to the types of people who die, the types of events that lead to their death, and their interactions with police and healthcare agencies. For the purposes of this discussion, however, I focus on the institutional response to Sean Rigg's death and the way it highlights how accountability construction is relational in cases of DAPC. This leads to an analysis of how his death has led to a reconsideration of how the IPCC investigates and reports on such cases that suggests an evolutionary shift in the processes of accountability construction in cases of DAPC in England and Wales.

Sean Rigg died in August 2008. The IPCC were referred to investigate the death by the DPS of the MPS. Their report was finally published 15 August 2012. The inquest into the death of Sean Rigg concluded on 1 August 2012. During the inquisition it became apparent that the evidence it considered was quite different to that examined by the IPCC. Much of this evidence had been gathered by Sean Rigg's family, and was apparently overlooked or ignored by the IPCC. Thus the findings of the jury in the narrative verdict were markedly different from those in the IPCC investigation report. This difference signified a crisis of legitimacy for the IPCC. Its chair, Anne Owers ordered an independent review into the IPCCs own independent investigation into Sean Rigg's death which would examine not only his case, but consider wider issues in how the IPCC investigated cases of DAPC. That review was chaired by Dr Silvia Casale of Bristol University's law school.

The Casale review was published in May 2013, fifty-eight months after Sean Rigg's death. It re-examined the available evidence and interviewed key individuals involved. One aim of the review was: 'to produce constructive criticism and recommendations for change' (Casale et al. 2013: 25). The preamble to the report stated the IPCC had a duty to 'fully and fearlessly' investigate cases of DAPC in order to secure public trust in the institution. It recognised that:

> 'When a death in custody occurs, the public needs to understand what went wrong and how similar events could be avoided in future.' (Ibid: 38)

This statement is remarkably similar to the quotation by Lord Bingham in the introduction to coroners' processes in Chap. 3 of this book. Furthermore, there was an expectation that the IPCC would ensure: 'the state … met its obligations arising from Article 2 of the European Convention on Human Rights' (Ibid: 18). Throughout the preamble there are strong parallels with the discussion in Chap. 3 about the role of the coronial system in investigating cases of DAPC. Casale noted that while an IPCC investigation report and narrative verdict will always have differences, there should be a degree of 'synergy' present (Ibid: 10). The review was commissioned by the IPCC at a point when its institutional legitimacy was clearly in crisis. Major reviews are generally not produced during periods of calm reflection within institutions (Gilsinan 2012; Chan and Dixon 2007). Consequently, the context in which the review was produced needs to be borne in mind when considering its findings. While Casale's findings are numerous and critical, the review is also at pains to emphasise how much progress the IPCC has made regarding practice and procedures since the death of Sean Rigg in 2008, an assertion that is critically evaluated in Chap. 7. The review noted that while the IPCC report into Sean Rigg's death was detailed in terms of narrative, it lacked a 'robust analysis of this information' (Casale et al. 2013: 2); thus mirroring the earlier discussion in this chapter about the difference between explanatory mode and investigatory mode.

The review was critical of officers' failure to identify Sean Rigg as an individual with mental health issues, and of the IPCC's inability to pose officers questions about their failure to check their MDT (Mobile Data Terminal) about his history, instead focusing in 'considerable detail [on] Mr Rigg's odd behaviour in public' (Ibid: 5). It was sceptical about the inability of the IPCC investigators to critically examine officers' assertions that Sean Rigg had no obvious mental health issues, stating that: '**the reasoning behind this statement does not bear examination**' (Ibid: 72, bold as original). These assertions meant that officers did not have to employ SOP (Standard Operating Practice) that should have been used when dealing with a person with mental health issues, such as conducting a risk assessment, prior to contact with the individual. Furthermore, it noted the failure of the IPCC to apply ACPO and Home Office guidance which stated that SOP should be used if officers: '*could reasonably have expected to have any suspicions*' (Ibid: 72, original italics); instead focusing on whether officers 'knew' he had mental health issues. Similarly, it noted the IPCC failure to consult an expert on mental health issues despite half of the cases of deaths in custody in 2011–12 relating to mental health issues (Ibid: 20). This underlines the issue of multi-agency contact in cases of DAPC as discussed in Chaps. 2 and 4. Furthermore, it observed that:

'During IPCC interviews, efforts to pose questions about recognising Mr Rigg's mental health condition were hampered by inappropriate conduct by Police Federation representatives'. (Ibid: 5)

It noted that no protocol existed for acceptable conduct by a Police Federation representative at such an interview. This appears to reflect Anne Owers' assertion that the initial IPCC investigation repeatedly faced obstruction (BBC 2013). Savage and Charman (2001) noted the role of the Police Federation in lobbying for its members and this supports Smith's (2009) observation that these cases are marked by an asymmetry of power in the investigatory process, that police typically possess more power than either the IPCC investigators or complainants in cases of DAPC.

The review criticised the conduct of the FME (Forensic Medical Examiner) in attendance and noted that he subsequently resigned based on a referral to the General Medical Council (GMC) by the IPCC (Casale et al. 2013: 6–7). This mirrors events in the Ian Tomlinson case where the initial pathologist was referred to the GMC for poor practice and subsequently struck off (Razak 2012); FMEs were also criticised and struck off in two other cases in the IPCC dataset. Furthermore, the IPCC report included a statement by the custody sergeant that he checked on Sean Rigg whilst in the police van (IPCC 2012: 57). This is a requirement by ACPO (2012) under its safer detention guidelines. The statement proved to be a falsehood in the inquest, due to evidence secured by the Rigg family, drawing the following comment:

> '**The review considers it regrettable that the IPCC was not able to deduce from the CCTV footage that the custody sergeant was lying about visiting Mr Rigg in the van.**' (Casale et al. 2013: 78–79, bold as in original)

The Casale review criticised the IPCC's handling of Sean Rigg's family, noting that it was inappropriate for IPCC investigators to research two family members on the Police National Computer (PNC). This echoes allegations that undercover officers researched members of Stephen Lawrence's family on the PNC in the aftermath of his death (Channel 4 2013). Finally, the review thanked the family for their tenacity and hard work in ensuring that more evidence came to light (Casale et al. 2013: 12). In this sense, the overt inclusion of the family in the process of investigating cases of DAPC appears to be similar to best practice expected in the coronial system as set out by the Chief Coroner (2013).

# Wider Issues in IPCC Investigations into Cases of DAPC

Casale then considered the wider role of the IPCC in cases of DAPC. She noted the unavoidable reliance of the IPCC on the police in the immediate aftermath of a DAPC, echoing Savage (2013a) and Smith (2009). The review stated that the arrest scene should be secured as a site of evidence, and that officers should be compelled to give statements, but: 'It appears to the review that full cooperation from the police is not always the case' (Casale et al. 2013: 15).

It recognised the IPCC's role in preventing further deaths by assessing and analysing trends and patterns of 'systemic weakness' in cases of DAPC and its potential to recommend changes in policy and operations to prevent possible recurrences (Ibid: 16). It stated that the IPCC lacked a system to store information in a way that could encourage analysis and reflective practice: 'so that there can be sustained organisational learning' (Ibid: 17). This reinforced evidence given to the HAC by a former IPCC commissioner, John Crawley, stating that the IPCC publishes reports that are essentially descriptive and therefore lacking in analysis (HAC 2010: 6). Having said this, it must be noted that organisational learning is as much an issue in the coronial system, as was made evident in Chap. 4. Two commonalities shared by the IPCC and coronial system are the inability to sanction police, and the lack of a system of national oversight to make effective use of the reports they generate in cases of DAPC, thus hindering organisational learning. It is unsurprising that campaign groups and families criticise the regulation of cases of DAPC for being toothless and ineffectual, and consequently being of questionable legitimacy to society.

The Casale review also suggested that the IPCC develop its own benchmarks for assessing police conduct rather than relying on those produced by the NPIA (National Police Improvement Agency) or ACPO. Rather than merely accepting policies were followed, the IPCC should consider whether they were adequate in the first place. Thus the measurement criteria that were a feature of the analysis in Chap. 4 are emphasised in terms of the relationality of accountability construction. This is a clear acknowledgement of the need to adopt processes that are cognitively legitimate to society rather than consequentially legitimate to the institution. Casale also encouraged the adoption of a more critical analysis by the IPCC. This reflects criteria established by Article 2 inquests in the consideration of 'in what circumstances' an individual meets their death. If the ECHR is considered to be a 'living instrument' it should reflect dynamic changes in societies rather than relying on established criteria for measuring events (Thomas et al. 2008).

Casale proceeded to list the component elements of an IPCC investigation necessary to satisfy the requirements of Article 2 of the ECHR. The investigation should be practically and hierarchically independent. It should be completed promptly and be effective in ascertaining the extent of state acts or omissions. The investigation should be open to public scrutiny in practice and not merely in theory. Finally, the next of kin should be sufficiently involved in the process. These criteria were tested by Smith (2009) as discussed in Chap. 3 who believed that the IPCC failed to meet all of these criteria. Casale went on to assert that in future investigations of DAPC:

> 'The IPCC look not only at police involvement in the circumstances surrounding the death but also more widely at other issues, including the possible contribution of other agencies to the circumstances surrounding the death before contact with the police.' (Casale et al. 2013: 13)

This suggests an approach remarkably similar to that used by Article 2 inquests. Indeed, a clear thread in the executive summary of the review is that the IPCC should adopt an approach more in keeping with coronial processes and recording practices. It also noted that the IPCC was 'severely' under-resourced and that all of the review's recommendations had resource implications (Ibid: 17). This has been highlighted by numerous sources (see, for example Savage 2013a, b; HAC 2010; Smith 2009). The lack of resources in both the IPCC and the coronial system was noted in Chap. 3. Announcements in 2015 by the Home Secretary to significantly increase the budget of the IPCC appear to reflect the government's determination to improve the effectiveness and legitimacy of the IPCC at a time when police funding, for example, is being significantly reduced (Dodd 2015).

# Aftermath: Reconstructing Legitimacy and Dialectical Relationships

I have argued throughout this book that the types of processes used in the construction of accountability determine the type of outcome recorded in cases of DAPC. It is beyond doubt that two different organisations employ different discursive processes when investigating DAPC. Until the Casale review, there was no official evaluation of the relevance and legitimacy of the respective organisations. How and why this state of affairs existed is discussed in more detail in the subsequent chapter as I examine why England and Wales has the system of regulation it does in cases of DAPC. The Casale review weighed up the processes and outcomes of both organisations and came down in favour of the coronial system. In the aftermath of the Casale review, the IPCC chair announced there would be a thorough review of the way in which the IPCC investigated and reported on cases of DAPC which would take into account Casale's findings and seek input from various stakeholder groups. This review published mid-term findings in late 2013 and a final report in spring of 2014. The IPCC (2014a) report represents the fourth stage of a process of accountability construction that began with the death of Sean Rigg. One investigation has informed and built upon another as accountability has been rearticulated by a succession of parties. The discursive turn is evident. The chapter now considers the latest stage of accountability construction to assess what it might mean in terms of understanding how the sphere of accountability construction is evolving in cases of DAPC.

The IPCC review is explicit in stating the importance of Article 2, for example:

'**Article 2 investigations should be thorough and wide-ranging, establishing what happened and why, and drawing conclusions beyond misconduct and criminal behaviour such as systemic problems or poor practice.**' (IPCC 2014a: 28, bold as in original)

This unequivocally replicates the approach taken by the coronial system in Article 2 inquests. It explicitly notes future 'Article 2 investigations' will demonstrate they have met the requirements of Article 2 (IPCC 2014a: 80). The IPCC report states that in future there will be more critical and rigorous investigations and the outcomes of these investigations will be made public (Ibid: 14), an implicit recognition that this is not currently the case. It makes clear the IPCC will use a wider variety of experts with knowledge in areas such as mental health and crime scene analysis (Ibid: 23). It pledges to use standardised investigation processes in cases of DAPC to ensure greater consistency (Ibid: 46). It notes the lack of critical learning during its ten-year history and laments the use of police as external consultants, particularly on restraint (Ibid: 54). Further to this, it states that IPCC investigation reports will be sent to chief police officers including recommendations for consideration. Under the Anti-Social Behaviour, Crime and Policing Act 2014 chief officers will be bound to reply to these recommendations within fifty-six days of receiving them (Ibid: 88). This is analogous to the coronial rule 43 report, even replicating the length of time allowed for reply. A process of evolution has occurred in the period 2004–15 illustrating Fairclough's (2010: 349) assertion that organisational discourse is constituted and reconstituted temporally.

Writing about police reform, Savage (2007a: 314) notes it is bound up with 'relative distributions of power and authority'. Moreover, he states that system failure can be the catalyst for 'institutional renewal' (Savage 2007b: 12). It would appear that both of these observations reflect a watershed in the regulatory sphere after the death of Sean Rigg. Language used by professions to create discourse depends on relations between actors and is fundamentally disciplinary (Gunnarson et al. 1997). Gunnarson et al. (1997) further posit that as discursive processes evolve, new genres of meaning replace old genres. The dialectical relationship in the construction of accountability is demonstrated in the case of Sean Rigg. Dynamic tensions between society, police and the state became manifest in the investigation of a suspicious death carried out by two different organisations. The dynamic tensions between those investigations led to a review of processes and outcomes culminating in a re-evaluation of the IPCC's purpose in terms of its role and function as a legitimate organisation. According to Black's (2008: 151) research on regulatory regimes, due to dialectical relationships: 'the organisation alters to bring itself closer into accord with the story it tells of itself, and indeed which it may be required to tell'. In this sense, there has been a redistribution of power in the sphere of accountability construction. In terms of both symbolic and practical accountability construction, *cognitive* legitimacy appears to have trumped *consequential* legitimacy in this 'game'. The idea that this process is a game, and involves the telling of stories is further explored in the following chapter as I examine how these processes might create a 'theatre of accountability', raising numerous questions such as who are the actors, who is the audience, and what relevance the script plays in these processes.

## Change and Continuity: Dialectical Processes

Developments in 2014–15 indicate that the Home Secretary is committed to reforming the IPCC and making it a more legitimate institution. Funding increases to the IPCC during these years mean that its annual budget is three times the size it was in 2013 when the Casale review was completed. At a time when police budgets are being significantly reduced, the IPCC's budget has been significantly increased (Dodd 2015). In the financial year 2014–15 it hired 100 more investigators and processed double the number of independent investigations than the previous year (Home Office 2015: 46). Clear demands from the Home Office are for the IPCC to better liaise with stakeholders; ensure that lessons are learned more effectively; and for it to work more closely with families (IPCC 2014b). The triennial review into the roles and functions of the IPCC states that the body is expected to become more organised, better governed and more responsive to the needs of stakeholders (Home Office 2015).

These developments occurred in tandem with a major review into the internal police disciplinary system chaired by Chip Chapman. It was commissioned by the Home Secretary with a remit to make the internal disciplinary system more public focused, transparent and independent (Chapman 2014). Chapman's numerous recommendations include the closer alignment of IPCC investigations and hearings with those of the force PSD, much as Reiner (2000) envisaged in Chap. 3 regarding the closer meshing of internal and external systems of complaints. Chapman also advocated disciplinary hearings occurring in public to ensure openness and transparency in order to promote a more legitimate system. Public hearings are currently a rarity, although one did occur in the DPS hearing into the death of Ian Tomlinson. While Chapman is clear about the need to change processes and rules to improve the disciplinary system, the main thrust of the report is that there needs to be cultural change in policing that accepts errors and mistakes occur. He states: 'Any process will not, by itself, make things better. Discipline is not a proxy for poor management of people where "what should we do about it" is often a better response than "did he (or she) do it"' (Chapman 2014: 63). This echoes the discussion in Chap. 2 about occupational cultures producing error rather than it being caused by individual officers (Shane 2013). Similarly, Chapman appears to embrace the concept of organisational learning noted in Chap. 2 by Coles and Shaw (2012) and Downham and Lingham (2009).

Responding to the Chapman review, the Home Office (2015) endorsed the majority of his recommendations. It stated a desire for the IPCC to dispose of managed and supervised investigations, with these being handed over to the relevant force's PSD. Instead, the IPCC should focus entirely on independent investigations. At the same time, the Home Office stated a desire for PCCs to take more of a role in deciding how complaints were referred and dealt with; it expected HMIC (Her Majesty's Inspectorate of Constabulary) to provide an overview of the complaints system as a whole; that HMIC could also hold Chief Constables to account in addition to the PCC (Police and Crime Commissioner) doing this; and that the College of Policing (CP) would be expected to produce benchmarks for the revised system of police complaints. Thus, while the desire to create a more legitimate police disciplinary system is laudable, it is difficult not to reflect that the overlapping system of regulation and accountability outlined in the discussions in Chaps. 2 and 3 is becoming increasingly complex. Indeed, the Home Office (2015: 13) noted concerns in the consultation phase post-Chapman that these developments might lead to a more 'fragmented system' and that there was a need to ensure consistency across the whole system, something that has been a feature of the discussion throughout the book thus far.

Finally, the Home Secretary announced in late 2015 that a further review into deaths in police custody would be chaired by Elish Angiolini.

Its purpose would be to examine wider systemic and organisational issues in cases of DAPC; consider how lessons could be better learned in these cases; and how the system could better respond to the needs of families (Gov.UK 2015). Deborah Coles of *Inquest* is a special adviser to this review. She stated: 'It is too early to tell if this is more about a public relations exercise than a real attempt to bring about effective systemic change' (Inquest 2015). When surveying developments in 2014–15 two observations occur. First, the production of documents, policies and reviews into the issue of DAPC shows no sign of abating. This illustrates the discursive practices apparent in the regulation of cases of DAPC, an issue that is examined in more detail in the following chapter. Second, that this production will not necessarily change the occupational culture of the police, or produce a more effective regulatory system that reduces the number of deaths in cases of DAPC.

## Conclusion

Relationships are key to understanding accountability and regulation in cases of DAPC. The evolutionary nature of the relationship between the coronial system and the IPCC has been examined in this chapter. The types of accountability the organisations construct are relational and determined by a wide variety of contexts. It is clear that not only are there differences between the two regulators in how they investigate and report on such deaths, but also that there are differences within each system, further emphasising the relationality of accountability construction in cases of DAPC. While the processes, measurement and benchmarking used by each regulator were often shown to be dissimilar, it is clear that there is an intention that in future they should be more closely aligned.

The chapter examined the diversity of the reports constructed by the IPCC and highlighted differing practises within the IPCC when investigating these deaths. The trend for the IPCC to explain how deaths occurred rather than critically investigate why they occurred was established. One similarity between the coronial and IPCC's construction of accountability was shown to the construction of individual characteristics in order to rationalise aspects of the death, and in two cases, why police officers were subsequently disciplined. The differences between correlate reports from both organisations were also emphasised in terms of what was presented and omitted from the respective narrative verdicts and IPCC investigation reports. These highlighted the trend of the IPCC to explain issues in detail, while the coronial system tended to be more critical and analytical in its approach.

The Casale review may mark a watershed in the practices of the IPCC with regards to investigating cases of DAPC. Throughout the review, there is a clear expectation that the IPCC should be more independent, critical, rigorous and analytical in cases of DAPC. All of these facets are present in an Article 2 jury inquest. The recognition that Article 2 needs to be carefully considered by the IPCC when producing investigation reports further suggests that coronial processes regarding organisational learning and the prevention of future deaths should be adopted by the IPCC. Evidently there is a dialectical relationship at work in the construction of accountability in cases of DAPC. In order to appear cognitively legitimate to the state and society, the IPCC is shifting towards the coronial system in adopting some of its principles and processes. The Home Secretary has enhanced the IPCC's resources and appears keen to integrate police disciplinary systems in an attempt to confer greater legitimacy on police activity. Having said this, it should still be noted that the coronial system and IPCC have commonalities in that they cannot sanction police, nor can they enforce recommendations they make. Thus, as established in Chap. 3, independence from the police has its own consequences when regulating deaths after police contact. Finally, it once again raises the question as to why these cases are heard by the two regulators in the first place, and why they are not considered in an alternate legal forum.

The relationships within the sphere of accountability construction are becoming increasingly complex and numerous. In terms of discourse, accountability construction has evolved within a system (coronial), then across a system (to the IPCC). This development appears to have been relatively unplanned, and to some degree organic. The next chapter considers how accountability construction relates to the discursive frameworks that the IPCC and coroners' courts function within. It investigates the role of agency in testing the boundaries of these discourses and considers what effect this might have in the construction of accountability. The discussion on structure and agency is examined in the context of their relationship with the police, state and society. These three entities represent audiences that consume the accountability constructed in cases of DAPC by the IPCC and coroner's court. Finally, these issues are analysed by examining discourse and its relationship with the discursive practices of both organisations.

# References

ACPO. (2006). *Guidance on the safer detention and handling of persons in police custody.* Available at: http://www.nacro.org.uk/data/files/nacro-2006021400-469.pdf. Accessed 9 Dec 2013.

ACPO. (2012). *Guidance on the safer detention and handling of persons in police custody* (2nd ed.). Available at: https://www.gov.uk/government/uploads/system/uploads/attachment_data/file/117555/safer-detention-guidance-2012.pdf. Accessed 5 Jan 2014.

Aiken, F., Duxbury, J., Dale, C., & Harbison, I. (2011). *Review of the medical theories and research relating to restraint deaths.* Available at: http://iapdeathsincustody.independent.gov.uk/wp-content/uploads/2011/11/Caring-Solutions-UK-Ltd-Review-of-Medical-Theories-of-Restraint-Deaths.pdf. Accessed 19 Dec 2013.

BBC News. (2013, May 17). Radio 4 Today programme. Available at: http://www.bbc.co.uk/news/uk-22554051. Accessed 17 May 2013.

Black, J. (2008). Constructing and contesting legitimacy and accountability in polycentric regulatory regimes. *Regulation and Governance, 2*(2), 137–164.

Bullock, K., & Johnson, P. (2012). The impact of the Human Rights Act 1998 on policing in England and Wales. *British Journal of Criminology, 52*(3), 630–650.

Casale, S., Corfe, M., & Lewis, J. (2013). *Report of the independent external review of the IPCC investigation into the death of Sean Rigg.* Available at: http://www.ipcc.gov.uk/news/Pages/pr_170513_Riggreview.aspx. Accessed 21 May 2013.

Chan, J., & Dixon, D. (2007). The politics of police reform: Ten years after the Royal Commission into the New South Wales Police Service. *Criminology and Criminal Justice, 7*(4), 443–468.

Channel 4. (2013). *Dispatches*: '*The police's dirty secret.*' Screened 24 June 2013.

Chapman, C. (2014). *Improving police integrity: Reforming the police complaints and disciplinary systems.* Available at: https://www.gov.uk/government/uploads/system/uploads/attachment_data/file/385900/45363_Cm_8976_Press.pdf. Accessed 10 Nov 2015.

Chief Coroner's Office. (2013). *The Chief Coroner's guide to the Coroners and Justice Act 2009.* Available at: http://www.judiciary.gov.uk/wp-content/uploads/JCO/Documents/coroners/guidance/chief-coroners-guide-to-act-sept2013.pdf. Accessed 20 Dec 2013.

Coles, D., & Shaw, H. (2012). *Learning from death in custody inquests: A new framework for action and accountability.* London: Russell Press.

Dodd, V. (2015). Police force could lose 22,000 jobs under new spending cuts. *The Guardian.* Available at: http://www.theguardian.com/uk-news/2015/aug/31/police-force-new-spending-cuts-22000-jobs. Accessed 8 Oct 2015.

Downham, G., & Lingham, R. (2009). Learning lessons: Using inquiries for change. *Journal of Mental Health Law, 18*(1), 57–69.

Fairclough, N. (2010). *Critical discourse analysis: The critical study of language* (2nd ed.). Harlow: Longman.

Gilsinan, J. (2012). The numbers dilemma: The chimera of modern police accountability systems. *Saint Louis University Public Law Review, 32,* 93–108.

Gov.UK. (2015). *Home Secretary announces chair for deaths in custody review.* Available at: https://www.gov.uk/government/news/home-secretary-announces-chair-for-deaths-in-custody-review. Accessed 25 Oct 2015.

Gunnarson, B.-L., Linell, P., & Nordberg, B. (Eds.). (1997). *The construction of professional discourse.* Harlow: Longman.

Home Office. (2015). *Improving police integrity: Reforming the police complaints and disciplinary systems.* London: HMSO.

House of Commons Home Affairs Committee. (2010). *The work of the independent police complaints commission.* London: TSO.

House of Commons Home Affairs Committee. (2013). *Independent police complaints commission.* London: TSO.

Inquest. (2015). *Independent review into deaths and serious incidents in custody must be effective and lead to real change.* Available at: http://www.inquest.org.uk/media/pr/independent-review-into-deaths-serious-incidents-in-custody-must-be-effective-and-lead-to-real-change. Accessed 31 July 2015.

IPCC. (2007). *Memorandum of understanding between the coroners' society of England and Wales and the IPCC.* Available at: www.ipcc.gov.uk/Documents/guidelines reports/mou.pdf. Accessed 22 May 2013.

IPCC. (2012). *IPCC Independent investigation into the death of Sean Rigg whilst in the custody of Brixton police.* Available at: http://www.ipcc.gov.uk/en/Pages/inv_reports_london_se_region.aspx. Accessed 21 May 2013.

IPCC. (2014a). *Review of the IPCC's work in investigating deaths: Final report.* Available at: http://www.ipcc.gov.uk/sites/default/files/Documents/deaths_review/Review_of_the_IPCCs_work_in_investigating_deaths_2014.pdf. Accessed 17 Mar 2014.

IPCC. (2014b). *Becoming the new IPCC: IPCC Corporate plan 2014/17.* Available at: https://www.ipcc.gov.uk/sites/default/files/documents/publications/corporate_plan_2014-17.pdf. Accessed 2 Dec 2015.

Kutcher, S., Bowes, M., Sanfold, F., Teehan, M., Ayer, S., Ross, J., Smith, L., & Thornhill, S. (2009). *Report of the panel of mental health and medical experts review of ED.* Available at: http://novascotia.ca/just/Public_Safety/_docs/Excited%20Delirium%20Report.pdf. Accessed 30 Sept 2013.

Marsh, D., Duque, L., Pablo, J., Qin, Y., Adi, N., Hearn, W., Hyma, B., Karch, S., Druid, H., & Wetli, C. (2009). Brain biomarkers for identifying excited delirium as a cause of sudden death. *Forensic Science International, 190*(3), 13–19.

Menaker, J., Farcy, D., Boswell, S., Stein, D., Dutton, R., Hess, J., & Scalea, T. (2011). Cocaine-induced agitated delirium with associated hyperthermia: A case report. *Journal of Emergency Medicine, 41*(3), 49–53.

Razak, R. (2012). G20 death pathologist Dr Freddy Patel is struck off. *London Evening Standard.* 23 Aug 2012.

Reiner, R. (1991). Multiple realities, divided worlds—Chief constables perspectives on the police complaints system. In A. J. Goldsmith (Ed.), *Complaints against the police: The trend to external review* (pp. 211–231). Oxford: Clarendon Press.

Reiner, R. (2000). *The politics of the police* (3rd ed.). Oxford: Oxford University Press.

Savage, S. (2007a). Give and take: The bifurcation of police reform in Britain. *Australian and New Zealand Journal of Criminology, 40*(3), 313–334.

Savage, S. (2007b). *Police reform: Forces for change.* Oxford: OUP.

Savage, S. (2013a). Thinking independence: Calling the police to account through the independent investigation of police complaints. *British Journal of Criminology, 53*(1), 94–112.

Savage, S. (2013b). Seeking 'civilianness': Police complaints and the civilian control model of oversight. *British Journal of Criminology, 53*(5), 886–904.

Savage, S., & Charman, S. (2001). The Bobby Lobby: Police associations and the policy process. In M. Ryan, S. Savage, & D. Wall (Eds.), *Policy networks in criminal justice* (pp. 24–54). Basingstoke: Palgrave.

Shane, J. (2013). *Learning from error in policing: A case study in organisational accident theory.* Heidelberg: Springer.

Smith, G. (2009). Why don't more people complain against the police? *European Journal of Criminology, 6*(3), 249–266.

Terpstra, J., & Trommel, W. (2009). Police, managerialisation and presentational strategies. *Policing: An International Journal of Police Strategies and Management, 32*(1), 128–143.

Thomas, L., Straw, A., & Friedman, D. (2008). *Inquests: A practitioner's guide* (2nd ed.). London: Legal Action Group.

Wadham, J. (2004). Investigations into deaths in police custody and the independent police complaints commission. *European Human Rights Law Review, 4*, 353–361.

# 6

## Discursive Practices and Systems

## Introduction

A number of complex factors affected the discursive relationship between the IPCC and coronial system as the method of accountability construction evolved during the period 2004–15. This chapter assesses the organisations as two *systems* of accountability production in terms of discourse and discursive practices. It considers the discourses of both systems and how they relate to each other, and to wider discourses that suffuse public, policing and governmental worlds. These relationships are critically evaluated in order to assess how they influence accountability construction in cases of DAPC. The production of findings in these cases is partly driven by the requirements of audiences, and consequently consideration is given to the nature of audiences that 'consume' the findings which have been produced. As such, discourse represents a cyclical process of production and consumption, and this relationship is also considered.

In Chaps. 3, 4 and 5 it was evident that not only do the coronial system and IPCC have different structures, but each of them employ different structures *within* their organisations to investigate these cases

© The Editor(s) (if applicable) and The Author(s) 2016     **137**
D. Baker, *Deaths After Police Contact*,
DOI 10.1057/978-1-137-58967-5_6

and record findings. Not only is the sphere of accountability construction relational, but individual organisations within it are characterised by relational processes and outcomes. Somewhat paradoxically, then, the discursive processes of regulation occur in an unregulated manner. The obligations imposed on the state by Article 2 might lead the approaches of the coronial system and IPCC to become more aligned (IPCC 2014; Casale et al. 2013). This chapter examines how and why these developments have occurred. It does this by evaluating the principles of discourse and how this affects accountability construction by considering the contexts of place, audiences and relationships. In particular, it argues that the means of accountability construction has become the end in itself. In this sense, the exhibition of agency that initially produced narrative verdicts in the Middleton case (note Chap. 3) has become a form of structure guiding future practices that construct accountability.

Although the apparent lack of structure in the sphere of accountability construction is criticised from a number of quarters (see, for example Beckett 1999; Shaw and Coles 2007; Smith 2009a) it might not necessarily be an impediment to producing accountability in these cases. The fact that tensions are manifest may be a recognition that the contested nature of these cases demand multiple audiences be served by the construction of accountability. Furthermore, it may illustrate the long-standing belief in political theory of governmental separation of powers (see, for example Montesquieu 1949; Locke 1966). In this sense, there appear to be competing discursive institutional regulatory structures within wider discursive societal structures that produce and construct accountability in cases of DAPC. This reflects Foucault's (1994) view that power is not a unified entity but one that is dispersed. He believed the state was not a unified function and that one should be wary of overestimating its reach and influence. This perspective is used to assess how, where and why diffusion exists in the discursive sphere of accountability construction.

The chapter examines the growth of hybrid regulatory systems in this sphere of governance and their impact on accountability construction. As has been demonstrated, the remit of organisations to construct accountability is relational and not always connected to other organisations within the same sphere of discursive practice. Furthermore, the reach and influence of these organisations appears, to some extent, to be circumscribed by each other's discursive processes and texts, and this further underlines the importance of understanding relationships in the discursive system of accountability construction. The chapter also considers the associated field of healthcare regulation as it seeks to understand similarities in the regulation of avoidable death in England and Wales, and suggests that issues such as ambiguous regulatory processes, a failure to learn lessons and failure to prevent avoidable deaths are not purely confined to the subject of death after police contact.

# Discursive Relationships

Accountability construction is a process manifest by multiple power bases and consequently dependent to a large extent on the types of discursive relationships between these power bases. The investigation of death is no exception. From the outset, it is important to establish that any investigation into death is a retrospective exercise that does not involve the participation of the deceased. Knowledge established about the deceased is open to contestation from a number of power bases, but notably not from the individual who died (Prior 1985). Hallam et al. (1999: 88) believe the dead body is a 'focus for discourse and practice'; and that 'bodies are sites of struggle over definitions over what is deemed normal and what deviant'. In the processes used by the IPCC and coroner a number of forms of evidence are sought—both physically and in the form of written and oral submissions.

The representation of bodies appears repeatedly in literature on policing, post-mortem inquiry and discourse generally. Young (1991: 129) notes the use of bodies in policing as: 'metaphors of disorder and potential chaos'. This is because they sustain a vision of order and control based on delimited categorisation that exists within police culture. Spitzer (1975: 645–46) identifies the categories of 'social junk' and 'social dynamite' that exist outside of such a vision, and it appears that both categories exist in the dataset. The former primarily as those dependent upon substances, and these are typically constructed as not representing a threat to the community. It might be argued that the 'social dynamite' group relates more to those with mental health issues who are perceived as unstable and consequently dangerous (note also, Razack 2015). Young (1991) would aver that both groups represent 'dirty work' in police culture. A similar point is made in Horsley's (2012) research suggesting pathology is the 'dirty work' of the medical profession. She goes on to assert that the body in post-mortem and inquests exists simultaneously as a body and as a person. This is paralleled by Foucault's (1976) view that bodies exist in discourse as both subjective entities and objective truths. The chapter aims to establish how *subjective* investigation effectively produces *objective* knowledge. Critically examining the relationships between power bases that produce this knowledge enables an understanding of how this affects the construction of accountability in these cases.

The number and variety of witnesses and evidential bases typically broadens in proportion to the level of contestation in the case. Hence, in the Sean Rigg case, the inquest used more witnesses and physical evidence than the original IPCC report, and this in turn led to the Casale review. Furthermore, the Casale review led to the IPCC commissioning its own fundamental review into how it investigates cases of DAPC. A more recent development, as noted in the previous chapter, is the appointment of Elish Angiolini to chair another independent review into deaths in police custody which began in early 2016. The relational aspect of accountability construction is well illustrated by this case, as is the fact that numerous power bases provided 'objective truths' about a single subject in different contexts. Foucault (1979a) believed that different contexts could produce three types of relationships between and within discourses, which he termed *oppositional, complementary* and *analogous.* First, the *oppositional.* It has been established that the coronial system and IPCC investigate cases of DAPC with different structures, processes and aims, and produce documents that reflect these respective differences. In this sense, they are not oppositional organisations, but different. This is examined in more detail in the following chapter using the concept of 'horizontal accountability' (Bovens 2007: 460). Second, Foucault (1979a) asserted that the discursive relationship could be *complementary.* The Sean Rigg case suggests that discursive processes driving accountability construction have altered the discursive relationship between the two organisations. The Casale review, supported by the IPCC (2014) report into investigating cases of DAPC explicitly stated that IPCC investigations into cases of DAPC should adopt significant aspects of coronial processes and practices. The third stage is yet to be determined at the time of writing—we are yet to see whether the IPCC system of accountability construction becomes *analogous* with the coronial system. Moreover, it cannot be presumed that the coronial system will remain unchanged as the Chief Coroner presses ahead with reforms based on standardising processes (see, for example, Chief Coroner 2015; Chief Coroner's Office 2013). Accountability construction evolved through the period 2004–15. The case of Sean Rigg exemplifies the constant process of discourse—of articulation and re-articulation based on shifting contexts and events, illustrating the concept of *complementary* discourse. This reflects Gunnarson et al.'s (1997: 1) view that discourse shapes and reshapes institutions and written discourse contributes to the 'historical creation of professional practices'.

Competing power bases ascribe knowledge onto the body and about the life of the deceased and events leading to their death. The knowledge codified as a result of these processes cannot be said to be the result of neutral or objective forms of inquiry. Different power bases bring different criteria to bear on the inquiry. Consequently, these need to be considered for what they say about why knowledge is produced and for whom it is produced. Hallam et al. (1999: 92) state that: 'the social significance of sudden death is that it threatens chaos: the notion that death may be random suggests lack of control'. Inquests and IPCC investigations seek to re-establish order over the process of death classification. The notions of classification and order creation can be seen in the processes of both organisations. When constructing findings, both organisations use benchmarking criteria that determine parameters for actions based on certain events. As discussed in the 'measurement' section of Chap. 4, these are typically manifest as policies or guidelines. Foucault (1979b) asserts that a triumvirate of power, knowledge and government combine to produce specific types of rationality that construct specific types of order in specific contexts.

Conversely, the role of individual agency and how it relates to discursive practices should not be overlooked. The Sean Rigg case demonstrated how different agents affected the structure of both the IPCC and coronial investigation. In the case of the IPCC, one manifestation was the alleged interference during questioning by Police Federation representatives. Furthermore, at the inquest, the Rigg family were assiduous in gathering evidence not considered by the IPCC that they wished to be heard in a public forum. Finally, the unparalleled decision of Anne Owers to order an independent inquiry into the IPCC's original report is an example of agency overcoming structure, or perhaps agency being used as a means of relegitimising an existing structure. These examples amply demonstrate the ability of individuals, or groups of individuals, to exert agency and affect the discursive practices that construct accountability in cases of DAPC.

## Means and Ends

Article 2 is a catalyst sparking evolutionary change in accountability construction. A focus on the structural means of the inquiry, via the Article 2 inquest, has produced unexpected ends in the shape of narrative verdicts. Consequently, those ends have become means in the process of subsequent inquiries through the structure of Coroners Rules. Polyvalence occurs when objective truths migrate across power bases via discursive practices (Foucault 1976), as manifest in the case of Sean Rigg. At first sight, this appears to be a paradoxical process. The initial use of agency in producing a narrative verdict has resulted in a form of structure that is increasingly used to record textual findings in cases of DAPC. This is an example of shifts within discursive practice affected by power relations, primarily caused by the requirements of the ECHR. In terms of discourse analysis, these processes relate to intertextuality (Foucault 1976). This concept states that the production of documents informs and contributes to the production of further documents in an area of knowledge. Winiecki (2008: 767), writing about discursive processes in courtrooms, notes that: 'Knowledge is maintained and created and made available for future use ... in particular contexts involving special rules or subsets of common social rules.' In this sense, narrative verdicts might be seen as a 'subset of rules' within the discourse that constructs accountability in these cases. It has been shown that the 'subset of rules' has spread from the coronial system to the IPCC via the Casale review, illustrating the fundamental importance of relationships between power bases and their influence in producing rational truths discussed earlier in this chapter (Foucault 1979b). A timeline of events that charts the evolution of accountability construction in cases of DAPC in the twenty-first century is set out on in Fig. 6.1. It illustrates the manifold events, publications, reviews and developments that occurred in the period covered by this book.

It could be argued that narrative verdicts and investigation reports fulfil the ultimate requirements of the ECHR in that the processes of an Article 2 inquest and IPCC investigation report become their purpose: the means become the end. Both organisations may be legitimising themselves to external audiences through discursive practices. In this sense, *cognitive* legitimacy, *procedural* legitimacy and *consequential* legitimacy are manifest (Terpstra and Trommel 2009). By constantly articulating and re-articulating the knowledge they produce, they can be seen to be producing rigorous, fair and meaningful findings to society when investigating cases of DAPC—thus constructing cognitive and procedural legitimacy. Satisfying the requirements set down by Article 2 constructs consequential legitimacy. Except that rather than consequential legitimacy being constructed merely in terms of adherence to benchmarking criteria, as discussed in Chaps. 4 and 5, it is also constructed in terms of fulfilling abstract principles embodied by Article 2. This effectively means that the discursive relationship has evolved so that benchmarking is a corollary to principle. Therefore benchmarking has altered from being an end itself, to the means through which the end of adherence to Article 2 is enabled.

In an article dealing with equal opportunities and the promotion of diversity within Higher Education providers in England and Wales, Ahmed (2007) considers how means become ends in this particular regulatory sphere. She asks the question: if documents are actors, what sort of acts do they perform? Are policies constructed to ensure compliance or to meet, or fulfil requirements? Effectively she asks: do policies exist to alter behaviour, or to create an audit trail that demonstrates the institution is actively striving to adhere to principles? Institutional desires to promote principles typically fall back to measurement criteria which aim to promote such principles, thus: 'you can become good at audit by

| | |
|---|---|
| 2001 | Middleton v Coroner for Avon |
| 2002 | Police Reform Act passed enabling creation of the IPCC |
| 2003 | Luce report: recommends complete overhaul of coronial system |
| 2004 | IPCC founded |
| 2004 | First known narrative verdict in cases of DAPC |
| 2005 | JCHR publishes first report into developments in the sphere of deaths in custody noting the changes required by Article 2 of the ECHR. |
| 2006 | ACPO and the NPIA publishes first guide for *Safer Detention in Custody* |
| 2008 | FFLM is formed, it has since produced numerous guideline documents with regards to cases of DAPC |
| 2008 | Fulton review into deaths in custody recommends the establishment of a Ministerial Board on Deaths in Custody |
| 2008 | NAO produces highly critical report into the work of the IPCC |
| 2009 | BMA publishes first guide for safer practices in the case of detainees in police custody |
| 2009 | Coroners and Justice Act passed by parliament, but not enacted. |
| 2010 | HAC produces highly critical analysis on the work of the IPCC |
| 2010 | IPCC produces its first 10 year review of patterns and trends in cases of DAPC |
| 2011 | Inquest into Ian Tomlinson's death is notable for using a purpose designed website with daily updates and all court transcripts posted on-line. |
| 2012 | Office of the Chief Coroner established |
| 2012 | ACPO publishes second edition of *Safer Detention in Custody* guidelines |
| 2013 | Casale review into the IPCC investigation of Sean Rigg's death, is highly critical of IPCC processes and practices as they relate to obligations under article 2 of the ECHR |
| 2013 | 2009 Coroners and Justice Act partially enacted |
| 2013 | Chief Coroner publishes public guidelines about how Article 2 inquests should be processed |
| 2014 | IPCC publishes full review into how it investigates cases of DAPC. It pledges to adopt a significant number of findings from the Casale review. |
| 2014 | Chapman review into internal police disciplinary systems |
| 2015 | Home Office Triennial Review into IPCC |
| 2015 | Home Secretary announces independent review into deaths in police custody |

**Fig. 6.1** Timeline of significant events affecting the construction of accountability in cases of DAPC

producing auditable documents' (Ahmed 2007: 319). This leads to an apparent paradox whereby having a good policy on race equality equates to being 'good' at race equality: '[the policy's] very existence is taken as evidence that the institutional world documented by the document … has been overcome' (Ahmed 2007: 320). Thus we end up in a situation where: 'Having good policies becomes a substitute for action' (Ahmed 2007: 321). This is a persuasive argument in light of the findings in Chaps. 4 and 5 of this book. The increasingly complex findings identified in narrative verdicts do not yet appear to have had a significant effect on the number of people who die in cases of DAPC. This suggests that the findings function more as a discursive practice that further informs policy formulation in the regulatory sphere.

The key functions fulfilled by coroners and the IPCC in these cases are to investigate, highlight issues of concern, report them and make recommendations with the aim of preventing future deaths. Given the observations above, this appears at best questionable, but effectiveness is not necessarily synonymous with legitimacy as was touched on in Chap. 2. Coroners' status as autonomous legal agents appears to ensure their *cognitive* legitimacy in both societal and governmental terms. The relative lack of connectivity or working relationships with other agencies in the sphere of DAPC marks coroners out as being functionally atypical, and possibly more legitimate. In the discursive sense, institutional systems might only appear legitimate when examined in their own procedural terms in the sense that they are produced through and within practice. They need not necessarily be fully integrated within the wider system of accountability in cases of DAPC, as is examined in more detail in the following chapter. Consequently, the coronial system may appear to be unusual and atypical, but this does not necessarily mean that it cannot perform a legitimate function in the construction of accountability in these cases, as was demonstrated in Chaps. 4 and 5.

As discussed in Chap. 5, narrative verdicts have begun to affect the construction of accountability by the IPCC. The Casale review was unequivocal in stating that the IPCC should refocus its approach based on processes and reporting mechanisms used by the coronial system in Article 2 inquests. The institutional reality of the IPCC is evolving in large part due to processes in another institution in the same discursive sphere. Somewhat perversely then, the lack of connectivity inherent in coronial practice as discussed above, has led to that practice being partially adopted by the IPCC as a result of a third party (Casale) identifying it as key in the construction of accountability. Practices produced by an inherent lack of connectivity have led ineluctably to shared practices via a third party, illustrating Foucault's (1979a) concept of polyvalence. It appears the IPCC's ability to legitimately construct accountability has been eroded by another organisation within the same discursive sphere. The crisis of legitimacy it faced in the aftermath of the Sean Rigg case led it to acknowledge the legitimacy gap and adopt discursive practices from the coronial system. As established earlier in the chapter, this reflects Foucault's (1979a) views on *complementary* relations between discourses. This raises the issue of why different organisations exist to construct accountability and why their processes vary.

## Ambiguity and Ambivalence

Ambiguity and ambivalence are easily conflated as they share the stem *'ambi'* which in Latin means 'the same'. Ambiguity has already been established as a key concept in police and coroners' roles, functions and use of discretion. To be ambiguous is to have more than one meaning, to be unclear, and/or to be unable to distinguish between alternatives. To be ambivalent is to possess mixed feelings or contradictory ideas about something or someone. Therefore, the principal difference between the two words is that while ambiguity relates to a lack of clarity about meaning, ambivalence means being unclear about feelings or ideas. In cases of DAPC ambiguity can be linked to the wording used to record findings; and to a lack of clarity about the roles and purposes of the regulatory organisations. These two issues have a commonality in that they relate to *discursive practices* in cases of DAPC, whereas ambivalence is manifest in the *organisation of the regulatory sphere* in which those practices are situated, in that it is not clear why both the coronial system and the IPCC investigate cases of DAPC. Thus ambiguity relates more typically to *practices* while the concept of ambivalence is more connected to the *systems* that enable practices to function within them.

It was established in Chap. 3 that police regulation occurs within a two-tier system. Chapter 5 demonstrated that regulation occurred on a number of levels specific to discursive systems. Hindess (1982: 503), writing about power struggles within specific arenas noted that: 'The constitution of an arena of struggle involves definite conditions, modes of action and possible effects which are all subject to variation within certain specifiable limitations.' To paraphrase Marx and Engels (1965), regulators construct accountability, but not in conditions of their own making. According to Hindess (1982) the type of arena where power is exercised is specific to the type of outcomes that are produced. Black notes that: 'Accountability relationships are discursive interactions with their own logics which draw on and thus reproduce particular structures of meaning' (2008: 152). What is less clear is why different regulatory arenas exist for the same object of regulation, and the chapter aims to examine the conditions that enable and facilitate this.

At the most basic level, ambivalence is manifest in the fact that more than one system is charged with investigating cases of DAPC. Weisbrode (2012) argues that ambivalence to some degree comes from an excess of ambition. For example, when we desire a solution to a problem and discover two possible alternatives, we are more likely to attempt both rather than stake all of our hopes on one. Similarly, choosing both might be a manifestation of wanting neither. Choice is an essential element of ambivalence, but so too is doubt. The inability of the state to actively choose between the coronial system and IPCC has led to them both investigating cases of DAPC. In this sense, Weisbrode (2012) posits that ambivalence does not only mean that choice is not exercised, but that the actual necessity of choosing need not be acknowledged; this might go some way to explaining the expansion of discourse on accountability in cases of DAPC. Moreover, this growth appears to exacerbate feelings of ambivalence, as Rudolph and Popp (2007) noted in their research into political parties and policy formulation. It might be argued then, that ambivalence begets further ambivalence in the system that constructs accountability in cases of DAPC. However, when a crisis of legitimacy occurs, ambivalence appears to be suspended while investigations are initiated and evaluations considered prior to strategic decisions being made, as was seen in Chap. 5.

Ambivalence pervades the notion of discourses with competing power bases. Ambivalence can mean that one simultaneously holds both positive and negative views of the same object (Weisbrode 2012). In this sense, the government may negatively view the coronial system as being overly autonomous and relatively unregulated (Luce 2003). At the same time, however, it may view the coronial system positively as providing a legitimate response to the demands of the ECHR (Chief Coroner 2015). In order to hold both views, it employs different discourses in respect of both views. The negative perspective could highlight discrepancies in discursive practice such as transparency and accountability, arguing the coronial system is short of both and in urgent need of reform (Luce 2003, Smith 2003). The positive perspective could stress the independence and autonomy of the coroner and jury in meeting obligations required by Article 2 of the ECHR (Matthews 2011). These perspectives do not sit comfortably beside one another, and do not obviously mesh. However, the reality is, in the coronial system, they *do* interlink. This is an example of discourses *opposing* one another while at the same time to some degree *complementing* each other, much as was discussed earlier in the chapter (Foucault 1979a).

This is not to say that ambivalence might preclude accountability. The growing number of organisations within the regulatory sphere is seen by Stone (2007) as a 'network' that encourages greater accountability and reduces the overall use of force by the police. It need not necessarily be the case that such a network be strategically planned or tightly linked and coherent in terms of organisational relationships, indeed, he states that it is not. Ambivalence may also be linked to ambiguity. The ambiguous nature of the wording used in narrative verdicts might represent a desire to express relatively contradictory findings within the same document. For example, to be critical of actions and omissions while stopping short of ascribing liability. The lack of clear purpose within the inquest process can produce an inquiry with such a broad degree of latitude that there might be no clear cut conclusions, as established with 'specific ambiguity' in Chap. 4. In this sense, ambivalence and ambiguity can be seen to be complementary. Narrative verdicts may have promoted greater accountability, but this does not mean they have necessarily promoted increased clarity in the wider sphere of police regulation. In order to consider how relationships between multiple regulatory organisations function, the chapter now examines systems of accountability, particularly 'hybrid' regulatory systems.

## Discursive Systems of Accountability

While using more than one accountability system to investigate the same subject might appear to embody ambivalence, it is not unusual in wider systems of governance. Numerous authors (see, for example Murphy et al. 2009; Black 2008; May 2007) have commented on the relatively recent emergence of multiple regulatory systems as a means of providing accountability. These are typically referred to as 'hybrid' regulatory systems (see, for example Halpern 2008). Hybrid regulation has emerged as the state moves away from being the primary regulator of organisations and attempts to encourage regulatory regimes that are more flexible and responsive (Black 2008). While hybrid systems have not entirely supplanted state regulation, they are increasingly used in numerous spheres that affect society such as food production and healthcare (May 2007). May (2007: 11) believes accountability must now therefore be considered as a: 'multilevel concept within a devolved regulatory state'. Although Smith (2009b: 421) notes evolving systems of regulation have 'transformed' numerous public services, the police appear to be an exception, perhaps underlining their unique status as discussed in Chap. 2. Halpern (2008: 86) states that: 'hybridity is a means of dispersing regulatory authority and, by so doing, fostering responsiveness and flexibility'.

A Foucauldian response might assert that hybridity could also create gaps and overlaps in knowledge and power. Hybrid regulation may exist on all, or any combination of the following levels: first, a combination of governmental and non-governmental organisations (NGOs) may be involved. On the subject of DAPC, examples of governmental actors are the coronial system and IPCC, examples of NGOs might be ACPO or the CP. Second, regulation may be provided by either central or regional providers. It was established in Chap. 3 that the coronial system is best imagined as a regional system, whereas the IPCC is unquestionably a national organisation. Third, Halpern (2008) asserts regulation may be provided by multiple policy actors. It is evident that this is the case in the sphere of accountability construction in cases of DAPC. Relatively recent entrants to this sphere are the BMA (British Medical Association) and the FFLM (Faculty of Forensic and Legal Medicine).

Murphy et al. (2009: 2) consider how regulation ensures compliance under hybrid systems. They posit that regulators have two options typically available to them. First, they can either sanction or use the threat of legal authority, they term this 'reactance'. Second, regulators can take an 'accommodative view' in seeking to secure future compliance by encouraging and disseminating best practice. This appears to mirror Smith's (2009a) view that while regulation is prospective (future oriented), accountability is constructed retrospectively. However, it must be remembered that in a hybrid system there are multiple actors and audiences, and many of the actors are *also* audiences. This suggests that maintaining or manufacturing cognitive and procedural legitimacy in one arena for one audience might not necessarily mean that a different audience within the regulatory sphere considers the construction to be legitimate, a point acknowledged by Black (2008).

Any regulatory regime must fit the circumstances within which accountability is constructed (May 2007). The goals and purposes of accountability must fit with the way in which regulation is designed to ensure that means and ends are met, using benchmarks to measure standards and outcomes. Three potential systems are posited by May (2007: 8–12): *rule* based, *goal* based and *system* based. He argues that if a goal-based system is pursued, then rules will not necessarily assist in goals being achieved, much as was underlined in the earlier discussion of Ahmed's (2007) article in this chapter. In a discussion that echoes Gilsinan (2012) and Chan (1999), May (2007) states that rules tend to become an end in themselves and mutate into a 'prescriptive' form of regulation. An example of this was manifest in Chap. 5 with the IPCC's *consequentialist* (Terpstra and Trommel 2009) form of accountability construction that effectively collapsed under the critical investigation of the Casale review. Furthermore, May (2007) notes that rule-based regulation is primarily based on legal enforcement, or *reactive* enforcement (Murphy et al. 2009: 2). In contrast, goal- and system-based regulation leans more towards *accommodative* encouragement (May 2007). Thus goal- and system-based

regulation focuses more on influencing working cultures as a way of promoting change. This links to concepts such as organisational learning
(Doyle 2010) and learning lessons (Downham and Lingham 2009) as
discussed in Chaps. 2 and 3. It suggests the hybrid system within which
accountability is constructed in cases of DAPC relies principally on
*goal-* and *system-*based regulation. According to May (2007) rule-based
regulation is used infrequently but still represents the ultimate mode
of regulation as it is primarily legal in nature. This observation might
underline the aftermath of the Sean Rigg case where the inquest was
regarded as more legitimate than the IPCC investigation. The discussion
above appears to reinforce May's (2007) point that regimes of accountability should be designed to fit the context within which accountability
is constructed. Therefore if Smith (2009b) is correct in his assumption
that some public services have been transformed by shifts in regulatory
structures, it might be the case that an appropriate structure has yet to be
identified that fits the police.

A more in-depth analysis of the hybrid system is set out by Black
(2008) who prefers the term 'polycentric' system. This highlights numerous aspects of the previous discussion regarding multiple actors and audiences, multiple types of regulation and the dispersal of regulators across
numerous levels. However, she takes the analysis further by examining
how dialectical processes, the use of narrative and language and the role
of discourse explain this polycentric system. In the discussion below, her
work is examined in some detail as it is particularly relevant in drawing
together significant elements highlighted in the book thus far. Echoing
numerous concepts analogous to Foucauldian thought, Black notes that
polycentric systems are: 'Marked by fragmentation, complexity and interdependence between actors ... their boundaries are marked by the issues
or problems which they are concerned with, rather than necessarily by a
common solution' (2008: 137). She asserts that *cognitive* legitimacy is of
central importance in the process of regulation, for without it audiences
question the right of the regulator to construct accountability. For this
reason, she notes that Power's (2004: 24) observation about organisations being 'turned inside out' is particularly relevant. In order to ensure
cognitive legitimacy, organisations are becoming increasingly transparent: 'the details of their internal decision-making structures and processes

… audit, and risk management processes, are seen as critically relevant to those outside them' (Black 2008: 141). The discussion in Chap. 5 demonstrated that in the aftermath of the Sean Rigg case the IPCC (2014) went to great lengths to demonstrate it could use transparent processes and structures in order to restore a patina of cognitive legitimacy.

Black believes this demonstrates the potentially transformative power that could be produced by relationships within a polycentric sphere of accountability. In the Sean Rigg case, the IPCC compared its role primarily with the role of the coronial system, supporting Black's (2008: 147) assertion that: 'Regulators can also seek to develop … cognitive legitimacy through, for example, linking themselves to other organisations which are perceived to be legitimate by those whose legitimacy claims they want to meet.' In this sense, as noted previously, regulatory actors are *also audiences* as they evaluate each other's processes and outcomes. This manifests itself in a process similar to jockeying for position in a dynamic and dialectical environment of accountability construction, or what Black (2008: 147) calls 'legitimacy networks'. The increasingly complex relationships within these legitimacy networks can lead to tensions and existential crises breaking out, not least because of what Koppel (2005: 2) terms 'multiple personality disorders'. These occur because it is not possible to simultaneously maintain legitimacy with all of the organisations within the sphere of accountability on the same issues or in the same contexts. This emphasises the convoluted and intricate nature of relationships that become increasingly manifest as the sphere of regulation expands. However, while the focus of authors has been on analysing how hybrid regimes work, Halpern (2008: 86) notes that: 'How constellations of policy actors are best organised for enhancing long-term regulatory flexibility remains largely unexplored.'

The increasing number of organisations within the sphere of accountability construction in these cases is also a feature of polycentric regimes according to Black (2008). Furthermore, this affects the complexity of the dialectical relationships discussed above. As each new organisation joins, it must evaluate other organisations in the network of legitimacy and consider how it forms a relationship with them. She notes that: 'Enrolment can also increase the regulator's need for legitimacy from a wider range of actors within the regulatory regime with whom it interacts in the performance of regulation' (Black 2008: 148). The way in which accountability is constructed, and the type of accountability that is constructed depends on the arena in which it is constructed, and the relationships that affect its construction, as was established in an earlier discussion incorporating Hindess (1982) and Foucault (1979a).

Black strikes a note of caution about the ability of one organisation within the sphere of regulation to replicate the processes of another in order to reinforce their cognitive legitimacy. Just because the accountability constructed by a different organisation in the same sphere is fixed on the same object does not mean each organisation is substitutable: 'Because different accountability relationships are grounded in different legitimacy claims' (Black 2008: 152). The sphere of accountability construction in cases of DAPC is heterogeneous rather than homogenous. Black's (2008: 156) view is that the composition of the 'field' in polycentric regulatory regimes is key to understanding the way they function and the types of accountability they construct. The polycentric system of regulation epitomises the way in which accountability is constructed in cases of DAPC in England and Wales, and the way the 'field' is organised is examined in more detail in the following chapter. This section has considered the manifold systems and dialectical relationships inherent within the polycentric sphere of accountability construction. While the observations above on the organisation and operation of regulators within a particular field clearly relate to the regulation of police in cases of DAPC, below I consider how they might apply to the regulation of healthcare agencies in cases of avoidable death. This suggests that the regulation of other public services is remarkably similar and demonstrates the same problems as those identified in the book thus far about policing and cases of DAPC.

# Accountability and Regulation in Healthcare: Discursive Systems and Practices

While the focus of this book is on accountability, governance and regulation of the police in cases of DAPC, it is clear that accountability, governance and regulation could also be considered in the sphere of healthcare agencies, particularly with what might be termed 'avoidable death' (see, for example Box 1983). At this stage I would like to pause to consider accountability, governance and regulation in the NHS in the context of the discussion throughout this book about police in cases of DAPC. Having established in this chapter that public services in England and Wales now exist in a 'post-regulatory state' (Halpern 2008: 87) and are overseen by hybrid regulatory systems, it is worth examining how this occurs in the realm of regulation and accountability for healthcare provision. The discussion in Chap. 2 underlined issues of multi-agency working in cases of DAPC. It noted the hierarchical and monolithic nature of these large scale organisations, and their inability to communicate effectively within their own structures, let alone with other public services. Chapter 4 established that half of the cases of DAPC considered in the dataset for this book involved other public services in addition to the police, and that juries were frequently critical of these services regarding failures in training, adherence to policy and practice, communication and risk assessments. Below, I examine events in the NHS in the twenty-first century in light of issues raised thus far in this book, in terms of avoidable death and lessons being learned; and in relation to the discussion in this chapter concerning regulatory regimes and discursive systems.

Numerous cases and public inquiries have highlighted healthcare practices which range from poor, to unethical, through to criminally liable. Inquiries into these cases have repeatedly highlighted failures in the regulation of practice due to failures in NHS accountability systems (see, for example Francis 2013; Smith 2003; Redfern 2001). Furthermore, these inquiries have stressed that such failures tend to occur due to systemic, organisational and cultural practices within the institution in question rather than due to individual malpractice or error. The Shipman case, officially uncovered in 2000, where a registered General Practitioner was found to have murdered at least fifteen patients and unlawfully killed 166 others sparked a major public inquiry. The Smith (2003) inquiry into Shipman found manifold failures in regulatory and oversight processes in fields from health provision to death investigation. In particular it highlighted the lack of analysis and evaluation of data that should have been able to stop Shipman killing so many of his patients at an earlier stage and hoped that in future: 'Knowledge gained from death investigation is applied for the prevention of avoidable death' (Smith 2003: 25).

The issue of large scale non-consensual organ retention at the Alder Hey children's hospital in Liverpool was highlighted by the Redfern (2001) inquiry. It found the systematic retention of significant numbers of hearts, brains and foetuses post-autopsy without parental consent occurred due to 'illegal and unethical' processes in medical practice, including the systematic falsification of records and statistics (Redfern 2001: 9). This occurred due to a failure by the hospital management to provide effective regulation that existed to curb clinical malpractice. In 2011, a BBC Panorama programme into the abuse and neglect of patients with learning disabilities in the Winterbourne View private hospital identified a culture of practice that eventually culminated with six staff being jailed (Plomin 2013). The then Care Services Minister, Norman Lamb, stated that the events revealed by the undercover BBC programme were a 'national scandal' and a 'shocking horror story' (Parish 2013: 8). These practices occurred despite frequent alerts to regulatory agencies being ignored. The aftermath of the case, while it resulted in numerous criminal trials, did not result in a public inquiry or any obvious form of institutional learning on the part of healthcare regulators (Plomin 2013).

The issue of avoidable deaths at the Mid-Staffordshire NHS trust hospital became apparent only after persistent whistle-blowing by staff and a vociferous media campaign led by family members who had witnessed the 'appalling suffering of many patients' (Francis 2013: 3). This led to three reviews, one in 2007, another in 2009, the last of which was the Francis inquiry (2013). It highlighted systematic failures within the hospital that it believed should have been identified due to the 'plethora of agencies, scrutiny groups, commissioners, regulators, and public bodies' notionally involved in the regulation of NHS services (Francis 2013: 3). Francis noted that nine different healthcare regulators had identified areas of significant concern at the hospital. For example, in 2004 there were 'warning signs' with a Commission for Healthcare Improvement re-rating the hospital from three stars to zero stars. In 2007 the Royal College of Surgeons labelled the surgical department 'dysfunctional' (Francis 2013: 41–42). While the regulators had overlapping areas of focus, they failed to share findings or communicate with each other, or with higher authorities, with each regulator apparently convinced that another would do so, leading to none eventually doing so.

In 2015 the principal healthcare regulator in England and Wales, the Care Quality Commission (CQC) was severely criticised by the House of Commons Committee of Public Accounts (2015: 3), noting that it was 'not yet an effective regulator of health and social care'. Criticisms covered its failure to meet inspection targets, failure to construct meaningful performance measurement criteria, and failure to respond to stakeholders concerns about specific healthcare trusts. This is not entirely surprising given that the Francis (2013: 57) report had noted two years previously that the CQC had a 'defensive institutional instinct to attack those who criticise it'. Such a mindset clearly does not bode well for organisational learning in issues relating to avoidable death.

Also in 2015, the Parliamentary and Health Service Ombudsman delivered a report criticising the inability of the NHS to 'adequately address' questions about 'serious and avoidable harms' identified by patient or family complaints. The report noted that nearly three-quarters of complaints it examined into incidents of avoidable deaths in NHS facilities should have triggered a 'serious incident investigation' by the relevant NHS trust but did not. It stated: 'There is no national guidance on patient safety incident investigations that sets out who should investigate and how independent they should be' (Parliamentary and Health Service Ombudsman 2015). At the time of writing, in late 2015, a leaked report commissioned in 2013 by NHS England into practices at the Southern Health NHS Trust revealed that it failed to adequately investigate in excess of 1,000 patient deaths in the period 2011–15 (Campbell 2015). These deaths were predominantly individuals with mental health needs or learning disabilities. The report highlighted the systematic lack of investigation of such deaths and the lack of any form of critical overview that could enable institutional learning into these deaths. Jeremy Hunt, the current Health Secretary stated that the government was 'profoundly shocked' by the findings which he believed were 'totally unacceptable' (BBC News 2015).

The examples above outline remarkably similar types of incidents, events and failures that have thus far been set out in this book about policing, accountability, regulation and governance in cases of DAPC. They predominantly affect people from marginalised groups within society: those who are aged, are seriously ill, have mental health issues or learning disabilities. The practices detailed occur principally because of organisational or cultural practices inside institutions rather than due to individuals or groups 'going rogue'. They highlight failures in hybrid regulatory regimes, failures to heed warning signs and whistle-blowers, and failures to learn lessons. I have deliberately limited this section to events uncovered in the twenty-first century in order to draw parallels with findings in the dataset for this book.

The issues raised above highlight the persistent and deep-seated failures of healthcare organisations and regulators to make headway on issues relating to poor practice and avoidable deaths. They also underscore the significance of official inquiries revealing serious failings in public in a way that regulators are often unable to do, thus echoing the example of the Casale review into the death of Sean Rigg. It is difficult, therefore, to avoid the observation that in critical cases that affect society hybrid regulation of public services is of questionable effectiveness; it often requires state intervention in the form of public inquiries, or legal intervention in civil or criminal courts. While it is the case that goal-based 'accommodative' regulation is more common in public service provision in England and Wales, it also appears to be the case that in critical cases, rule-based 'reactive' regulation is favoured in order to ensure cognitive legitimacy is constructed in societal terms (Black 2008, May 2007).

## Discourses of Accountability

Having discussed regulatory systems and their discursive relationships, the chapter now returns to consider the discourse of language and its role in constructing objective truths within these systems. To some extent, narrative structures appear to dictate how 'the story' of the deceased can be told, in such a way as to explain how the death occurred. The inquisition process that precedes the construction of narrative verdicts must be expressed through the processes and structure of narrative. The explanation produced by members of the public is partly for other members of the public—both in terms of *cognitive* and *procedural* legitimacy (Terpstra and Trommel 2009). However, it is also directed at other agencies involved in the sphere of accountability construction—Terpstra and Trommel's (2009) conception of *consequential* legitimacy. The state can be seen to have met its obligations to the ECHR by ensuring a rigorous, independent and public investigation into the loss of a citizen's life. However, in some cases, the death is explained as a series of failures, usually through omissions, but sometimes through actions. The latter are typically cases that capture public imagination and indignation due to apparently being examples of unfair or unjust treatment—Ian Tomlinson and Sean Rigg illustrate this (see, for example Greer and McLaughlin 2012; Hirschfield and Simon 2010). In these cases, *all* forms of legitimacy are critically questioned and a legitimacy crisis may flare.

Therefore, the construction of accountability might fulfil the demands of the state on all levels. In the cases of Sean Rigg and Ian Tomlinson, misconduct is identified in the inquest, and subsequently dealt with in the criminal court and/or by the officer or FME resigning, being dismissed or struck off the medical register. Albeit this process appears to take a grindingly long time, as Benn and Worpole (1986) note. In cases where omission is a cause of death, more guidelines are produced, best practice is sought as a way of preventing such future 'tragedies' and agencies attempt to 'learn the lessons'. Measurements are tested to ensure that state agencies did everything they could, based on benchmarking criteria, to ensure that the individual did not die. These observations fit with Chan's (1999) belief, discussed in Chaps. 2 and 3, that there is an essentially performative aspect to police accountability. Moreover, this echoes Innes's (2003: 163) view, outlined in Chap. 4, that events are constructed as: 'dramaturgically [displaying] a moral message within a given cultural context'. In this sense, it is necessary to consider who the performance is for in order to understand the nature of its content and purpose within its specific context.

Fairclough (1992) views discourse as a system of knowledge and belief that exists on more than one level. He asserts that discourse exists *relationally*, in that social relationships between the participants in discourse are negotiated. One example of this in Chap. 4 was the observation that juries tend to focus on criticisms of non-police agencies where they are present, but are also more likely to be critical of police when other agencies are not present. Furthermore, Fairclough (1992) states that discourse exists on an *ideational* level in terms of how texts signify processes and relations to the wider world, mirroring Terpstra and Trommel's concepts of *cognitive* and *procedural* legitimacy. This was seen in Chap. 4 regarding the use of multiple agencies and documents to produce a system of measurement that could be used as benchmarks to explicate complex events incorporating actions or omissions. The use of a jury to produce such documents appears fundamental in ensuring that the text constructed is comprehensible to lay-persons.

Implicitness is a consistent property within texts (Fairclough 2003). Narratives contain shared meanings that link the producers of text to the consumers of it. Implicitness is manifest as shared assumptions and these occur in three forms. First, as *existential* assumptions: assumptions about what exists. In any account of a case of DAPC there are undisputed facts shared by the coronial and IPCC construction of accountability, for example; who died, where they died and when they died. Second, there are *propositional* assumptions. These are assumptions about what can or will be the case. In cases of DAPC this appears to relate to measurement criteria used by the coronial system and IPCC. Some sort of shared benchmarking must be used in order to create a framework within which actions or omissions are assessed. Finally, there are *value* assumptions. They are: 'assumptions about what is good or desirable' (Fairclough 2003: 55). This appears to relate to the tendency of accountability construction documents to establish conditions or characteristics in the deceased as a way of situating them within a system of values.

Discursive processes construct accountability by making it appear plausible, legitimate and independent. However, it has been demonstrated that legitimacy and independence are relational concepts throughout this book. The processes represent *one* way in which accountability can be constructed. As Hyden (1997: 261) notes, the construction of institutional narrative: '[excludes] another potential story'. Although discursive systems are marked by change and continuity, it is important to distinguish the relationship between change and continuity. It appears that change is manifest in processes and discourses primarily driven by the requirements of the ECHR. Continuity has occurred because the state and its agents are still able to avoid prosecution based on the arenas and systems in place that investigate cases of DAPC. In Chap. 3 of this book, Gilsinan (2012) noted that police accountability systems tended to be 'isomorphic' in that the façade of accountability evolved, but the outcome of their processes remained the same. It might be argued that in the great majority of cases, the construction of accountability in these cases acts as a shield that protects the state and its agents. Periodically, cases that cause public outrage lead to state agents being identified and their actions being further scrutinised in other fora. These might be viewed as sacrificial cases, necessary to ensure the overall legitimacy of a system that constructs accountability in cases of DAPC. The reality, after all of the contexts have been stripped away, after polyvalence and intertextuality have been acknowledged and discursive practices noted, is that the text remains (see, for example Smith 1974). As Hyden (1997: 260) notes, reality has been codified in text: 'The text abides and later can become the "object" of renewed interpretations.'

It could be argued that the accumulation of discourse in the area of accountability construction is based partly on rational knowledge and partly on will. Will comes from the ECHR as an absolute principle. First, it holds that the right to life is the ultimate right of humans. Second, it considers this right to be a positive right that should be *enabled* as distinct from *protected* and challenges states to demonstrate that this occurs within their borders. The state uses specific rational processes and mechanisms based on measurement criteria constructed from diverse bodies of knowledge to ensure this is the case. As Rickert (1926: 79) notes: 'The man of action can only derive his means from knowledge. His goals depend not on his knowledge but on his will.' The ECHR requires a principle to be aimed for, but accountability construction appears to be based not on principles but on rationally measurable criteria. As has been established throughout this chapter, it appears that the construction of accountability in these cases exists in a series of uneasy equilibria. The 'end' of the ECHR principle enshrined by Article 2 is expressed in qualitative terms while the 'means' are constructed principally by more quantitative measurements, most typically though benchmarking criteria.

The issue of measurement is relational as it depends on the contextual criteria used to evaluate acts and omissions. In Chap. 5 discrepancies were established between narrative verdicts and IPCC reports based on the relative assessment criteria used. Arendt (1998) believed that the ability to measure was based on the capacity of human imagination to conceive of measurement criteria. She posited that measurements were based on what is known and what 'works'—rather than measurements based on ideals, morals or ethics. This led to a situation whereby the capacity to construct measurement was inherently delimited by how a subject was known and represented. The absolute goal of the right to life is measured against relative measurement criteria produced by discursive practices. Absolute ends have an uncertain relationship with relative means.

## Conclusion

The cyclical nature of discourse production reveals two related issues: means and ends, and ambiguity and ambivalence. The former related to the fact that processes and practices constructing accountability in cases of DAPC have largely become the end product of accountability construction rather than merely its means. This was seen as being a by-product of the obligations of the state in responding to the requirements of the ECHR, and of the need to construct rationally measurable criteria in order to satisfy abstract principles enshrined in Article 2. Relationships that characterise the sphere of accountability construction are complex and multi-faceted, as established during the discussion on hybrid regulatory systems. The concept of 'networks of legitimacy' illustrates the complexity of these dialectical relationships and highlights the fact that typically, actors are also audiences in the construction of accountability. This affects how they represent themselves to audiences in terms of the legitimacy they wish to construct. Thus, what appears, at first sight, to be a relatively homogenous system of accountability construction is in fact anything but. It is a heterogeneous system that should be considered in terms of dialectical relationships in order to be better understood with regards to its processes and outcomes.

These observations were discussed by considering the concepts of ambiguity and ambivalence. Ambiguity is manifest in the discursive practices and processes of organisations in the regulatory sphere, for example, in terms of recording texts that tend to lack cohesive clarity due to the complex and contested issues often involved in these cases. Ambivalence characterises the complex system of organisations that exist in the sphere of accountability construction in DAPC. The diffuse and disconnected nature of these organisations suggest the state is ambivalent about how these cases should be investigated and reported on. The lack of connections between different organisations within the system of hybrid regulation amply illustrated this, and was further demonstrated to be manifest in the sphere of healthcare regulation. This underlined the fact that the regulatory system applied to policing and cases of DAPC is not unique, but widespread in the regulation of public services in England and Wales.

Finally, the role of discourse in shaping language demonstrated how it is not only the discursive practices of organisations that are marked by dialectical relationships. The types of language used to construct narrative were examined by considering the space in which it was constructed and the audiences for whom it was constructed. In this sense, discursive practices exist in relation to organisational dynamics and to the production of meaning through texts. The latter demonstrated that meaning is determined and constructed in specific contexts and uses forms of rationality specific to those contexts. This means rationally objective meanings are constructed from relatively subjective bases of knowledge and the relationship between the two determines the type of accountability constructed. The following chapter examines how these relational processes manifest themselves as different forms of accountability that address different types of audiences. It considers how accountability, regulation and discourse coexist with governance in the contexts of wider society and what this says about how accountability is constructed in cases of DAPC.

# References

Ahmed, S. (2007). "You end up doing the document rather than doing the doing": Diversity, race equality and the politics of documentation. *Ethnic and Racial Studies, 30*(4), 590–609.

Arendt, H. (1998). *The human condition.* Chicago: University of Chicago Press.

BBC News. (2015). NHS failure to probe deaths 'shocking'. Available at: http://www.bbc.co.uk/news/health-35061716. Accessed 14 Dec 2015.

Beckett, C. (1999). Deaths in custody and the inquest system. *Critical Social Policy, 19*(2), 271–280.

Benn, M., & Worpole, K. (1986). *Death in the city*. London: Canary Press.

Black, J. (2008). Constructing and contesting legitimacy and accountability in polycentric regulatory regimes. *Regulation and Governance, 2*(2), 137–164.

Bovens, M. (2007). Analysing and assessing accountability: A conceptual framework. *European Law Journal, 13*(4), 447–468.

Box, S. (1983). *Power, crime, and mystification*. London: Routledge.

Campbell, D. (2015). NHS trust failed to properly investigate deaths of more than 1,000 patients. *The Guardian*. Available at: http://www.theguardian.com/society/2015/dec/09/southern-health-nhs-trust-failed-investigate-patient-deaths-inquiry. Accessed 11 Dec 2015.

Casale, S., Corfe, M., & Lewis, J. (2013). *Report of the independent external review of the IPCC investigation into the death of Sean Rigg*. Available at: http://www.ipcc.gov.uk/news/Pages/pr_170513_Riggreview.aspx. Accessed 21 May 2013.

Chan, J. (1999). Governing police practice: Limits of the new accountability. *British Journal of Sociology, 50*(2), 251–270.

Chief Coroner. (2015). *Report of the Chief Coroner to the Lord Chancellor.* Second Annual Report: 2014–2015. Available at: https://www.judiciary.gov.uk/wp-content/uploads/2014/07/ann-report-chief-coroner-to-the-lord-chancellor-2014-5.pdf. Accessed 12 Oct 2015.

Chief Coroner's Office. (2013). *The Chief Coroner's guide to the Coroners and Justice Act 2009.* Available at: http://www.judiciary.gov.uk/wp-content/uploads/JCO/Documents/coroners/guidance/chief-coroners-guide-to-act-sept2013.pdf. Accessed 20 Dec 2013.

Downham, G., & Lingham, R. (2009). Learning lessons: Using inquiries for change. *Journal of Mental Health Law, 18*(1), 57–69.

Doyle, J. (2010). Learning from error in American criminal justice. *Journal of Criminal Law and Criminology, 100*(1), 109–149.

Fairclough, N. (1992). *Discourse and social change*. Cambridge: Polity.

Fairclough, N. (2003). *Analysing discourse: Textual analysis for social research.* Oxford: Routledge.

Foucault, M. (1976). *The will to knowledge: The history of sexuality volume one* (F. Hurley, Trans.). London: Penguin.

Foucault, M. (1979a). *The archaeology of knowledge* (A. Sheridan, Trans.). London: Routledge.

Foucault, M. (1979b). *Omnes et singulatim: Towards a criticism of political reason.* Available at: http://tannerlectures.utah.edu/_documents/a-to-z/f/foucault81. pdf. Accessed 3 June 2014.

Foucault, M. (1994). Truth and juridical forms. In J. D. Faubion (Ed.), *Michel Foucault—power: Essential works of Foucault 1954–1984 vol 3* (pp. 1–89). London: Penguin.

Francis, R. (2013). *Report of the Mid Staffordshire NHS Foundation Trust Public Inquiry.* London: TSO.

Gilsinan, J. (2012). The numbers dilemma: The chimera of modern police accountability systems. *Saint Louis University Public Law Review, 32,* 93–108.

Greer, C., & McLaughlin, E. (2012). This is not justice: Ian Tomlinson, institutional failure and the press politics of outrage. *British Journal of Criminology, 52*(2), 274–293.

Gunnarson, B.-L., Linell, P., & Nordberg, B. (Eds.). (1997). *The construction of professional discourse.* Harlow: Longman.

Hallam, E., Hockey, J., & Howarth, G. (1999). *Beyond the body: Death and social identity.* London: Routledge.

Halpern, S. (2008). Hybrid design, systemic rigidity: Institutional dynamics in human research oversight. *Regulation and Governance, 2*(1), 85–102.

Hindess, B. (1982). Power, interests and the outcomes of struggles. *Sociology, 16*(4), 498–511.

Hirschfield, P., & Simon, D. (2010). Legitimating police violence—Newspaper narratives of deadly force. *Theoretical Criminology, 14*(2), 155–182.

Horsley, P. (2012). "How dead dead the dead are": Sensing the science of death. *Qualitative Research, 12*(5), 540–553.

House of Commons Committee of Public Accounts. (2015). *Care quality commission. Twelfth report of session 2015–16.* Available at: http://www.publications.parliament.uk/pa/cm201516/cmselect/cmpubacc/501/501.pdf. Accessed 11 Dec 2015.

Hyden, L.C. (1997). The institutional narrative as drama. In B.-L. Gunnarson, P. Linell, & B. Nordberg (Eds.), *The construction of professional discourse* (pp. 245–264). Harlow: Longman.

Innes, M. (2003). *Investigating murder: Detective work and the police response to criminal homicide.* Oxford: Oxford University Press.

IPCC. (2014). *Review of the IPCC's work in investigating deaths: Final report.* Available at: http://www.ipcc.gov.uk/sites/default/files/Documents/deaths_review/Review_of_the_IPCCs_work_in_investigating_deaths_2014.pdf. Accessed 17 Mar 2014.

Koppel, J. (2005). Pathologies of accountability: ICANN and the challenge of "multiple accountabilities disorder"'. *Public Administration Review, 65*(1), 94–108.

Locke, J. (1966). *The second treatise of government: (An essay concerning the true original, extent and end of civil government), and a letter concerning toleration.* Oxford: Blackwell.

Luce, T. (2003). *Death certification and investigation in England, Wales and Northern Ireland: The report of a fundamental review.* London: The Stationery Office.

Marx, K., & Engels, F. (1965). *The German ideology.* London: Lawrence and Wishart.

Matthews, P. (2011). *Jervis on the office and duties of coroners: With forms and precedents. Fourth cumulative supplement to the twelfth edition.* London: Sweet and Maxwell.

May, P. (2007). Regulatory regimes and accountability. *Regulation and Governance, 1*(1), 8–26.

Montesquieu, C. (1949). *The spirit of the laws* (T. Nugent, Trans.). New York: Hafner.

Murphy, K., Tyler, T., & Curtis, A. (2009). Nurturing regulatory compliance: Is procedural justice effective when people question the legitimacy of the law? *Regulation and Governance, 3*(1), 1–26.

Parish, C. (2013). Government pledges to act on Winterbourne 'catastrophe'. *Learning Disability Practice, 16*(2), 8–10.

Parliamentary and Health Service Ombudsman. (2015). *A review into the quality of NHS complaints investigations where serious or avoidable harm has been alleged.* Available at: http://www.ombudsman.org.uk/reports-and-consultations/reports/ health/a-review-into-the-quality-of-nhs-complaints-investigations-where-serious-or-avoidable-harm-has-been-alleged/1. Accessed 8 Dec 2015.

Plomin, J. (2013). The abuse of vulnerable adults at Winterbourne view hospital: The lessons to be learned. *Journal of Adult Protection, 15*(4), 182–191.

Power, M (2004) The Risk Management of Everything: Rethinking the Politics of Uncertainty. Available at: http://www.demos.co.uk/files/riskmanage-mentofeverything.pdf. Accessed 12/6/14.

Prior, L. (1985). Making sense of mortality. *Sociology of Health and Illness, 7*(2), 167–190.

Razack, S. (2015). *Dying from improvement: Inquests and inquiries into indigenous deaths in custody.* Toronto: University of Toronto Press.

Redfern, M. (2001). *The Royal Liverpool Children's Inquiry: Summary and recommendations.* London: TSO.

Rickert, H. (R. Spiers, Trans.). (1926). 'Max Weber's view of science.' In P. Lassman, & I. Velody (Eds.). (1989) *Max Weber's "Science as a vocation"* (pp. 76–86). London: Unwin.

Rudolph, T., & Popp, E. (2007). An information processing theory of ambivalence. *Political Psychology, 28*(5), 563–585.

Shaw, H., & Coles, D. (2007). *Unlocking the truth: Families' experiences of the investigation of deaths in custody.* London: Inquest.

Smith, D. (1974). The social construction of documentary reality. *Sociological Inquiry, 44*(4), 257–267.

Smith, J. (2003). *The shipman inquiry (third report): Death certification and the investigation of deaths by Coroners.* London: The Stationery Office.

Smith, G. (2009a). Why don't more people complain against the police? *European Journal of Criminology, 6*(3), 249–266.

Smith, G. (2009b). Citizen oversight of independent police services: Bifurcated accountability, regulation creep, and lesson learning. *Regulation and Governance, 3*(4), 421–441.

Spitzer, S. (1975). Toward a Marxian theory of deviance. *Social Problems, 22*(5), 638–651.

Stone, C. (2007). Training police accountability in theory and practice: From Philadelphia to Abuja and Sao Paolo. *Theoretical Criminology, 11*(2), 245–259.

Terpstra, J., & Trommel, W. (2009). Police, managerialisation and presentational strategies. *Policing: An International Journal of Police Strategies and Management, 32*(1), 128–143.

Weisbrode, K. (2012). *On ambivalence: The problems and pleasures of having it both ways.* London: MIT Press.

Winiecki, D. (2008). The expert witness and courtroom discourse: Applying micro and macro forms of discourse analysis to study process and the "doing of doings" for individuals and for society. *Discourse Society, 19*(6), 765–781.

Young, M. (1991). *An inside job.* Oxford: Oxford University Press.

# 7

# Accountability, Governance and Audiences

## Introduction

Relationality has been a consistent theme in this book. Concepts such as independence, legitimacy and consensus have been shown to be largely dependent upon contextual interpretations. Similarly, these concepts are marked by their ability to trigger other concepts by association. For example, legitimacy tends to infer fairness and justness, and consensus speaks of public confidence and legitimacy. Key issues relating to the role and function of policing and its regulatory sphere are relational, contain other concepts, and subsequently self-support other related notions within the conceptual realm of policing. It is unproblematic to assert that Foucault's views on intertextuality and polyvalence, discussed in previous chapters, are relevant to this discussion.

That the concept of accountability is reflective of the conceptual realm above should be no surprise. It is therefore of fundamental importance to analyse and evaluate what the concept of accountability means with respect to policing in England and Wales in these cases as it directly relates to how police justify actions or omissions in cases of DAPC. This chapter

© The Editor(s) (if applicable) and The Author(s) 2016
D. Baker, *Deaths After Police Contact*,
DOI 10.1057/978-1-137-58967-5_7

builds on the previous chapter where systems of regulation were analysed. Various types of accountability are discussed in the light of regulatory systems and their applicability to key issues highlighted thus far in this book about cases of DAPC. The chapter gives particular consideration to legal, procedural and moral types of accountability. It assesses the types of relationships that exist within the sphere of accountability construction and considers how they depend upon shifting contingencies that affect the creation of accountability. The diffusion of accountability is examined in the context of wider changes in governance and accountability in the public sphere.

The diffusion of regulation and accountability represents an evolving landscape of governance. While this is typified by more devolution and marked by a growing body of independent organisations, there is a dichotomy in that it has also led to an 'audit explosion' whereby those organisations are subject to increasing oversight and regulation by auditory bodies. This apparently dichotomous state of affairs is considered with specific regard to the sphere that constructs accountability in cases of DAPC. Temporality is examined to consider how accountability construction is affected by an apparent focus on the past and future as distinct to the present, how this affects the production of texts, and the subsequent reproduction of texts throughout the sphere of accountability.

The epistemology of accountability is evaluated in terms of its relationality and subjectivity. The construction of benchmarking criteria that enable measurement in large part affects the type of accountability that is constructed. This is analysed through the dyad of means and ends as discussed in the previous chapter. In order to produce the *end* of accountability, *means* have been adopted in the form of processes. The end, supplied by the two principal organisations considered in this book, is the narrative verdict or IPCC investigation report. The means are the Article 2 inquest and the IPCC independent investigation. This section of the chapter analyses whether the means have effectively become ends due to the focus on measurement criteria produced by organisations in the sphere of accountability. In this sense, the process may have subsumed the outcome in a desire to meet the obligations of the ECHR. If this is the case it would affect the type of accountability constructed in cases of DAPC.

The ECHR represents a significant part of the audience that consumes accountability in these cases, but it represents one actor in that audience. The chapter examines how other audiences relate to the production and consumption of accountability. It evaluates the notion that the audience of accountability might simultaneously be the producers and consumers in a theatre of accountability construction. This leads to a critical discussion that considers the public nature of accountability construction in cases of DAPC. Finally, the chapter tests different conceptual frameworks that might enable an understanding of how the multiple organisations in the accountability sphere might relate to one another.

# Accountability: A Relational Concept

'Accountability is one of those golden concepts that no one can be against. It is increasingly used in political discourse and policy documents because it conveys an image of transparency and trustworthiness. However, its evocative powers make it also a very elusive concept because it can mean many different things to different people.'(Bovens 2007: 448)

The quotation above unequivocally highlights a number of relational issues that characterise accountability. First, it has become a leitmotif for governance in the public sphere. Second, it is a concept that is subject to contextual relationships and thus socially constructed. Third, as a cluster concept it further invokes a number of other socially constructed concepts such as transparency, openness, and legitimacy. These issues serve to illustrate Chan's (1999) observations discussed in Chaps. 2, 3 and 5 that police accountability is performative in that it seeks to secure consent by addressing the requirements of specific audiences. In this sense, the question of what accountability is *for* needs to be examined.

As a relational concept, accountability might be considered from a number of perspectives: for example, procedural, or financial; in terms of effectiveness or legality; or possibly in terms of value for money. The two most obvious perspectives are procedural and legal forms of accountability as the primary purpose of the coronial system and the IPCC when investigating and reporting on these cases is to fulfil the requirements of the

ECHR (Matthews 2014; Casale et al. 2013). In this sense, the procedural and legal forms are linked as they must demonstrably fit the requirements of the ECHR in order for the state to be seen to rigorously and independently investigate the death of its citizens (Thomas et al. 2008), an example of procedural legitimacy (Terpstra and Trommel 2009). Similar to Bovens, Gilsinan (2012) notes that there is an assumed relationship between accountability and transparency, and consequently transparency with robust democratic structures. These observations appear to be consistent with principles laid down by the ECHR that the state is obliged to follow when investigating cases of DAPC. If procedure-driven accountability is the means that satisfies the ends of legal accountability, then the nature of the procedures used are of fundamental importance to understanding how accountability is constructed in cases of DAPC.

In this section of the chapter, different types of accountability are discussed as they relate to different organisations within the sphere of accountability construction. Accountability is considered as types, for example: legal, political, administrative, organisational, public, financial or moral in nature. Bovens (2007), writing about public governance and accountability believes *legal* accountability to be the least ambiguous type, reflecting May's (2007) findings in the previous chapter. This occurs where organisations are held to account in legal proceedings: 'as the legal scrutiny will be based on detailed legal standards' (Bovens 2007: 456). In this sense Bovens refers to precedent or legal principles. The latter effectively produced narrative verdicts and the former has perpetuated them. Legal, or 'rule based' (May 2007: 11) regulation was demonstrated to be the most effective form when regulators are faced with critical incidents in healthcare.

Bovens (2007) further posits that *political* accountability to elected representatives can produce accountability in the public sphere. In this case, the HAC (2013, 2010, 1980) and JCHR (Joint Committee on Human Rights) (2004) appear relevant; both committees have produced reports on this issue for parliament. The latter was instrumental in setting up the Fulton review (2008) which subsequently established the IAP (Independent Advisory Panel on Deaths in Custody) on deaths in custody. It was established in Chap. 5 that the Home Secretary is increasingly focusing on the issue of DAPC and the work of the IPCC, not least in commissioning another independent report into the issue. Bovens asserts that *administrative* accountability is held to be produced by external auditory and regulatory functions, reflecting Terpstra and Trommel's (2009) concept of consequential legitimacy. One might consider organisations such as the NAO (National Audit Office) and to some extent the IPCC as fitting this category. In the discussion in Chap. 3 it was established that the NAO (2008) performs an administrative function upon the IPCC as they perform administrative accountability on the police, further underlining the dialectical nature of accountability construction in this sphere.

A similar view of consequential legitimacy is outlined by Yesufu (2013), as *organisational* accountability. This is defined as being an internal system of codes and conditions whereby sanctions can be imposed and behaviour regulated. It might be best imagined as the work of the PSD (Professional Standards Department) within each police force (Dillon 2013). Furthermore, Yesufu (2013) views *public* accountability as being measured by how effectively complaints are dealt with. As discussed in Chap. 5, this has been the subject of focus by the Chapman (2014) review regarding how police disciplinary systems could be improved. It could also be associated with the coronial service in cases of DAPC, although the IPCC also play a part in the construction of what Terpstra and Trommel (2009) would term cognitive legitimacy. Moreover, Yesufu (2013) states that *financial* accountability is manifest in terms of how business-like or efficient the police are, and this appears to fit the remit of HMIC reflecting Terpstra and Trommel's (2009) concept of consequential legitimacy based on performance management (see, for example HMIC 2014). All of this being said, it should be noted that all of these accountability types and regulatory agencies are not entirely discrete. The discussion in Chap. 5 demonstrated that current developments show the possibility of mission creep and overlapping responsibilities with HMIC expected to oversee aspects of the IPCC's role, and PCCs (Police and Crime Commissioners) likely to take more of a role in the police complaints process (Home Office 2015).

Kaldor (2003) defines *moral* accountability as ensuring the mission of the agency is adhered to with regards to its activities. It is the concept of *moral* accountability that does not appear to have an organisational monitor in cases of DAPC. This may be because the previously discussed definitions of accountability rest on observable—which is to say, quantifiable—measurement criteria. Perhaps the nearest representation is the coroner's court jury, in that their verdict represents the view of laypeople who effectively construct procedural, consequential *and* cognitive legitimacy (Terpstra and Trommel 2009). Narrative verdicts do not only take into account these criteria, for it was established in Chap. 1 and in Chap. 5 that on numerous occasions juries have constructed quite different findings to those of the IPCC. Thus the means by which ends are constructed in these cases relate to the type of accountability used in the method of construction.

Moral criteria would be subjective, but it has already been established that quantifiable or not, other concepts of accountability are also freighted with subjective interpretations. Kaldor's (2003) focus is on third-sector agencies; she believes moral accountability to be a necessary anchoring principle that ensures the organisation does not lose its focus on core principles that drive it. It may be less useful when applied to policing, for it was established in Chap. 2 that the police role is ambiguous and complex. However, it could be argued that the preservation of life could be a core principle of policing, much as Shane (2013) envisages police officers as 'safety officers'. The fundamental focus of Article 2 suggests that preservation of life is increasingly important as a way of defining acts and omissions in cases of DAPC (Matthews 2011: 180–81).

Currently, the requirements of the ECHR are addressed in terms of procedural, organisational, legal and administrative forms of accountability. A shift of focus to ensuring life is preserved as a moral principle, rather than through a series of post-facto measurement criteria might produce qualitatively different results. This appears to be close to Shircore (2006) and McIvor's (2010) evaluation of the extremely limited liability of the police in cases of DAPC. Similar to Reiner's (2000) observations in Chap. 3 of this book, they assert that rather than focus on shielding the police from civil prosecution in cases of death, it might be more productive if the police were more proactive in preventing death, or enabling life, in the first place. An alternate point of view is that if police were more often subject to criminal trial, and more prosecutions occurred, then this could represent a more effective correction to police actions and omissions in these cases. If Bovens (2007) is correct, and legal sanction represents the most effective form of accountability, it would support the assertions of families and campaign groups that the most effective deterrent to people dying after contact with the police could be through the criminal court system in England and Wales. In order for this to occur, there would need to be cultural and legal shifts within the organisations that construct accountability in these cases in terms of how they are investigated in the first place.

## Relationships of Accountability

In considering relationships of accountability, Bovens (2007) analyses the nature of the obligation under which an account is provided. First, he asserts that there is *vertical* accountability in the relationship between political and legal entities. The state is impelled to demonstrably respect Article 2 of the ECHR. Second, there is *horizontal* accountability between organisations that exist on a similar footing, for example the relationship between the IPCC and the coronial system, as evinced by their memorandum of understanding (IPCC 2007). Third, there is *diagonal* accountability, whereby an organisation has no power to censure the body it regulates, but can forward reports to an organisation that has such power. An example of this would be the IPCC and/or coroner passing reports to the CPS to consider the case for prosecution of state agents. This discussion underscores Black's (2008) view, expounded in the previous chapter, that understanding the composition of the regulatory 'field' and its dialectical relationships are key to understanding how accountability is constructed.

Accountability is a multi-faceted and socially constructed concept. Furthermore, it is enacted before an increasing number of actors contingent upon its definition, as discussed above. This means accountability is played out before and on behalf of multiple actors and audiences, all of whom have particular criteria with which they measure the production of accountability. Foucault (1976) asserted that discursive processes drove power based on aims and objectives, but that these were not necessarily inscribed at a strategic level. He believed that the aims and objectives existed at a level that was more circumscribed: 'The rationality of power is characterised by tactics that are often quite explicit at the restricted level where they are inscribed' (Foucault 1976: 95). Therefore, power is not exercised at a meta-level, but is more localised and consequently less likely to be connective. Given this analysis, it is not surprising that accountability construction is neither consistent nor straightforward, being made up of multiple contingencies and foci. Dubnick (2003: 19), echoing Chan (1999) notes: 'Account giving is contingent on the nature of, the reasons for, the mode of, and the places where accounts are provided. In other words, there is a performative nature to account giving.' The distribution of accountability construction is diffuse, and this leads to a dispersal of power, regulation and accountability.

## Between Past and Future

Accountability occurs retrospectively while regulation occurs prospectively (Smith 2009). Shane (2013: 69) notes that: 'It is hindsight that enables police policymakers to shape the future.' Narrative verdicts and IPCC investigation reports have dual functions that aim to hold actors to account *and* to prevent future deaths. In this sense, regulation and accountability are conflated. Komter (2006) also notes that looking back in order to look forward is characteristic of police record keeping. It summons up a vision of organisations re-evaluating their actions or omissions as a result of looking back, in order to reformulate aspects of practice for the future. This appears to chime with Shaw and Coles's (2007) view of 'accountable learning' discussed in Chaps. 2 and 3, also noted by Dillon (2013), Shane (2013), Spray et al. (2012) and Doyle (2010) with their view of 'organisational learning'. An emerging trend in the literature is that of institutional learning.

On the other hand, this tendency of 'looking back in order to look forwards' could indicate an inherently ambivalent aspect at the heart of accountability construction in cases of DAPC. Arendt (1977) noted society's uncertain relationship with the present in *Between Past and Future*. She believed that our preoccupation with past events and future possibilities had a tendency to debilitate us in the present. Weisbrode

(2012: 27) notes that: 'ambivalence makes us think more of movement than of destination or direction'. In this sense, it might be said that accountability construction in these cases is more preoccupied with past and future even while it is dealing with the present, or as Foucault puts it: 'One must take into account not the past offence, but the future disorder' (1991: 93). This might account for a theme that appears to be consistent in the sphere of police accountability—that standards will improve based on reports, investigations, inquiries and guidelines being commissioned and produced. Such documents consistently state that there are problems to be addressed, but they *are* being addressed and it is hoped that improved performance will occur as a result. Savage (2007) is sceptical of this, believing that the state might not want to learn, or even *acknowledge* the need to learn. Indeed, there is an aspirational undertow to these documents, while at the same time a recognition that in practice improved performance might not be possible. For example, the last major review into healthcare in custody unequivocally advocated that healthcare be provided equivalent to that delivered to the non-incarcerated population. However, the BMA noted towards the conclusion of the document: 'The BMA and FFLM support these principles but fear in practice they may not be achieved' (BMA 2009: 32). These fears appear to be borne out by a London Assembly Police and Crime Committee (2014: 5) report into healthcare in MPS custody which stated that the system was not working as intended and results were 'patchy'.

One case that illustrates this discussion is the death of Mark Duggan. His death can be compared directly to aspects of Sean Rigg's case. The inquest into Mark Duggan's death occurred after Casale's (2013) review. As discussed in Chap. 5, amongst her numerous findings were failures on the part of the IPCC: a failure to secure the scene of death; to communicate clearly and consistently with the deceased's family; and to prevent collusion between officers giving evidence to IPCC investigators. Casale (2013) went on to state that significant improvements had been made by the IPCC since Sean Rigg's death in 2008 about these issues. Mark Duggan died in 2011, and the IPCC was found, once again, to have failed in all three areas listed above (Dodd 2014).

Aspiration, temporality and ambivalence appear to reflect the current zeitgeist that represents processes as 'journeys'. The then prime minister,

David Cameron, speaking the day after the Mark Duggan verdict of 'lawful killing' was delivered, noted that 'we are on a journey' with regards to police legitimacy amongst black communities in London (Bloomberg 2014). In principle, it might not be problematic to suggest that a goal might never be reached, or acknowledging that learning processes are inherently open-ended. In practice, however, processes of regulation in cases of DAPC are fundamentally situated in the measurement of past occurrences. A consistent theme throughout this book has been the inability of organisations to learn lessons from past deaths based on analyses of trends and patterns (see, for example Downham and Lingham 2009; Fulton 2008; Shaw and Coles 2007). This suggests that it is not looking back per se that is a problem, but looking back at individual cases as distinct from the wider case book of these deaths. Members of marginalised groups, in particular, can be forgiven for wondering how long this 'journey' might take, and where, if at all, it will end. Or whether 'the journey' is an institutional exercise that perpetually kicks the can down the road, as Stafford Scott (2015: 60) notes: 'We are a community that some people describe as hard to reach. But the reality is that we've become easy to ignore.'

The relationship between past and future appears to be bound up with the relationship between principles and practice in that principles are measured against past performance and future expected practice, but current practice is effectively dealt with retrospectively. This process of retrospection also occurs with a significant delay as established in Chap. 4: nearly half of cases in the dataset were inquests held thirty-six months or more after the individual's death. There are echoes here of the discussion in Chap. 5 regarding the official recognition of a consistent inability to identify trends in cases of DAPC that stretches back over fifteen years yet continues to be identified in any major report that touches on the subject (see, for example, Leigh et al. 1998; Casale et al. 2013). Similarly, the previous chapter demonstrated that this phenomenon is not limited to regulating these cases, but also applies to healthcare and avoidable death (see, for example Smith 2003; Francis 2013). The relationship between time and accountability reflects the ambiguity and ambivalence that characterises accountability construction in these cases.

# The Landscape of Accountability

The chapter now moves on to consider the wider landscape within which accountability is constructed in cases of DAPC. Smith (2013) asserts that cycles of scandal and reform have contributed to a growing discourse around police accountability. The evolution of accountability construction has not occurred in a vacuum, it reflects changes in wider governmental discourses about accountability (Bovens 2007). By governmental discourses, I do not mean exclusive to the government, but in the wider sense of state governance of a sphere of influence, much as envisaged by Foucault (1994). In the area of DAPC there are non-state organisations that play a role in accountability production by publishing guidelines that provide parameters whereby actions or omissions might be evaluated. Examples of these include (but are not limited to) ACPO (Association of Chief Police Officers), the BMA and the FFLM (Faculty of Forensic and Legal Medicine); these represent 'multiple policy actors' envisaged by Halpern (2008: 86) in the previous chapter. Furthermore, there are organisations that are funded by the state but could not be considered to be a branch of government—the IPCC and the coronial system fit into this category. Then there are organisations that are demonstrably branches of government such as the HAC and the NAO. Finally, at a supra-national level there is the ECHR, which, as has been demonstrated throughout this book, has had a catalytic effect on the way in which these cases are investigated. Governance incorporating a growing number of norms generated from a growing number of power bases has been noted by Barendrecht (2011). These developments support Foucault's (1994: 73) view that: 'This great pyramid of gazes [constitutes] the new form of the judicial process.'

The field of accountability construction has broadened and deepened, with successively more organisations becoming involved, as noted by Smith (2013), and Savage (2013). Charman and Savage (2008: 111) observe the state's need for more 'joined up' public services that are closely monitored by performance management. The culture of auditing, inspecting, reporting and guidance more commonly seen in public governance has produced a more complex 'institutional architecture'

(Clarke et al. 2007: 101). The development of more regulatory mechanisms while the government effectively devolves and decentralises power appears to be paradoxical, and to some degree illustrates what Halpern (2008: 87) terms 'the post-regulatory state'. Foucault (1976) might suggest it is an example of discursive power as it is diffuse and decentred; an increasing number of frameworks and organisations enable more 'space for interpretation' as there is increasing ambiguity over which framework, guideline or policy is most relevant in any given context. On the other hand, the proliferation of organisations regulating accountability in cases of DAPC ensures more focus on the subject (Stone 2007). Thus, when Bovens (2007) asserts that accountability is to some degree a mechanism of control, a key issue is how the 'degree' is interpreted and based on what context/s. The apparently ambivalent relationship between the coronial system and the IPCC in cases of DAPC was not addressed until the crisis of legitimacy sparked by the death of Sean Rigg. The Casale review unequivocally tilted the construction of accountability in favour of the coronial system, a view emphatically endorsed by the IPCC (2014) as it sought to re-establish its legitimacy. Not only are there different types of accountability, and different types of relationships in the sphere of accountability, but there are different types of landscape that can construct accountability, or 'institutional architecture'. However, it could be argued that ambivalence in the sense discussed above could be more accurately represented as a state of dynamic tension within the governmental sphere which has long been advocated as a way of ensuring power is decentralised through a process of checks and balances, as was noted in the previous chapter.

Numerous authors have noted the shift from governing to governance since the mid-1990s (see, for example Clarke et al. 2007; Mulderring 2011). The area of police accountability is held to be particularly sensitive due to the complex balance between governance, effective policing, the rule of law, transparency and democracy (Puddister and Riddell 2012). Mulderring (2011: 45) believes that governance reflects the move away from rigid hierarchies of bureaucracies to what she terms 'soft power'. Governance no longer necessarily has clear lines of control and/ or accountability, but 'complex networks of self-governing actors'. These changes are not necessarily planned or overseen, and are not part of a strategic vision of one organisation. They occur partly within the organisational discourse that has produced them, but also in the context of textual construction by other organisations (Fairclough 2008; Clarke et al. 2007). This raises the issue of how relatively subjective means produce 'objective truths' and leads to the consideration of epistemological issues inherent in accountability construction.

# Epistemology of Accountability

The construction of guidelines that measure acts or omissions is not only an example of intertextuality or of discursive patterns. It is an example of an increasingly rationalised system of governance that constructs measurable criteria by which these acts and omissions might be evaluated, as noted by Punch (2009: 48): 'accountability and rationality go hand in hand—to be accountable you have to show that your actions were rational, therefore it is seen as a form of justification which creates legitimacy'. To some extent, this represents a shift from professional judgement towards managerialism and risk management, echoing Foucault's (1994: 209–13) views on governmentality and the relative nature of rationality. The discussion in Chap. 5 about the Casale review into the IPCC investigation of the Sean Rigg case demonstrates some examples of how this shift might be critiqued. As discussed in the previous chapter, Arendt (1998) noted that the human ability to construct measurement criteria is immanently limited to our ability to initially conceive of such criteria. Or as Weber puts it: 'so-called objectivity … rests on one foundation and one alone, namely, the ordering of a reality which is given, according to certain subjective categories—subjective in the specific sense that they represent the presupposition on which our knowledge is based' (cited in Löwith 1993: 146).

Thus, the IPCC was able to produce independent investigation reports for some years using observable measurement criteria that tended to be uncritical of police actions or omissions in these cases, an example of Terpstra and Trommel's (2009) *consequential* legitimacy. The IPCC is a relative newcomer to the arena of accountability construction in these cases. It was purpose-designed to address issues of police complaints and public confidence in the police. In contrast, the coronial system is the longest established part of the legal system in England and Wales. It is well known for its decentralised, ambiguous and arcane systems and procedures. In the Sean Rigg case it appears that the inquest was able to provide a more accurate and critical version of events than the IPCC independent investigation. This led to another party becoming involved in order to critically analyse the processes of the investigation and the criteria used to measure acts and omissions. To some extent this echoes Den Boer's (2002) view that accountability construction in policing increasingly focuses on quantitative measurement as distinct from qualitative concerns which might provide a better context within which actions or omissions occurred. In the death of Sean Rigg it is unproblematic to assert that the coronial process represented a more qualitative approach while the IPCC's investigation leaned more toward the quantitative. Gilsinan (2012: 94) views this as a tendency of regulatory agencies to arrive at conclusions while overlooking the effectiveness of the processes that produced them, a condition he terms 'process amnesia'. He asserts this is a condition whereby the producer and consumer of these documents implicitly takes their factual content at face value without considering the process that produced the facts. As Fairclough (2003: 55) notes: 'Implicitness is a pervasive property of texts.' While the IPCC reports appear to be precise, packed as they are with empirical detail, they are not necessarily accurate, as was established in Chap. 5. Precision relates to the reproducibility of measurement, whereas accuracy relates to the proximity of measurement results to a set value. While IPCC reports lend themselves to reproducibility of measurement, it is not clear how useful the set values are that the measurements are being tested against.

If police are to be seen to use their power appropriately—to be legitimate in their function, and be seen to be held accountable—then they will most likely operate with processes that demonstrate these qualities in a way that meets legal and procedural requirements (Bullock and Johnson 2012). That is not to say that the police may attempt to fulfil these functions in a purposefully fabricated or manufactured way, rather it is to say that they are aware of the fundamental importance of these terms being satisfied in order to allow them to function legitimately. Writing more generally about police accountability, Reiner (2013) notes that a populist focus on local accountability has ensured, for example, that previous concerns about holding the police accountable for the use of force has shifted to a more 'calculative and contractual' form of accountability. Similarly, the organisations charged with regulating police actions or omissions in cases of DAPC look for benchmarking frameworks within which these can be assessed and evaluated, albeit that most of these policies and frameworks are formulated by the self-same organisations that use them to measure acts or omissions of their own agents in cases of DAPC. This raises the issue of whether the broadening sphere of accountability construction is to some extent a closed sphere. New organisations may be admitted to the sphere, but once they are admitted they appear to abide by the same types of measurement criteria that already exist and to a large extent perpetuate a similar body of discursive knowledge on cases of DAPC. An exception to this appears to be the ability of the jury to record decisions that contradict expert opinions about whether policies or guidelines were adhered to, as was established in Chap. 4. Van Sluis et al. (2009: 160–2) assert that systems of police accountability are more marked by continuity than change, but that 'windows of opportunity' for change occur. It might be that the case of Sean Rigg represents such an opportunity.

## Means and Ends

If accountability is a relatively closed sphere this might support the previous discussion that the means used within it have become its ends. Bovens (2007: 449) notes that although accountability: 'started as an instrument to enhance the effectiveness ... of public governance, [it] has gradually become a goal in itself'. The increased focus on accountability means that the performance of the organisation held to account is increasingly driven by criteria dictated by those who hold that organisation to account (Gilsinan 2012). Therefore more attention is paid to the criteria than to whether the organisation is working effectively, another example of Terpstra and Trommel's (2009) *consequential* legitimacy. This relates to the apparent dichotomy of 'doing the right thing' or 'doing things right' as identified by Clarke (1998). He notes that even though organisations may not believe in the criteria they are measured by, they are bound to work within them and aim to meet them, primarily because they know they are measured against them. As Foucault (1994: 14) observes: 'Knowledge is always a certain strategic relation in which man [*sic*] is placed.'

In a similar way, in Chap. 3 of this book, it was established that independence was revered with 'near totemic status' (Savage 2013: 95) while being a highly relational concept. The symbolic and organisational ends that the concepts of independence and accountability represent may have become subsumed into means that are intended to produce improved ends, much as was noted by Ahmed (2007) in the previous chapter. Geisler (2001) notes the tendency for complex organisations to make texts public that were previously private, but that this does not necessarily ensure improved transparency. Gilsinan (2012: 109) observes, somewhat gloomily: 'Once systems of accountability and transparency become part of the standard operating procedure of an organisation, they lessen their ability to enhance either accountability or transparency'. Terpstra and Trommel (2009: 138) echo this view, positing that accountability and audit systems tend to become part of standard operating procedures, become ritualistic, largely symbolic and ultimately provide the means that enable police to leave 'the essential machinery of the organisation intact'. The research of Chan and Dixon (2007: 450) into the aftermath of the Wood commission into corruption in the New South Wales police appears to support this assertion. They found that after an initial wave of cultural reform based on qualitative issues had been implemented, police reverted to quantitative measurements of performance and replaced 'reform' in its corporate objectives with 'continuous business improvement'.

In the case of the IPCC there is an irony in that the totemic independence with which it was imbued in order to meet its intended ends has been somewhat eroded as an increasing number of regulatory organisations insist on auditing it or holding it to account. The more accountability (as a form of control) is demanded of an organisation, the less likely it is able to exercise the expert judgement that it was intended and expected to possess (Busuioc et al. 2011). Similarly, Hewitt (1993) notes that in relation to social policy, state power and reach tends to grow via related and semi-related agencies. In this book this could refer to agencies such as ACPO, HMIC and the BMA. The observations in this section of the chapter suggest manifest ambivalence. The state desires organisations to be demonstrably independent, but simultaneously expects them to be increasingly subject to oversight—by other organisations. It appears that the ends of regulatory agencies have increasingly become means by which they rearticulate processes and are constituted within the wider discourse of accountability in cases of DAPC. The diffusion of regulation has led to a dispersal of responsibility. Chan (1999) states that this tendency represents a managerial as distinct to a legal focus. She believed that if criteria could be satisfied, and accounts given then audiences would typically be satisfied—that essentially the process would be more important than the outcome. This raises the issue of who the audiences are that require satisfaction and how they relate to both one another and the subject of DAPC.

## Acknowledging Audiences

There is a combination of issues that all point to the relatively low level of importance conferred by the state on the inquest process. The non-standardised manner of recording the death via the 'inquisition sheet' is an example, as discussed in Chap. 4. Then there is the non-standardised manner of recording the narrative, with some inquests using hand-written narratives, some using typed narratives, and others using questionnaires of varying lengths and types. Finally, errors in spelling and grammar are not uncommon, as are basic omissions such as the date of birth of the deceased, and the date or place of the inquest (note also Razack 2015).

The relative level of importance conferred on the inquest process can also be seen in the location of the inquest. Within the dataset, one was conducted in a conference centre, two in hotels, one in a town hall, one in a disused NHS building and one at a football club. When the various factors previously discussed are considered in the context of the practices, processes and environment of a criminal court, it appears to reinforce the view held by many authors (see, for example Luce 2003; Davis et al. 2002; Tarling 1998) that the coronial system is the forgotten service within the legal system in England and Wales. It suggests a degree of ambivalence on the part of the state about the significance of the coronial system. On the one hand the state tasks it with fulfilling obligations under Article 2 of the ECHR, on the other hand it is noted for being significantly under-resourced (see, for example Matthews 2011; Smith 2003).

Institutional audiences primarily appear to be the other organisations that exist within the increasingly dispersed and hybrid regulatory sphere in cases of DAPC. The organisations participating as producers of knowledge in this forum are also consumers of knowledge constructed by other organisations. In order to keep up to date with the evolving discourse and intertextuality in the construction of accountability it is necessary for each organisation to stay abreast of developments to update their guidelines and demonstrate adherence to these criteria. Thus the participants make up what might best be imagined as a 'theatre of regulation' in cases of DAPC. Each organisational participant plays a part in the construction of the overall narrative in each case. A narrative verdict is a form of micro-narrative about the death of an individual, as was demonstrated in Chaps. 3 and 4. In the construction of each narrative a wealth of other discourse is considered that informs it. These individual narratives form a body of knowledge at a meta-level that consists of individual cases and policies, guidelines and reports. Thus it appears that the theatre itself is the audience to its own knowledge production. To some degree this reflects McLuhan's (2005) well-known dictum about the role of television—the medium of the process has become the message of accountability construction. The issue of audiences has been discussed throughout this chapter; and the concept of relationality has been a thread throughout this book, for example regarding accountability, legitimacy and independence. The section below considers how 'the public' is a relational concept in the construction of accountability in cases of DAPC.

## 'Beware of the Leopard'

In *The Hitchhikers' Guide to the Galaxy* the protagonist, Arthur Dent, discovers that his house is to be demolished to make way for a new road. Distraught, he complains to a council official who tells him that the plans had been on public display for a considerable time, which gave him ample opportunity to lodge a complaint. Dent replies the plans were indeed on public display when he searched for them: in a cellar to which there were no stairs, with no lighting, in a locked filing cabinet situated in a disused toilet on which hung the sign 'beware of the leopard' (Adams 1980). This literary reference questions the public nature of investigations into cases of DAPC and the way in which their findings are recorded (Williams and Emsley 2006). Chapter 2 established that police are granted the legitimate right to use force on the basis of public consent. This consent is subject to being held to account when force is used. That being given, a logical question is to consider the nature of what is 'public' in these cases. For example, it would appear reasonable to assume that the IPCC investigates cases of DAPC and produces a report into each case. However, in comparison with the narrative verdicts used throughout this book, only one-third of the IPCC reports existed in the public domain. It appears to be an example that challenges their ability to construct both *cognitive* and *procedural* legitimacy, as conceived of by Terpstra and Trommel (2009). Furthermore, given that a key function of the IPCC is to promote public confidence in the police, the level of transparency this demonstrates is questionable. Moreover, in light of the discussion in Chaps. 3 and 5, there are concerns as to what extent the IPCC reflect public concerns about transparency and promoting public confidence in the police.

In the coronial system, while inquests are held in public, it is relatively rare for the public to be in attendance. Part of the reason for this might be that it is often unclear where or when inquests will be held. The coronial system has long been criticised for being insufficiently 'public facing' in its operations, particularly when compared with similar functions in Australia or Canada (Luce 2003). This relates to issues such as a lack of dedicated websites, a lack of basic information over where an inquest is being held, and a general disinterest in informing the public about the functions of the coroner's court. Furthermore, while narrative verdicts are notionally public documents, in reality they are public only if the public are present when the verdict is read aloud.[1] The most common

---

[1] There are a few exceptions to this. The Ian Tomlinson inquest is notable for all transcripts being available on the coroner's dedicated website. However, it is relatively unusual for a coroner to have

way they become public knowledge is by media reportage—and this is typically in a highly edited form. Consequently, for a narrative verdict to become publicly known, there must be either public or media present when they are delivered.[2] Should a member of public wish to see a narrative verdict, they need to satisfy the coroner that they fulfil the criteria of being a 'properly interested person' in the case (Levine 1999). The coroner makes this judgement using discretion which cannot be subsequently challenged or appealed (Dorries 2004; Matthews 2011). Narrative verdicts are not publicly available in a collated form. Similar to the IPCC, the public nature of recorded findings is equivocal. This discussion underlines that 'public' is a relational concept in the production and construction of accountability in these cases.

It is a matter of speculation as to whether the distressing issues raised by individual cases are more effective in focusing agencies on making improvements than assessing more abstract quantitative data. On the one hand it might be argued that quantitative data could enable a more straightforward platform from which to analyse and identify trends, although there seems to be little improvement in this regard, given the consistent output of IPCC research identifying key issues of concern and the publication of the 'Learning the Lessons' series. On the other, it might be argued that individual cases highlighted by coroners' juries have produced more change. The verdict in the case of Sean Rigg appears to have been catalytic in producing changes in the sphere of accountability construction that a significant number of reports from diverse agencies over a ten-year period did not. Hall et al. (1978) posited that exceptions do exist in the criminal justice system whereby state agents may be publicly criticised, or even prosecuted, as a result of their actions. However, these exceptions were effectively bracketed off from the majority of actions and events in the criminal justice system by being situationally and contextually constructed as exceptional, a point echoed by Hindess (1982) and Box (1983). In the Sean Rigg case force was used by the police, it was

---

a dedicated website, let alone post information regarding inquests on it.

[2] I attended an Article 2 inquest in London in July 2013 that produced a highly critical verdict. There was no representation at the inquest by either family members or media. The story was first reported by the media two weeks after the fact by the *London Evening Standard* based on a press release by the NGO *Inquest* regarding the narrative verdict and subsequent coroner's rule 43 report.

captured on camera and made public. In this case, it appears that the public nature of these incidents create a different climate of accountability construction, similar to the deaths of Walter Scott[3] and Eric Garner[4] in the US, much as identified by Greer and McLaughlin (2012) and Hirschfield and Simon (2010).

## Conceptual Systems of Accountability

A consistent theme in this and the previous chapter has been the broadening of the hybrid discursive sphere that constructs accountability in cases of DAPC. In this section I critically discuss the concept of the 'system' of accountability construction, by considering possible conceptual frameworks that might provide a way of better understanding the sphere of accountability that surrounds police accountability in these cases.

Stone (2007) asserts that a *network* of accountability has increasingly built up around police misconduct and their use of force. He believes that the network is not systematic in the sense that it is strategically constructed. Nor does he believe that it is systematic in highlighting all cases of misconduct or the abuse of force. However, he does believe that the growth and spread of organisations has increased focus on these issues and that in some unidentifiable, yet quantifiable way this has led to a small but steady decrease in cases of DAPC. However, whether the word 'network' is entirely accurate is questionable. A network implies interconnectivity, for example if one considers electricity, the internet or a series of nerves or arteries. These networks are notable for their fluidity, interchangeability and effectiveness. While it is fair to state that to some degree the organisations within the sphere of accountability construction have connectivity in some respect, it is a stretch, given the discussion in Chaps. 5 and 6 to believe that they interconnect. They may refer to each other, or inform

---

[3] Died after being shot in the back by a police officer in North Charleston, South Carolina in 2015. His family have been offered $6.5M in damages by North Charleston City Council that precludes any further civil claims over his death.

[4] Died after being restrained in a choke hold by police officers on Staten Island in 2014. His family have been offered $5.9M in damages from the city of New York that precludes any further civil claims over his death.

one another's practice. This is not the same as performing a relatively unified function as a result of remote elements focused on one centre. Stone's (2007) analysis focuses on organisations that provide regulation of the police; he does not explicitly consider medical organisations, for example. The number of organisations demonstrably involved in accountability construction means that there are a number of organisational agendas present in any interaction, so it might be more accurate to state that there is the illusion of a network. It was established in Chap. 4 that 'deaths after police contact' is somewhat of a misnomer. A more accurate term might be 'deaths after multi-agency involvement'. In this sense, the issue is not so much whether there is a network that ensures police accountability, but whether there is a network that covers all of these agencies with regards to the construction of accountability in these cases.

Brodeur (2010), writing more generally about developments in policing prefers the term *web*. This term might also be useful in examining the construction of accountability in cases of DAPC. A web has a centre and is flexible in terms of its construction—it can expand and contract. It catches objects, but its size and strength dictates the number of objects it can catch. It might also be considered to be a structure that is marked by gaps as well as substance. These characteristics appear to reflect Foucault's view of discursive power—that is marked by limit and lack, by fissures and inconsistencies, and that it is made and remade. However, whether it accurately characterises the sphere of accountability construction is debatable. One might argue that the coronial system is a web in that it has the inquest at its centre and the process of the inquisition is remade for each case; and that the size and scope of the expanded Article 2 inquest increases the possibility of a broader range of findings being reached. Similarly, the narrative verdict is something that is made and remade specific to the particular case under consideration. However, the wider sphere of regulatory agencies are less of a web in that they often lack connectivity.

A more useful way of viewing the sphere of accountability construction might be to imagine it as an orbital system in which bodies revolve around a focal star (see Fig. 7.1). I aim to explore this using the notion of orbits in a symbolic and allegorical way in order to test it as a framework that may help explain the complex relations manifest in the sphere of accountability construction. The initial uncertainty about the functioning

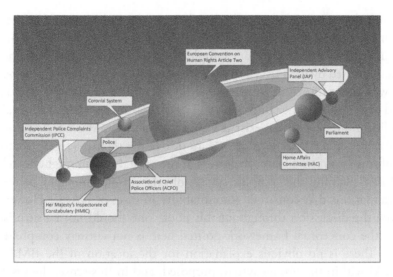

**Fig. 7.1**  An orbital system of accountability

of our solar system was due to the inability to correctly identify what the focal point of the system was (Wyatt 1977). We now know that the Earth is not the centre of the solar system, and that this failure in identification led to a significant misunderstanding of the system as a whole. I suggest that a similar state of affairs might exist in the sphere of accountability construction in cases of DAPC.

The focus of academic attention in this sphere is on the police, perhaps because of the symbolic role they play as an institution within society. However, if the focal star is identified as the ECHR and Article 2 asserting the right to life, the system can be symbolically conceived of in terms of it being an orbital system of accountability (note Fig. 7.1). The planets are represented by the various bodies that affect the construction of accountability in cases of DAPC. Their orbits are determined by the focal presence of the ECHR. We might imagine bodies orbiting the ECHR to be the coroner's court, constructing legal accountability; parliament, constructing political accountability; and the police PSD, constructing administrative accountability. These bodies affect each other's orbits in relation to one another and the focal object of the ECHR. All of them co-exist and interact to some degree but do not necessarily connect or intersect. They inform the existence of other bodies, but are also independent entities in their own right. In addition, some of these bodies have satellites in orbit around them. Parliament, for example, orbits the ECHR, but Parliament is also orbited by the HAC and the IAP, as without Parliament, these bodies would not function. Similarly, the IPCC, ACPO and HMIC could be said to be orbiting the police. Snow (1991: 166–67) asserts that the major bodies of the solar system exist as a fluid system that conform to some general trends in terms of location and motion rather than as a rigid structure conforming to strict laws. I believe that the orbital system might be helpful in explaining the complex system of relationships inherent between organisations that construct accountability in cases of DAPC. However, given the discussion throughout this book, one should not be surprised that the conceptual framework posited here is not entirely comprehensive. There is no obvious explanation for the location of the BMA or FFLM within the orbital system proposed, and in this sense, the system remains a relatively non-unified and diffuse framework.

## Conclusion

After considering the organisational structures, texts and discourses that hold police accountable in cases of DAPC, this chapter analysed and evaluated the different ways in which accountability may be conceived and measured. It considered the relationship between the different organisations in the theatre of accountability construction that has coalesced around the issue of DAPC. This involved an assessment of the landscape of accountability that has developed around the subject and how it relates to wider discursive developments of governance, the state and society. Finally, it considered a possible explanatory framework that might help make sense of the complex and interconnected system of relationships between organisations, the state and society in cases of DAPC.

Accountability is a relational concept that has become firmly ensconced in organisational discourse as governance and has been devolved to a growing number of organisations. It has been shown to be a concept that appears ever-present yet difficult to define. Its definition depends, to some degree, on the type of accountability that is imagined. It encapsulates other relational terms such as legitimacy, regulation and transparency. Types of accountability included legal, political, procedural, public, financial, administrative and moral forms. In cases of DAPC legal accountability is provided principally by the coroner's court, while political accountability is provided by agencies in the parliamentary realm such as the HAC and IAP. Administrative and procedural accountability are similar and constructed by the IPCC, and to some extent the police themselves through each force's PSD. Financial responsibility, while less relevant to this book is provided by police governance structures and HMIC. Finally, the concept of moral accountability was discussed as having the potential to provide a principle-based form of accountability that might be qualitatively different to the other types of accountability discussed. Whereas other types of accountability relate to measurement criteria often based on quantitative principles, moral accountability might be considered as a way of meeting the obligations of Article 2 of the ECHR in enabling the right to life.

With such a complex system of accountability types and organisations the relationship between them was considered in an attempt to understand the various interactions that may occur as accountability is constructed in cases of DAPC. Understanding the interactional discourses could help to better analyse and evaluate the different processes used and texts produced in these cases. It was established that these relationships are not always clear, or connected, and do not always occur as a result of strategic planning. In this sense, the Foucauldian concept of power being dispersed and affecting discourses in a non-strategic manner was demonstrated as being relevant to understanding accountability construction in these cases. The landscape of accountability has become more complex in this sphere as more organisations have become involved in the construction of accountability in cases of DAPC. It has led to a broadening and deepening of accountability construction as a growing number of texts, processes and policies are applied to the subject. The development of an increasing number of measurement criteria appears to have led to the processes that construct accountability becoming ends in themselves as the various organisations involved scramble to demonstrate that they meet the requirements set down by Article 2 of the ECHR. Thus, as the discourse of accountability evolves and becomes more embedded in standard operational practices, the ends it aims to achieve becomes subsumed by the processes that drive it.

The ambivalence that exists in systems of accountability construction was demonstrated as it is unclear how each organisation relates to one another, or in some cases how part of one organisation relates with another part of the same organisation. This produces processes that are often ambiguous and lead to overlaps or disconnects between the different organisations involved in the sphere of accountability construction. In part, this is because there are multiple audiences that consume this accountability that demand different forms of accountability in terms of the processes employed and the documents constructed. One aspect of this discussion highlighted the questionable assertion that the sphere of accountability construction is public. The concept of 'public' is relational in a similar way to which independence and accountability were demonstrated as being relational.

An attempt was made to contextualise the complex system that comprises accountability construction in cases of DAPC in England and Wales. Explanatory frameworks were considered as a way of better understanding this system, first as a network and secondly as a web. While both of these frameworks have their merits, they also have limitations. This is possibly due to the limited amount of research that has been conducted into this subject. I concluded by offering a new conceptual system that might help explain how accountability might function in cases of DAPC. The orbital system proposes that rather than view police at the centre of the accountability system, it might be more helpful to consider Article 2 of the ECHR as the focal point of the accountability system. In this way, while the organisations providing regulation for cases of DAPC do not connect as a network, they might be seen to relate to one another as orbital bodies, regulated to some degree by the focal point of Article 2, and to some degree by each other's trajectories.

# References

Adams, D. (1980). *The hitchhiker's guide to the galaxy*. London: Pan.

Ahmed, S. (2007). "You end up doing the document rather than doing the doing": Diversity, race equality and the politics of documentation. *Ethnic and Racial Studies, 30*(4), 590–609.

Arendt, H. (1977). *Between past and future: Eight exercises in political thought.* New York: Penguin.

Arendt, H. (1998). *The human condition.* Chicago: University of Chicago Press.

Barendrecht, M. (2011). Rule of law, measuring and accountability: Problems to be solved bottom up. *Hague Journal on the Rule of Law, 3*(2), 281–304.

Black, J. (2008). Constructing and contesting legitimacy and accountability in polycentric regulatory regimes. *Regulation and Governance, 2*(2), 137–164.

Bloomberg. (2014). *Cameron tells protestors in London riot shooting to respect law.* Available at: http://www.bloomberg.com/news/2014-01-09/cameron-tells-protesters-in-london-riot-shooting-to-respect-law.html. Accessed 24 Jan 2014.

Bovens, M. (2007). Analysing and assessing accountability: A conceptual framework. *European Law Journal, 13*(4), 447–468.

Box, S. (1983). *Power, crime, and mystification.* London: Routledge.

British Medical Association. (2009). *Health care of detainees in police stations.* Available at: http://bma.org.uk/-/media/Files/PDFs/.../Ethics/healthdetainees0209.pdf. Accessed 6 Sept 2013.

Brodeur, J.-P. (2010). *The policing web.* New York: Oxford University Press.

Bullock, K., & Johnson, P. (2012). The impact of the Human Rights Act 1998 on policing in England and Wales. *British Journal of Criminology, 52*(3), 630–650.

Busuioc, M., Curtin, C., & Groenleer, M. (2011). Agency growth between autonomy and accountability: The European Police Office as a 'living institution'. *Journal of European Public Policy, 18*(6), 848–867.

Casale, S., Corfe, M., & Lewis, J. (2013). *Report of the independent external review of the IPCC investigation into the death of Sean Rigg.* Available at: http://www.ipcc.gov.uk/news/Pages/pr_170513_Riggreview.aspx. Accessed 21 May 2013.

Chan, J. (1999). Governing police practice: Limits of the new accountability. *British Journal of Sociology, 50*(2), 251–270.

Chan, J., & Dixon, D. (2007). The politics of police reform: Ten years after the Royal Commission into the New South Wales Police Service. *Criminology and Criminal Justice, 7*(4), 443–468.

Chapman, C. (2014). *Improving police integrity: Reforming the police complaints and disciplinary systems.* Available at: https://www.gov.uk/government/uploads/system/uploads/attachment_data/file/385900/45363_Cm_8976_Press.pdf. Accessed 10 Nov 2015.

Charman, S., & Savage, S. (2008). Controlling crime and disorder: The labour legacy. In M. Powell (Ed.), *Modernising the welfare state* (pp. 105–124). Bristol: Policy Press.

Clarke, J. (1998). Doing the right thing? Managerialism and social welfare. In P. Abbott & L. Meerabeau (Eds.), *The sociology of caring professions* (2nd ed., pp. 234–254). London: UCL Press.

Clarke, J., Newman, J., Smith, N., Vidler, E., & Westmarland, L. (2007). *Creating citizen consumers: Changing publics and changing public services.* London: Sage.

Davis, G., Lindsey, R., Seabourne, G., & Griffiths-Baker, J. (2002). *Experiencing inquests. Home office research study,* 241. Home Office Research, Development and Statistics Directorate.

Den Boer, M. (2002). Towards an accountability regime for an emerging European policing governance. *Policing and Society, 12*(4), 278–289.

Dillon, B. (2013). Prevention and organisational learning: A new paradigm in professional standards. In A. MacVean, P. Spindler, & C. Solf (Eds.), *Handbook of policing, ethics and professional standards* (pp. 193–203). Abingdon: Routledge.

Dodd, V. (2014, January 8). Mark Duggan's death: two shots fired and two conflicting stories. *The Guardian.*

Dorries, C. (2004). *Coroners' courts: A guide to law and practice* (2nd ed.). Oxford: Oxford University Press.

Downham, G., & Lingham, R. (2009). Learning lessons: Using inquiries for change. *Journal of Mental Health Law, 18*(1), 57–69.

Doyle, J. (2010). Learning from error in American criminal justice. *Journal of Criminal Law and Criminology, 100*(1), 109–149.

Dubnick, M. J. (2003). Accountability and the promise of performance: In search of the mechanisms. Conference paper for American Political Science Association, August 28–31, 2003. Available at: https://www.qub.ie/schools/SchoolofLaw/Research/InstituteofGovernance/Publications/briefingpapers/Filetoupload,47656,en.pdf. Accessed 22 Feb 2013.

Fairclough, N. (2003). *Analysing discourse: Textual analysis for social research.* Oxford: Routledge.

Fairclough, N. (2008). The discourse of new labour: Critical discourse analysis. In M. Wetherell, S. Taylor, & S. Yates (Eds.), *Discourse as data* (pp. 229–266). London: Sage.

Foucault, M. (1976). *The will to knowledge: The history of sexuality volume one* (F. Hurley, Trans.). London: Penguin.

Foucault, M. (1991). *Discipline and punish: The birth of the prison* (A. Sheridan, Trans.). London: Penguin.

Foucault, M. (1994). Truth and juridical forms. In J. D. Faubion (Ed.), *Michel Foucault—power: Essential works of Foucault 1954–1984 vol 3* (pp. 1–89). London: Penguin.

Francis, R. (2013). *Report of the Mid Staffordshire NHS Foundation Trust Public Inquiry*. London: TSO.

Fulton, R. (2008). Review of the forum for preventing deaths in custody: Report of the independent reviewer.

Geisler, C. (2001). Textual objects: Accounting for the role of texts in the everyday life of complex organisations. *Written Communication, 18*(3), 296–325.

Gilsinan, J. (2012). The numbers dilemma: The chimera of modern police accountability systems. *Saint Louis University Public Law Review, 32*, 93–108.

Greer, C., & McLaughlin, E. (2012). This is not justice: Ian Tomlinson, institutional failure and the press politics of outrage. *British Journal of Criminology, 52*(2), 274–293.

Hall, S., Critcher, C., Jefferson, T., Clarke, J., & Roberts, B. (1978). *Policing the crisis: Mugging, the state and law and order*. Basingstoke: MacMillan.

Halpern, S. (2008). Hybrid design, systemic rigidity: Institutional dynamics in human research oversight. *Regulation and Governance, 2*(1), 85–102.

Hewitt, M. (1993). Bio-politics and social policy: Foucault's account of welfare. In M. Featherstone, M. Hepworth, & B. Turner (Eds.), *The body: Social process and cultural theory* (pp. 225–253). London: Sage.

Hindess, B. (1982). Power, interests and the outcomes of struggles. *Sociology, 16*(4), 498–511.

Hirschfield, P., & Simon, D. (2010). Legitimating police violence—Newspaper narratives of deadly force. *Theoretical Criminology, 14*(2), 155–182.

HMIC. (2014). *Value for money profiles 2013*. Available at: http://www.hmic. gov.uk/wp-content/uploads/2013/12/value-for-money-profiles-2013-updated-figures.pdf. Accessed 31 Mar 2014.

Home Office. (2015). *Improving police integrity: Reforming the police complaints and disciplinary systems*. London: HMSO.

House of Commons Home Affairs Committee. (1980). *Deaths in police custody: Together with the proceedings of the Committee, and the minutes of evidence and appendices*. London: HMSO.

House of Commons Home Affairs Committee. (2010). *The work of the independent police complaints commission*. London: TSO.

House of Commons Home Affairs Committee. (2013). *Independent police complaints commission*. London: TSO.

IPCC. (2007). *Memorandum of understanding between the coroners' society of England and Wales and the IPCC*. Available at: www.ipcc.gov.uk/Documents/ guidelines reports/mou.pdf. Accessed 22 May 2013.

IPCC. (2014). *Review of the IPCC's work in investigating deaths: Final report*. Available at: http://www.ipcc.gov.uk/sites/default/files/Documents/deaths_

review/Review_of_the_IPCCs_work_in_investigating_deaths_2014.pdf. Accessed 17 Mar 2014.

Joint Committee on Human Rights. (2004). *Third report: Session 2004–05.* Available at: http://www.publications.parliament.uk/pa/jt200405/jtselect/jtrights/15/1510.htm#a46. Accessed 17 June 2013.

Kaldor, M. (2003). Civil society and accountability. *Journal of Human Development, 4*(1), 5–27.

Komter, M. (2006). From talk to text: The interactional construction of a police record. *Research on Language and Social Interaction, 39*(3), 201–228.

Leigh, A., Johnson, G., & Ingram, A. (1998). *Deaths in custody: Learning the lessons* (Police research series paper 26). London: Crown.

Levine, M. (1999). *Levine on coroners' courts.* London: Sweet and Maxwell.

London Assembly Police and Crime Committee. (2014). *Falling short: The met's healthcare of detainees in custody.* Available at: http://www.london.gov.uk/sites/default/files/14-01-27-Falling%20short%20the%20Met%27s%20healthcare%20of%20detainees%20in%20custody_Jan%202014.pdf. Accessed 18 Feb 2014.

Löwith, K. (1993). *Karl Marx and Max Weber.* London: Routledge.

Luce, T. (2003). *Death certification and investigation in England, Wales and Northern Ireland: The report of a fundamental review.* London: The Stationery Office.

Matthews, P. (2011). *Jervis on the office and duties of coroners: With forms and precedents. Fourth cumulative supplement to the twelfth edition.* London: Sweet and Maxwell.

Matthews, P. (2014). *Jervis on the office and duties of coroners; with forms and precedents. Thirteenth edition.* London: Sweet and Maxwell.

May, P. (2007). Regulatory regimes and accountability. *Regulation and Governance, 1*(1), 8–26.

McIvor, C. (2010). Getting defensive about police negligence: The *Hill* principle, The Human Rights Act 1998 and The House of Lords. *Cambridge Law Journal, 69*(1), 133–150.

McLuhan, M. (2005). *Understanding media.* London: Routledge.

Mulderring, J. (2011). The grammar of governance. *Critical Discourse Studies, 8*(1), 45–68.

National Audit Office. (2008). *The independent police complaints commission.* London: TSO.

Puddister, K., & Riddell, T. (2012). The RCMP's 'Mr Big' sting operation: A case study in police independence, accountability and oversight. *Canadian Public Administration, 55*(3), 385–409.

Punch, M. (2009). *Police corruption: Deviance, accountability and reform in policing*. Cullompton: Willan.

Razack, S. (2015). *Dying from improvement: Inquests and inquiries into indigenous deaths in custody*. Toronto: University of Toronto Press.

Reiner, R. (2000). *The politics of the police* (3rd ed.). Oxford: Oxford University Press.

Reiner, R. (2013). Who governs? Democracy, plutocracy, science and prophecy in policing. *Criminology and Criminal Justice, 13*(2), 161–180.

Savage, S. (2007). Restoring justice: Campaigns against miscarriages of justice and the restorative justice process. *European Journal of Criminology, 4*(2), 195–216.

Savage, S. (2013). Thinking independence: Calling the police to account through the independent investigation of police complaints. *British Journal of Criminology, 53*(1), 94–112.

Scott, S. (2015). 'There is no justice; there is just us.' In H. Athwal & J. Bourne J. (Eds), *Dying for justice* (pp. 59–61).

Shane, J. (2013). *Learning from error in policing: A case study in organisational accident theory*. Heidelberg: Springer.

Shaw, H., & Coles, D. (2007). *Unlocking the truth: Families' experiences of the investigation of deaths in custody*. London: Inquest.

Shircore, M. (2006). Police liability for negligent investigations: When will a duty of care arise? *Deakin Law Review, 11*(1), 33–62.

Smith, J. (2003). *The shipman inquiry (third report): Death certification and the investigation of deaths by Coroners*. London: The Stationery Office.

Smith, G. (2009). Citizen oversight of independent police services: Bifurcated accountability, regulation creep, and lesson learning. *Regulation and Governance, 3*(4), 421–441.

Smith, G. (2013). Oversight of the police and residual complaints dilemmas: Independence, effectiveness and accountability in the United Kingdom. *Police Practice and Research: An International Journal, 14*(2), 92–103.

Snow, T. (1991). *The dynamic universe: An introduction to astronomy* (4th ed.). St Paul: West Publishing.

Spray, J., Draycott, S., & Taylor, C. (2012). *Deaths in custody: The impact of rule 43 reports on organisational learning*. Available at: http://iapdeathsincustody.independent.gov.uk/wp-content/uploads/2012/10/IAP-Impact-of-R43-analysis.pdf. Accessed 20 Feb 2014.

Stone, C. (2007). Training police accountability in theory and practice: From Philadelphia to Abuja and Sao Paolo. *Theoretical Criminology, 11*(2), 245–259.

Tarling, R. (1998). *Coroner service survey. Home Office research study 181*. London: Home Office.

Terpstra, J., & Trommel, W. (2009). Police, managerialisation and presentational strategies. *Policing: An International Journal of Police Strategies and Management, 32*(1), 128–143.

Thomas, L., Straw, A., & Friedman, D. (2008). *Inquests: A practitioner's guide* (2nd ed.). London: Legal Action Group.

Van Sluis, A., Ringeling, A., & Frevel, B. (2009). Evolving patterns in the police systems of North Rhine-Westphalia, the Netherlands and England & Wales. *German Policy Studies, 5*(2), 145–168.

Weisbrode, K. (2012). *On ambivalence: The problems and pleasures of having it both ways*. London: MIT Press.

Williams, C., & Emsley, C. (2006). Beware of the leopard? Police archives in Great Britain. In M. Proctor, M. Cook, & C. Williams (Eds.), *Political pressure and the archival record* (pp. 227–235). Chicago: Society of American Archivists.

Wyatt, S. (1977). *Principles of astronomy* (3rd ed.). Boston: Allyn and Bacon.

Yesufu, S. (2013). The development of policing in Britain in the next five years. *Police Journal, 86*(1), 66–82.

# 8

# Conclusion

This book began with an end, with the death of Sean Rigg. It looked back at how he came to meet his death. It considered the accountability that was constructed in the aftermath of his death, and how this evolved through time, and different iterations of accountability construction. The book has followed the pattern of death investigations in cases of DAPC, retrospectively analysed events that led to such deaths and evaluated the systems and processes used to construct accountability. As the book reaches its conclusion it reconsiders the key findings identified from this retrospective research process and uses them as a way to look forward in an attempt to ascertain how accountability construction might continue to evolve in cases of DAPC.

The system of accountability construction that aims to provide a legitimate response to these deaths is a simulacrum of a system. It is marked by ambiguity of process, purpose and of the relationships between organisations that participate in accountability construction in these cases. While cases of DAPC are investigated in a more rigorous way due to Article 2 of the ECHR, there are still significant disparities in the processes used by the coronial system and the IPCC, and by processes used within each

© The Editor(s) (if applicable) and The Author(s) 2016
D. Baker, *Deaths After Police Contact*,
DOI 10.1057/978-1-137-58967-5_8

organisation. Investigations into these deaths are consistently inconsistent; one certain observation about narrative verdicts is that they are typically atypical. The type of outcome produced by these investigations, whether in the coronial system or the IPCC, is relatively arbitrary. This is perhaps unsurprising given the relationality and ambiguity that is present in the system of accountability construction in cases of DAPC. Accountability, legitimacy, regulation, independence and transparency are clearly highly relational concepts. They are relational dependent upon multiple contexts and perspectives, as has been demonstrated throughout this book. Thus understanding relationships has been key to understanding how accountability is constructed in cases of DAPC.

The lack of central oversight of the regulation constructed in these cases means that there is a lack of analysis that could enable patterns and trends in these deaths to be established from the rich seam of findings evident in the outcomes of death investigations. Consequently, lessons are seldom learned and this must at least partially explain the relatively stable number of deaths over time (see Fig. 2.1), and the persistent over-representation of marginalised groups in these deaths. It also validates the view that accountability construction occurs within the simulacrum of a system. Treating these deaths as individual cases is at best misguided and at worst potentially negligent. They are clearly the result of organisational cultures and practices as much as the result of individual actions or omissions by individuals working for public services. Much of this suggests that currently, accountability construction in cases of DAPC is principally of symbolic value to the state and society. The construction of accountability in these cases has a façade of verisimilitude, yet this tends to shatter in critical cases if pressure is applied, as was particularly notable in the case of Sean Rigg.

## Change and Continuity

Article 2 of the ECHR has effected significant change in the way these cases are investigated and the way that findings are constructed as a result. The construction of accountability in cases of DAPC is evolving. The move to consider these deaths 'in what circumstances' has clearly enabled juries to focus on more holistic issues relating to the death of individuals. This has led to a number of findings being identified that might be helpful in learning lessons to prevent future deaths. In particular it has identified the relevance of other public services in these deaths, and highlighted wider organisational practices and processes that go beyond what individual officers did or did not do when the deceased met their death. The increased focus on measurement of actions or omissions has enabled failure to be noted more frequently in narrative verdicts, and this is linked to the wider scope enabled by Article 2 noted above. The focus on omission means that many of these cases are now identified in terms of inaction rather than action, underlining the significance of Article 2 in promoting the right to life of citizens as distinct to preventing their death.

While there has been change in the evolution of accountability construction in the twenty-first century, there has also been continuity. Evidently there is more focus on these cases; more critical findings are being recorded, in greater detail, and more frequently; the IPCC is being encouraged to be more critical and given increased resources to do so; the police disciplinary system is being overhauled; and the Home Secretary appears earnest in her desire to hold police more accountable in these cases. On the other hand, the number of criminal prosecutions does not appear to have altered; the IPCC and coronial system still have no power to enforce recommendations or press charges; and the ability to learn lessons appears stubbornly unchanged from the findings of the 1998 PCA (Police Complaints Authority) review into cases of DAPC (see Leigh et al. 1998). It seems perverse that measurement is so entrenched in the construction of accountability in terms of findings recorded, but that the measurement of effective progress in reducing the number of deaths over a period of years is apparently lacking.

The inability to learn lessons and effect change appears to reflect the ambivalence and ambiguity that characterise the sphere of accountability construction. Given the relational nature of many of the key issues discussed throughout this book that is not entirely surprising. Ambivalence is manifest in the state's apparent inability to choose between the coronial system or IPCC, or indeed even to acknowledge such a choice exists. Similarly, the choice of both might indicate a desire to have neither. The long-mooted reforms to both systems which have been subject to consistent and focused criticism over the last ten years indicate that this is by no means an idle thought. Ambivalence is also manifest in the wider constellation of the hybrid regulatory sphere that encompasses police activities. Many of the relationships in this constellation are uncertain, leading the observer to ponder why the system exists in its present form. Ambiguity is manifest in the roles and functions of the police, and also in the regulatory sphere in terms of role, function and processes. It should not necessarily be a surprise that a system of accountability construction characterised by ambiguity has its bases in processes that appear marked by vacillation. Nor should it be a surprise that lessons are not learned as a result, as there is a lack of clarity over what is being regulated and how it should be regulated. Thus the symbolic nature of regulation means the simulacrum of a system of accountability is sufficient for most of society and the state, for much of the time. The practical reality of regulation means that there is little evidence of meaningful lessons being learned in these cases. If effectiveness, in terms of reducing the number of people who die by learning meaningful lessons was the key measurement tool on this issue, then the practical reality of regulation in these cases might be different.

The legitimacy of accountability was examined in Chap. 7 where it was considered in relation to the wider discourse of governance. An over-arching issue in this book is that there are numerous organisations involved in the construction of accountability in cases of DAPC, and that the number of organisations in this sphere has grown over time. These organisations are producing an increasing number of documents about the issue of DAPC, and these documents have both an inter-referential aspect and a self-referential aspect. Thus the widening of discourse has produced a widening of discursive texts on the issue. The growth of discourse and discursive texts does not appear to be part of any strategic system of overview on the part of the state. The time period from which the dataset has been drawn is significant in demonstrating the dynamic tensions and inconsistencies apparent in the way that the construction of accountability has evolved in these cases. The discourse of accountability has evolved in the twenty-first century and this has affected discursive practices and the texts they produce. The ambivalence inherent in the system of accountability construction, coupled with the ambiguous roles and processes that characterise the regulatory sphere, means that this expansion of discursive knowledge does not necessarily create effective lesson learning in cases of DAPC. One is left contemplating whether, similar to the banking system 'crash' in 2008, the system of accountability construction in cases of DAPC has simply become 'too big to fail'; that the resources and belief invested in it in both real and symbolic terms are so great the state must ensure its survival.

This book has argued that the relationship between the police, state and society is complex and dynamic. The effectiveness of the relationship relies on police being viewed as legitimate by both state and society. In order for this to occur, accountability has to be both present, and seen to be present. Accountability occurs as a result of the relationship between a number of bodies, and its production and construction is consequently complex and dynamic. The ambiguity present in the role and function of the police, and their subsequent relationship with the state and society is mirrored in the way in which accountability is constructed. An analysis of the processes, relationships, power bases and structures that characterise this state of affairs has illustrated that understanding relationality is key to understanding the subject of DAPC. The finding that the construction of accountability is consistent in its inconsistency underscores this observation. The apparent web or network of accountability that appears to surround the issue of DAPC is neither strategic nor systematic. Instead it is marked by gaps and overlaps of knowledge; ambiguity and ambivalence as to the purpose and function of accountability construction; lack of overall analysis of key issues; and dysfunctional or non-complementary relationships. One question to ask at this point is: is this situation unique to policing and cases of DAPC, or does it exist elsewhere in other regulatory spheres that construct accountability?

## Wider Issues in Accountability and Regulation

Chapter 6 demonstrated that many of the key issues highlighted in the regulation of cases of DAPC were also present in the regulatory sphere charged with holding healthcare agencies accountable. The failure to accurately compile data; to analyse available data; to communicate effectively between regulators; to learn lessons; and to rely on questionable bench-marking criteria were all commonalities between the regulatory spheres of policing and healthcare agencies.

But what of the wider world of accountability and governance? Is it purely public services that are stricken with the problems and failures listed above and considered throughout this book? A cursory glance at all manner of areas suggests that one does not have to look far to see significant failures of regulation, accountability and governance across numerous fields at national and transnational levels. In finance, the collapse of the banking sector in 2008 was widely held to be the result of insufficiently robust regulatory frameworks. Its problems were endemic, deep-seated and grounded in the organisational cultures and practices that pervaded the finance sector (Canova 2009). In sport, the travails of FIFA, the world governing body of football have been heavily documented by the media throughout 2015. Its corrupt practices were held to stem from its own organisational structures and practices throughout the world, combined with what we now know to be an almost non-existent regulatory regime that enabled such practices to prosper (Jennings 2011). The scandal led to the surreal spectacle of the International Olympic Committee criticising FIFA for failing to reform and deal with allegations of corruption (BBC Sport 2015).

In the UK, the Leveson inquiry into press standards was established in 2011, sparked by a phone hacking scandal initially exposed by the *Guardian* newspaper. Leveson noted a weak regulatory system overseeing the UK media that often failed to protect individual citizens (Gibbons 2013). The report from the inquiry was published in 2012. In the first line of the report Leveson states that his is the seventh report into press standards in the UK in less than seventy years, noting that this: 'requires me to consider the extent to which there was a failure to act on previous warnings as to the conduct of the press, the way in which the press has been regulated (if it has) and, in any event, how regulation should work in the future' (Leveson 2012: 3). Evidently, Leveson himself doubted the capacity of the state, media and regulators to learn lessons, even after a full-scale public inquiry. Similarly, the failure of UK Parliamentary authorities to provide regulatory oversight was a feature of the MPs 'expenses scandal' primarily exposed by the

*Daily Telegraph* in 2009. This eventually led to seven MPs being jailed (Martin 2014). Once again, the abuse of parliamentary expenses by MPs was found to be the result of systemic organisational practices within the UK Parliament combined with weak and ineffective regulatory oversight (Allen and Birch 2011).

Evidently there are numerous issues highlighted in this book that go beyond policing and the issue of death after police contact. The burgeoning of hybrid regulatory regimes in the 'post-regulatory' state appears to reflect the present state of account-giving and regulation in England and Wales. Regulation is provided by increasingly 'accommodative' means (Murphy et al. 2009), based on an increasingly complex system of regulators whose relationships are often unclear, both with the body that is subject to regulation, and the other regulators in the hybrid regulatory regime. Legal and political forms of 'reactive' regulation (Murphy et al. 2009) seem to re-emerge when accommodative regulatory regimes fail, in order to re-establish societal legitimacy in times of crises. This supports Bovens' (2007) observation about vertical and legal account-giving trumping all other forms accountability in the final analysis. There is a gap between the policies and practices of organisations that appears to reflect an increasing desire to respect the rights of individuals yet at the same time focus on evaluations based on audit to protect the organisation from blame. This state of affairs is characterised by the ambivalence which appears to be at the heart of accountability construction. It creates a concomitant legitimacy gap between organisations and sections of society as a result. The issues identified here apply to healthcare, finance, media, sport and Parliament itself. Given more space and time I could have provided many more examples. My point is that the construction of accountability in cases of DAPC is marked by issues that go beyond policing and its regulators. This suggests that the issue of DAPC is perhaps not as unique as it is currently presented as being.

All of the above, however, must also be considered in the context of issues related to death after police contact. People die, they do not return. They leave behind families and friends who are grief stricken because of the death, and often doubly traumatised because they feel the accountability process does not construct legitimate outcomes. The police work increasingly as an agency of last resort, expected to do more with less, facing the outcomes of austerity both in terms of their reduced capacity but also the reduced capacity of associated services that puts a greater onus on the police to provide a service for marginalised groups in society. Where does this leave us? How might meaningful change be effected?

## Future Directions

On the basis of this research, in order for there to be meaningful reductions in the number of deaths after police contact three changes are proposed. First, the issue of DAPC needs to be re-imagined as a crisis of healthcare. Half of the people who die have been in contact with more than one public service, and more than half have either mental health issues, and/or issues with substance dependency. Not considering the role of other public services in how these deaths occur is blinkered and unhelpful. On the one hand, individuals from marginalised groups deserve better support from healthcare agencies. On the other, those agencies need to work more effectively in partnership with police in England and Wales to better enable the right to life of *all* citizens. How likely this might be is debatable given the significant and repeated cuts to public services and the long running problems of providing effective multi-agency working due to the issues outlined in Chaps. 2 and 4.

Second, the role of the police needs to be re-imagined as 'peace' officers, or 'safety officers'. The majority of people who died in the dataset were not being violent or resisting arrest. If police view themselves as enforcers of criminal justice they are less likely to consider the preservation of life as a number one priority when approaching vulnerable individuals. In order for this to occur there needs to be a reconsideration of the police ethos in England and Wales that stresses the 'service' aspect of the police role. Producing more and more detailed policies on safer detention and dealing with marginalised groups will at best deliver incremental change on the issue of DAPC. Focusing on officers' training, education and respect for the right to life is likely to have more effect in the long run. Again, how likely these changes might be is doubtful given the resistance to change within policing organisations as documented throughout this book, and the difficulty in having sufficient will to drive through cultural change in working practices. Change in policing often appears to be manifest at a symbolic rather than a practical level.

The first two proposed changes relate to refocusing the service provision so that it might result in fewer people dying in cases of DAPC. The final change relates to the way in which these cases are regulated. It appears from the discussion in Chaps. 6 and 7 that the most effective modes of regulation are legal and political. Hybrid systems of regulation may have their place in the wider field of regulation, but in extreme cases they lack power primarily because they do not lead to organisations or individuals being sanctioned. Changes to the legal mode of accountability first need to begin with the creation of a database that can enable an analysis of patterns and trends recorded by the coronial system and the IPCC. Once patterns and trends have been identified, it might be possible to mobilise the political will to organise a forum that brings together the IPCC, the Chief Coroner, the Home Office, the IAP and the CPS (Crown Prosecution Service) on an annual basis. Two results from that annual forum could be: First, that findings are disseminated among the bodies that make up the wider police 'family' such as the NCPC (National College of Police Chiefs), PCCs (Police and Crime Commissioners), CP (College of Policing) and HMIC. This would be similar to the IPCC's 'Learning the Lessons' bulletins, but would be backed up by more analysis and information about the outcomes of particular cases. This could enable accountable learning driven by internal managerial and regulatory mechanisms in policing organisations.

The second purpose of this forum would be to agree with the CPS on potential courses of action to be taken when certain types of actions or omissions are identified in future cases; in short, that officers would be prosecuted more frequently in these cases due to the national analysis of the issue backed up by the political will to enforce change. The results could then be reviewed on an annual basis at each successive forum. In this sense, accountable learning could exist on two levels—within the police organisation, and external to it. This is similar to Chapman's (2014) recommendations to mesh the internal and external aspects of police disciplinary systems, much as was imagined by Reiner (2000).

Of the three proposals, this might appear the least likely, but evidence from the USA suggests that this is not necessarily the case. A number of police officers are currently undergoing or awaiting trial,[1] apparently as a result of the increased media focus on deaths after police contact driven by movements such as #blacklivesmatter, 'Hands Up United' and 'The Counted'. These developments would have seemed highly unlikely even one year ago. Consequently, developments in technology should also be taken into account when considering future directions for accountability in cases of DAPC. The increasing likelihood of body cameras being adopted by police; the increasing frequency with which citizens record events on camera phones; and the ability of social media to highlight the issue of DAPC—these developments might also effect change in the construction of accountability in cases of DAPC. Similarly, the case of Sean Rigg, re-examined below, demonstrates that if the will exists, and the demands are persistent, then prosecutions might eventually follow.

At the time of writing, in late 2015, the construction of accountability into Sean Rigg's death is still incomplete, despite his death occurring seven and a half years ago. In the aftermath of the Casale review, Sean's case file was returned to the IPCC who, in December 2013, began to reconsider their investigation into his death. In May 2014, a re-investigation into the events leading to Sean's death began, eventually becoming two separate investigations. In one case, all four officers involved in the arrest, restraint and detention of Sean Rigg, in addition to the custody sergeant at Brixton police station when Sean died are still under investigation. In the other case, two officers, PC Birks and PS White (both of whom are also part of the other investigation into Sean Rigg's death) were under investigation for, respectively, perverting the course of justice, and perjury. PC Birks attempted to resign from the MPS (Metropolitan Police Service). The attempted resignation was challenged by the Rigg family. This led to PC Birks' resignation being rescinded by the MPS. He subsequently launched a judicial review to challenge this decision, partly based on the fact that he had secured a place to become a minister in the Church of England, and needed to resign in order to take up this role. In September 2014 his review failed on the basis that it was in the public

---

[1] Note, for example, officer William Rankin in Virginia, on trial for first-degree murder for the death of William Chapman, an unarmed 18 year old in April 2015 (Swain 2015). Similarly, in Chicago in November 2015, officer Jason Van Dyke was indicted on charges of the first-degree murder of 17 year old Laquan McDonald (Davey and Smith 2015).

interest to identify potential wrongdoers in cases of death in police custody (High Court of Justice 2014).

In October 2014, the CPS announced that it would not prosecute the two officers identified as having allegedly perverted the course of justice and committed perjury. It reversed this decision in July 2015 based on the Victim's Right to Review scheme, pursued and initiated by the Rigg family. One officer has now been charged. PS Paul White, the custody sergeant who claimed to have visited Sean while in the police van, has been charged with perjury and is awaiting trial. PS White was initially on 'restricted duty' rather than being suspended during this time despite having allegedly lied under oath to the inquest. This decision was overturned by the MPS commissioner after calls from Marcia Rigg to suspend PS White. It is expected that PS White's trial will commence in autumn 2016. Eight years after Sean's death, Marcia Rigg and her family still await some form of closure.

# References

Allen, N., & Birch, S. (2011). Political conduct and misconduct: Probing public opinion 1. *Parliamentary Affairs, 64*(1), 61–81.

BBC Sport. (2015). Fifa: Sepp Blatter should be replaced by external president. Available at: http://www.bbc.co.uk/sport/0/football/34476100. Accessed 14 Dec 2015.

Bovens, M. (2007). Analysing and assessing accountability: A conceptual framework. *European Law Journal, 13*(4), 447–468.

Canova, A. (2009). Financial market failure as a crisis in the rule of law: From market fundamentalism to a new Keynesian regulatory model. *Harvard Law and Policy Review, 3*(2), 369–396.

Chapman, C. (2014). *Improving police integrity: Reforming the police complaints and disciplinary systems.* Available at: https://www.gov.uk/government/uploads/system/uploads/attachment_data/file/385900/45363_Cm_8976_Press.pdf. Accessed 10 Nov 2015.

Davey, M., & Smith, M. (2015). Chicago protests mostly peaceful after video of police shooting is released. *New York Times.* Available at: http://www.nytimes.com/2015/11/25/us/chicago-officer-charged-in-death-of-black-teenager-official-says.html?_r=0. Accessed 15 Dec 2015.

Gibbons, T. (2013). Building trust in press regulation: Opportunities and obstacles. *Journal of Media Law, 5*(2), 202–219.

High Court of Justice. (2014). *Judgements—Regina (Birks) v Commissioner of Police for the Metropolis and others.* Available at: http://www.11kbw.com/uploads/files/R_Birks_vCommissionerofPoliceApprovedJudgmentCS-Sept2014.pdf. Accessed 21 Dec 2015.

Jennings, A. (2011). Investigating corruption in corporate sport: The IOC and FIFA. *International Review for the Sociology of Sport, 46*(4), 387–398.

Leigh, A., Johnson, G., & Ingram, A. (1998). *Deaths in custody: Learning the lessons* (Police research series paper 26). London: Crown.

Leveson, B. (2012). *An Inquiry into the culture, practices and ethics of the press: Executive summary and recommendations.* London: TSO.

Martin, I. (2014). MPs' expenses: A scandal that will not die. *The Daily Telegraph.* Available at: http://www.telegraph.co.uk/news/newstopics/mps-expenses/10761548/MPs-expenses-A-scandal-that-will-not-die.html. Accessed 14 Dec 2015.

Murphy, K., Tyler, T., & Curtis, A. (2009). Nurturing regulatory compliance: Is procedural justice effective when people question the legitimacy of the law? *Regulation and Governance, 3*(1), 1–26.

Reiner, R. (2000). *The politics of the police* (3rd ed.). Oxford: Oxford University Press.

Swain, J. (2015). Police officer indicted for first-degree murder in death of unarmed teenager. *The Guardian.* Available at: http://www.theguardian.com/us-news/2015/sep/03/virginia-police-officer-indicted-william-chapman. Accessed 15 Dec 2015.

# Appendix: Overview of Narrative Verdicts Used in This Book

Set out below is a very brief overview of each case considered in the dataset for this book. The intention is to provide the reader with some context for the material in this book. For the sake of brevity it has been necessary to reduce each case to key issues identified in this book, any quotations are taken direct from the narrative verdict in the case. Coroners' inquisition sheets do not record the ethnicity of individuals, consequently this information is not included below.

| Case number | Months elapsed to inquest | Sex | Circumstances |
|---|---|---|---|
| 1 | 25 | M | Mental health issues, restraint, died in custody with mental health team present. '172cm tall considered medically obese … and exhibited considerable strength when restrained.' |
| 2 | 8 | M | Restraint, swallowed drugs 'died when he attempted to conceal a package of herbal cannabis in his mouth.' |
| 3 | 24 | M | Mental health issues, failure of mental health team, shot after waving gun at police. '[The deceased] was incorrectly diagnosed with "Acute Stress Disorder."' |

© The Editor(s) (if applicable) and The Author(s) 2016
D. Baker, *Deaths After Police Contact*,
DOI 10.1057/978-1-137-58967-5

| Case number | Months elapsed to inquest | Sex | Circumstances |
|---|---|---|---|
| 4 | 38 | M | Restraint, died in custody after being arrested for shop-lifting. 'His physical distress and complaints of being unwell were not properly addressed.' |
| 5 | 63 | M | Alcohol, head injury, died in hospital after 2nd admission in 24 hours. 'His behaviour after the fall was mistaken for his habit of lying on the floor.' |
| 6 | 29 | M | Died after being struck by taxi during police vehicle pursuit. |
| 7 | 27 | M | Mental health issues, restraint, police called to support mental health team. Died in ambulance. '[The deceased] was a 28 year old male suffering from schizophrenia and diabetes.' |
| 8 | 27 | M | Alcohol and drugs involved, detained for own safety, died in custody. 'The deceased was a long term user of alcohol and had been on a program of opiate therapy for many years.' |
| 9 | 49 | F | Swallowed drugs, died in custody after police raid. 'Had the appropriate precautions and actions been taken death may have been prevented.' |
| 10 | 36 | M | Alcohol involved, died in hospital or in police van 'as a result of a pre-existing medical condition following heavy alcohol intake and violent exertion.' |
| 11 | 27 | M | Arrested for breaching peace. 'Died of hypertensive heart disease accelerated by the trauma and the necessary operations to correct a fracture sustained during a lawful arrest.' |
| 12 | 27 | M | Alcohol involved, died in hospital after transfer from custody. 'He was on occasion found … drunk, doubly incontinent and infested.' |
| 13 | 12 | M | Died after colliding with another car during police pursuit. |
| 14 | 9 | M | Homeless, drugs involved, arrested on outstanding warrant. Suicide in custody. |
| 15 | 24 | M | Swallowed drugs, alcohol involved, died in custody. 'We would like to express our sympathy to the family and friends of the deceased who died so tragically.' |
| 16 | 38 | M | Drugs involved, suicide in custody, failure of doctor and police supervision. 'The mis-typing of [the deceased's] surname failed to display previous custody records.' |

| Case number | Months elapsed to inquest | Sex | Circumstances |
|---|---|---|---|
| 17 | 62 | M | Drugs and alcohol involved, threatened suicide, police restraint, died in hospital. |
| 18 | 45 | M | Health issues, incorrectly identified as drunk and disorderly. Failure of medical staff and police, died in hospital. 'With reference to the comparison of custody and CCTV records we observed that dishonest entries had been made.' |
| 19 | 9 | M | Alcohol involved, police pursued on foot leading to death by fall from height. |
| 20 | 42 | M | Mental health issues, swallowed drugs, failure of mental health team to provide adequate care. '[The deceased] was a young man with a long history of complex and complicated psychological and psychiatric difficulties.' |
| 21 | 12 | M | Alcohol involved police pursuit death |
| 22 | 26 | M | Drugs involved, mental health issues, died in custody after self-administered overdose. |
| 23 | 20 | M | Police responded to call from hostel staff. Drugs involved, restraint, died in hospital. '[The deceased] was found in his room which was in disarray and very hot. He was on his back, sweating, naked and had blood on his forehead.' |
| 24 | 35 | M | Mental health issues, shot on 'A' road after 'psychotic episode'. |
| 25 | 47 | M | Drugs involved, 'excited delirium', restraint, died in custody. |
| 26 | 74 | M | Police called by deceased's mother. Restraint, CS gas and baton used, died in police vehicle. |
| 27 | 29 | M | Deceased was armed and under police surveillance. Shot outside restaurant. |
| 28 | 6 | F | Mental health issues, died after being transferred from hospital to custody. |
| 29 | 25 | M | Drugs involved, died partially dressed on open ground in winter. 'He was in receipt of daily methadone and prescribed diazepam.' |
| 30 | 36 | M | Swallowed drugs, police criticised for duty of care, died in custody. |
| 31 | 32 | M | Collapsed after being confronted by police at home address. Died of 'stress related factors'. |
| 32 | 55 | M | Drugs involved, 'excited delirium', restraint. Failure of police and medical staff, died in custody. |

| Case number | Months elapsed to inquest | Sex | Circumstances |
|---|---|---|---|
| 33 | 34 | M | Police requested by deceased's neighbours. Drugs involved, 'excited delirium', restraint, died in custody. |
| 34 | 26 | M | Arrested during burglary whilst on bail. Restraint by security guards then police. |
| 35 | 46 | M | Swallowed drugs after police raid based on 'gross failure of intelligence systems'. |
| 36 | 43 | M | Police called to disturbance. Restraint, use of CS gas and baton. 'He was heavily built and in good health.' |
| 37 | 44 | M | Alcohol involved, ambulance in attendance, died in custody. 'Gross failure to provide basic medical attention.' |
| 38 | 28 | M | Mental health issues, alcohol involved, shot after day-long siege. |
| 39 | 63 | M | Arrested during burglary. Drugs and alcohol involved, died in custody. 'Despite heroic efforts by all concerned [the deceased] was eventually pronounced dead.' |
| 40 | 17 | M | Alcohol involved, armed, shot after short siege. '[The deceased] had been drinking that day and had a recent history of drinking heavily.' |
| 41 | 38 | M | Arrested for alleged assault on wife. Alcohol involved, died in custody with neglect as contributory factor. |
| 42 | 46 | M | Arrested after running from 'suspected crack house.' Swallowed drugs, restraint. |
| 43 | 48 | F | Swallowed drugs, believed to be 'pseudo/ feigning', died in custody. 'Her convulsions continued in the cell and were interpreted as resistance.' |
| 44 | 56 | M | Drugs involved, died in custody after 'gross failings in system'. |
| 45 | 29 | M | Alcohol involved, died in custody, neglect as contributory factor. '[The deceased] was not known as a heavy drinker.' |
| 46 | 16 | M | Brandishing knife when arrested. Alcohol and drugs involved, 'excited delirium', restraint, died in hospital. 'He continued to shout incoherently, moaning groaning and growling.' |
| 47 | 20 | M | Mental health issues, waving three guns. Shot in public area. |

| Case number | Months elapsed to inquest | Sex | Circumstances |
|---|---|---|---|
| 48 | 13 | M | Alcohol involved, head wound. Died in hospital after delayed transfer from custody suite. '[The deceased] was left in his cell alone for 21 minutes until the ambulance arrived.' |
| 49 | 25 | M | Alcohol involved, struck with baton whilst 'walking peaceably' in public area. |
| 50 | 58 | M | Mental health issues, police called to hospital to restrain patient, died in hospital. 'There was no identified lead person from clinical staff or the police to take charge of the situation.' |
| 51 | 12 | M | Health issues, died in custody after 'joint failings of police, medics and translation procedures.' |
| 52 | 46 | M | Mental health issues, restraint, died in custody after failures by mental health team, police and FME. |
| 53 | 14 | M | Drugs involved, 'excited delirium', use of pepper spray and restraint, died in custody. |
| 54 | 34 | M | Mental health issues, drugs involved, restraint, died in custody. 'He struggled violently against necessary restraint.' |
| 55 | 54 | M | Alcohol involved, head wound, died in custody after 'gross failures' by police and medical teams. '[The deceased] did not receive an appropriate examination from the M.E due to the omission of basic medical assessment.' |
| 56 | 27 | M | Suicide during police raid. '[The deceased] … was on bail facing criminal proceedings the following week.' |
| 57 | 13 | M | Swallowed drugs, died in hospital after transfer from custody suite. |
| 58 | 22 | M | Alcohol involved, restrained after being taken to mental health institution. Died later in hospital. |
| 59 | 29 | M | 'Acute behavioural disturbance' caused by cocaine intoxication. Died partly due to restraint, partly because of delayed ambulance response caused by errors in CAD. |
| 60 | 30 | M | Alcohol involved, 'unfit for detention'. Died due to 'inadequate care' caused partly by insufficient medical assessment whilst in custody. |
| 61 | 16 | M | Epileptic seizure whilst in custody. 'There was a lack of understanding between individuals within the same agency and between the different agencies as to the observations [the deceased] was on and why.' |

| Case number | Months elapsed to inquest | Sex | Circumstances |
|---|---|---|---|
| 62 | 34 | M | Lawfully shot dead by police officer. 'There was no emphasis on exhausting all avenues which could have affected reaction and subsequent actions.' |
| 63 | 19 | M | Mental health issues. Died due to misadventure: an unintended overdose of prescribed medication. Psychiatrists prescribing medication to deceased were unaware of medication prescribed by GPs. |
| 64 | 10 | M | Mental health issues, alcohol involved. 'He had a history of alcoholism and psychiatric problems.' Despite multi-agency contact on day of death, he 'was left alone in his home ... with a lot of alcohol in the property.' Died of alcohol poisoning. |
| 65 | 29 | M | Died of 'amphetamine induced delirium in association with prolonged struggle'. Taken to A and E by police car. It 'became clear that the Senior Registrar was not familiar with the dangers of prolonged restraint of a patient in the prone (face- down) position. |
| 66 | 78 | M | Died due to restraint, cocaine toxicity and airway obstruction. 'The jury believes that the officers could have considered alternative ways of dealing with [the deceased] without using force.' |
| 67 | 20 | M | Died due to acute alcohol poisoning in custody. |
| 68 | 47 | M | Mental health issues. Died due to 'acute behavioural disturbance' and restraint in an A and E setting. The jury found that 'periods of restraint were unreasonable and contributed to [the deceased's] death.' |

# Bibliography

Athwal, H., & Bourne, J. (Eds.). (2015). *Dying for justice.* Available at: http://www.irr.org.uk/wp-content/uploads/2015/03/Dying_for_Justice_web.pdf. Accessed 18 June 2015.

Baker, D. (2015). *Analysing the construction of accountability in cases of death after police contact.* Unpublished PhD thesis, Open University, Milton Keynes.

Beggs, J., & Davies, H. (2009). *Police misconduct, complaints, and public regulation.* Oxford: Oxford University Press.

Brecht, B. (1958). *Life of Galileo* (C. Laughton, Trans.). London. Methuen.

Cashmore, E., & McLaughlin, E. (Eds.). (1991). *Out of order: Policing black people.* London: Routledge.

Charman, S., & Savage, S. (2009). Mothers for justice? Gender and campaigns against miscarriages of justice. *British Journal of Criminology, 49*(6), 900–915.

Dean, G., & Gottschalk, P. (2011). Continuum of police crime: An empirical study of court cases. *International Journal of Police Science and Management, 13*(1), 16–28.

Dyson, S., & Boswell, G. (2006). Sickle cell anaemia and deaths in custody in the UK and the USA. *The Howard Journal, 45*(1), 14–28.

European Court of Human Rights. (2010). *European convention on human rights.* Available at: http://www.echr.coe.int/Documents/Convention_ENG.pdf. Accessed 1 June 2014.

© The Editor(s) (if applicable) and The Author(s) 2016
D. Baker, *Deaths After Police Contact*,
DOI 10.1057/978-1-137-58967-5

Findlay, M. (2001). Juror comprehension and complexity: Strategies to enhance understanding. *British Journal of Criminology, 41*(1), 56–76.

Hannan, M. (2013). Deaths in or following police custody: An examination of cases from 1998/00–2008/09. In A. MacVean, P. Spindler, & C. Solf (Eds.), *Handbook of policing, ethics and professional standards* (pp. 56–67). Abingdon: Routledge.

Home Office. (2008). *The review of policing by Sir Ronnie Flanagan: Final report.* London: HMSO.

Höpfl, H. (1999). Organisations: Breaking the body of the text. In I. Parker (Ed.), *Critical textwork: An introduction to varieties of discourse and analysis* (pp. 129–140). Buckingham: Open University Press.

House of Lords. (2004). *Judgments—Regina v. Her Majesty's Coroner for the Western District of Somerset (Respondent) and another (Appellant) ex parte Middleton (FC) (Respondent).* Available at: http://www.publications.parliament.uk/pa/ld200304/ldjudgmt/jd040311/midd-1.htm. Accessed 2 Oct 2012.

Hyvärinen, M. (2009). Analysing narratives and story-telling. In P. Alasuutari, L. Bickman, & J. Brannen (Eds.), *The sage handbook of social research methods* (pp. 447–460). London: Sage.

Inquest. (2012). *Inquest into the death of Sean Rigg begins 11 June 2012.* Available at: http://www.inquest.org.uk/press-releases/press-releases-2012/inquest-into-death-of-sean-rigg-begins-monday-11-june-2012. Accessed 22 June 2013.

IPCC. (2015). *Submission to the Home Office regarding triennial review of the IPCC.* Available at: https://www.ipcc.gov.uk/sites/default/files/Documents/speeches/IPCC_response_to_the_Triennial_Review_report_June_2015.pdf. Accessed 29 Sept 2015.

Jackson, L. (2013). Policing the police: Investigating professional standards. In A. MacVean, P. Spindler, & C. Solf (Eds.), *Handbook of policing, ethics and professional standards* (pp. 32–39). Abingdon: Routledge.

Klockars, C. (1985). *The idea of the police.* Beverly Hills: Sage.

Lawrence, R. (2000). *The politics of force: Media and the construction of police brutality.* Berkley: University of California Press.

Lee, B., Vittinghof, E., Whiteman, D., Park, M., Lau, L., & Tseng, Z. (2009). Relation of Taser (electrical stun gun) deployment to increase in in-custody sudden deaths. *The American Journal of Cardiology, 103*(6), 877–880.

Llewellin, P., Arendts, G., Weeden, J., & Pethebridge, A. (2011). Involuntary psychiatric attendances at an Australasian emergency department: A comparison of police and health-care worker initiated presentations. *Emergency Medicine Australia, 23*(5), 593–599.

Loader, I. (2006). Fall of the "Platonic Guardians": Liberalism, criminology and political responses to crime in England and Wales. *British Journal of Criminology, 46*(4), 561–586.

Loader, I., & Mulcahy, A. (2001). The power of legitimate naming: Part II—Making sense of the elite police voice. *British Journal of Criminology, 41*(2), 252–265.

Loader, I., & Mulcahy, A. (2003). *Policing and the condition of England: Memory, politics and culture.* Oxford: Oxford University Press.

Manning, P. (2003). *Policing contingencies.* Chicago: University of Chicago Press.

Moscovici, S. (2000). *Social representations: Explorations in social psychology.* Cambridge: Polity.

National Confidential Enquiry into Perioperative Deaths. (2001). *Changing the way we operate.* Available at: http://www.ncepod.org.uk/pdf/2001/01sum.pdf. Accessed 29 Oct 2012.

Newburn, T., & Peay, J. (Eds.). (2011). *Policing: Politics, culture and control.* Oxford: Hart.

Noble, A., Best, D., Stark, M., & Marshall, E. (2001). *The role of the forensic medical examiner with 'Drunken Detainees' in police custody* (Police research series: paper 146). London: Home Office.

Parliament. (2010). *Memorandum submitted by the Police Action Lawyers Group.* Available at: http://www.publications.parliament.uk/pa/cm200910/cmselect/cmhaff/366/10022309.htm. Accessed 17 July 2013.

Powell, R., Weber, L., & Pickering, S. (2013). Counting and accounting for deaths in Australian immigration custody. *Homicide Studies, 17*(4), 391–417.

Reiner, R. (1992). Policing a postmodern society. *Modern Law Review, 55*(6), 761–781.

Rogers, M. (2003). Police force! An examination of the use of force, firearms and less-lethal weapons by British police. *Police Journal, 76*(3), 189–203.

Samuel, E., Williams, R., & Ferrell, R. (2009). Excited delirium: Consideration of selected medical and psychiatric issues. *Neuropsychiatric Disease and Treatment, 5*, 61–66.

Scott, R. (2013). The duty of care owed to a mentally ill person in the community who may require involuntary apprehension. *Psychiatry, Psychology and Law, 20*(5), 660–685.

Scraton, P., & Chadwick, K. (1987). *In the arms of the law: Coroners' inquests and deaths in custody.* London: Pluto.

Smith, G. (2005). A most enduring problem: Police complaints reform in England and Wales. *Journal of Social Policy, 35*(1), 121–141.

Smith, G. (2006). Police complaints in the reform era. *Criminal Justice Matters,* *63*(1), 26–27.

Smith, G. (2010). Every complaint matters: Human Rights Commissioner's opinion concerning independent and effective determination of complaints against the police. *International Journal of Law, Crime and Justice, 38*(4), 59–74.

Smith, E., & Jacobs, K. (1973). *Introductory astronomy and astrophysics.* London: W.B Saunders.

Starmer, K. (2000). *European human rights law: The Human Rights Act 1998 and the European Convention on Human Rights.* London: Legal Action Group.

Vilke, G., Payne-James, J., & Karch, S. (2012). Excited delirium syndrome (ExDS): Redefining an old diagnosis. *Journal of Forensic and Legal Medicine, 19*(1), 7–11.

Wall, I. (2008). Lack of training in custodial medicine in the UK—A cause for concern? *Journal of Forensic and Legal Medicine, 15*(6), 378–381.

Wells, K. (2011). *Narrative inquiry.* Oxford: Oxford University Press.

Wetli, C., & Fishbain, D. (1985). Cocaine-induced psychosis and sudden death in recreational cocaine users. *Journal of Forensic Science, 30*(3), 873–880.

Willig, C. (Ed.). (1999). *Applied discourse analysis: Social and psychological interventions.* Buckingham: Open University Press.

# Index

© The Editor(s) (if applicable) and The Author(s) 2016
D. Baker, *Deaths After Police Contact*,
DOI 10.1057/978-1-137-58967-5

Farrell, A., 61
Fédération Internationale de Football
    Association (FIFA), 204
FFLM. *See* Faculty of Forensic and
    Legal Medicine (FFLM)
firearms, 81, 99, 113, 119. *See also*
    shooting
FME. *See* Forensic Medical
    Examiner (FME)
force, use of by police
    and 'accidents', 25
    legitimisation of in shooting, 81
    restrictions, 31
    and role of police, 24, 25
    sanctioned, 93
    as subjective, 5, 29, 32
Forensic Medical Examiner (FME),
    2, 2n1, 86, 124, 158
Foucault, Michel
    on bodies, 140
    on knowledge, 140–3, 179, 182
    on power, 14, 138, 140–3, 148,
        173, 174, 177, 178, 188
Francis report 2013, 156, 176
Fulton review 2008, 42, 170

G

Garner, Eric, 187
Geisler, C., 182
Gilsinan, J., 31, 41, 69, 119, 123,
    150, 160, 170, 180–2
Givelber, D., 61
Goldsmith, A., 30, 37, 40, 71
governance, systems of, 149
'gross failure' 86, 88, 92, 93
guidelines, enactment of on ground,
    28
Gunnarson, B-L., 128, 141

H

Haggerty, K., 88
Hallam, E., 58, 139, 141
Hall, S., 186
Halpern, S., 149, 152, 154, 177, 178
handcuffs, use of, 2
Hardwick, Nick, 71
healthcare, 16, 34–6, 44, 63, 80, 88,
    93, 96, 99, 103, 121, 139,
    149, 153–7, 162, 170, 175,
    176, 203–6
Her Majesty's Inspectorate of
    Constabulary (HMIC), 27,
    28, 37, 41, 67, 72, 89, 95,
    130, 171, 183, 190, 191,
    207
Hewitt, M., 182
Hillsborough stadium, 25
Hindess, B., 147, 153, 186
Hirschfield, P., 32, 33, 41, 90, 94,
    95, 158, 187
'*The Hitchhikers' Guide to the Galaxy*'
    (Adams), 184
HMIC. *See* Her Majesty's
    Inspectorate of
    Constabulary (HMIC)
Home Office, 27n4, 59, 59n3, 123,
    129, 130, 207
Home Secretary, 37, 66, 72, 126,
    129, 130, 132, 170, 201
Horsley, P., 140
House of Commons Committee of
    Public Accounts, 156
House of Commons Home Affairs
    Select Committee (HAC),
    37
Human Rights Act (HRA) 1998, 14,
    55
human rights laws, international, 40

CPI Antony Rowe
Eastbourne, UK
November 05, 2019